POKÉMON ORIGAMI

First published in the UK by Scholastic, 2024
1 London Bridge, London, SE1 9BA
Scholastic Ireland, 89E Lagan Road, Dublin Industrial Estate,
Glasnevin, Dublin, D11 HP5F

First published in the US by The Pokémon Company International, 2024

ISBN 978 0702 33851 9

A CIP catalogue record for this book is available from the British Library.

Printed and bound in China

Paper made from wood grown in sustainable forests and other controlled sources.

2 4 6 8 10 9 7 5 3 1

www.scholastic.co.uk

How This Book Works

The paper templates you should use to fold the characters are on pages 57-120. This book offers fun for even newcomers to origami, and the designs have been kept simple, sometimes using two or more sheets of paper.

Each project tells you which template should be used to make the character. There is an asterisk on the back of each template that tells you how the paper should be oriented when you begin to fold. Then it's just a matter of following the folding instructions.

Occasionally, you will need to make cuts or use tape or glue. This is indicated by scissor, tape, or glue symbols (see Key to Symbols below).

The projects are also rated for difficulty: one (1) Poké Ball for beginner projects, two (2) for intermediate, and three (3) for advanced. If you don't have much experience folding origami, we recommend starting with a character like Alolan Diglett first, as it's one of the easier characters to fold. Once you gain more experience under your belt, you can try folding one of the more challenging Pokémon—like Pikachu!

How to Understand the Folding Instructions

Origami folding instructions show you how to fold the paper correctly through step-by-step illustrations and text so you can create your own Pokémon characters. Here's how it works:

Let's begin with a simple sequence of the three steps with written explanations that show you how to make just one simple fold.

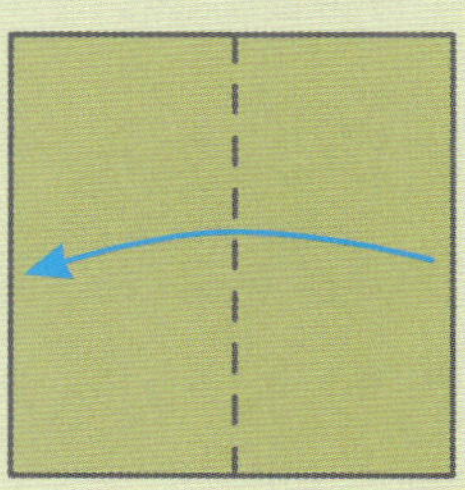

1 Fold in half sideways.

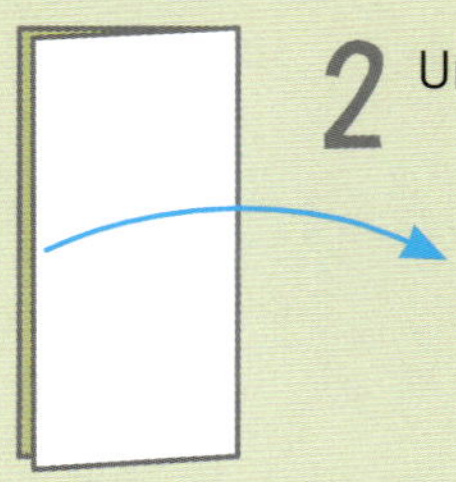

2 Unfold.

3 Finished.

Key to Symbols

- This push arrow symbol tells you that you need to turn a corner or a point inside out.
- This symbol tells you to turn the paper over, usually sideways.
- This symbol tells you that the next diagram has been drawn on a larger scale.
- This symbol tells you to pleat the paper in a zigzag shape.
- A circle is used to highlight particular areas mentioned in the instructions.
- You will need to use glue where you see this symbol.
- You will need to use scissors where you see this symbol.
- You will need to use adhesive tape where you see this symbol.

Here Are the Things You Need to Know to Follow the Folding Steps:

The edges of the paper are shown as thick solid lines. The front of the paper is shown as shaded, and the back of the paper is shown as white. It's important to check that your paper looks the same as the illustrations both before and after every fold you make.

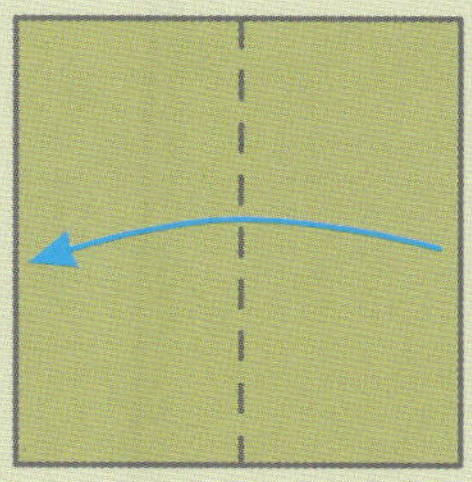

STEP 1 is made up of two parts: a movement arrow and a fold line. The movement arrow tells you which part of the paper moves, which direction it moves in, and how it should be positioned at the end of the step. In this case, the movement arrow tells you to pick up the right edge of the paper and fold it across so that it rests on top of the left edge.

When you make a fold, you will need to flatten it to make a crease. The fold line shows you where this crease will form. It's always a good idea to flatten the paper completely, press it down firmly with the soft part of a finger, then run a fingernail along the edge to make your crease really sharp.

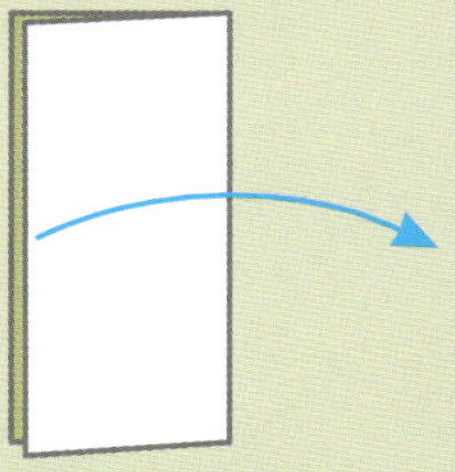

STEP 2 shows you what the result of making the first fold will look like. When necessary, edges that lie exactly on top of each other as a result of a fold are shown slightly offset on the "after" diagram so that you can see they are there.

Sometimes, a movement arrow without a fold line is used to indicate that you should use the crease you have already made to "open out" the design. Every illustration in a folding sequence (apart from the first and the last) can be thought of as both an "after" picture for the step before and a "before" picture for the step after. So, Step 2 shows you the result of the folding instruction in Step 1, but it also gives you another instruction that leads to Step 3.

STEP 3 shows the crease you made as a thin line. The trick to following folding instructions is to always look one step ahead. Doing so ensures that you know what the results of making a fold should look like before you begin to make it.

Here Are a Few More Things You Need to Know about the Folding Symbols and How They Work:

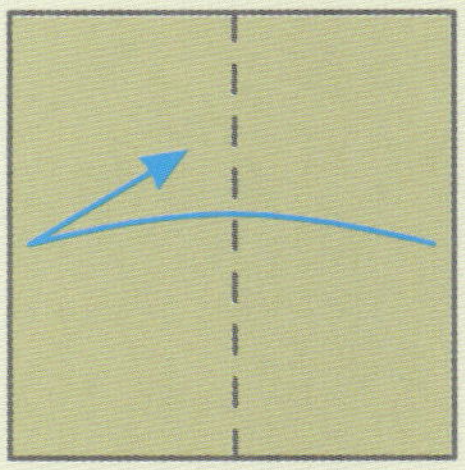

This version of the movement arrow means fold, crease firmly, then unfold. This illustration is a combination of Steps 1 and 2, and it is used to save space in the book.

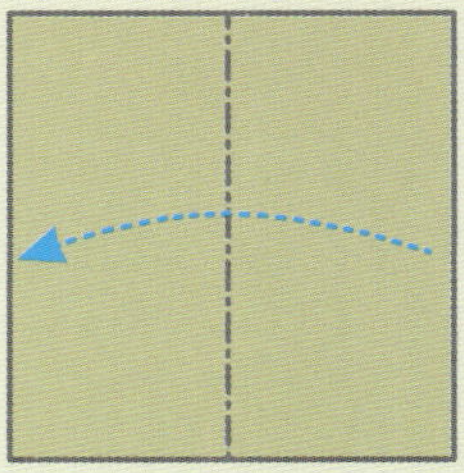

A dashed-and-dotted fold line with a dotted movement arrow means that the fold should be made away from you, behind the paper. So, this folding instruction means fold the right edge backward behind the paper onto the back of the left edge, then flatten to crease.

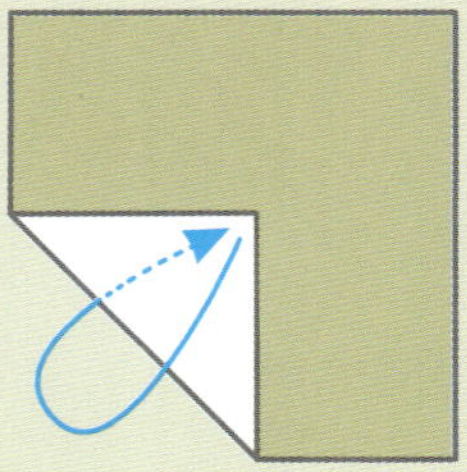

An illustration of this kind tells you to swivel the white triangular flap to the back by reversing the direction of the existing crease. The crease acts like a hinge when you do this.

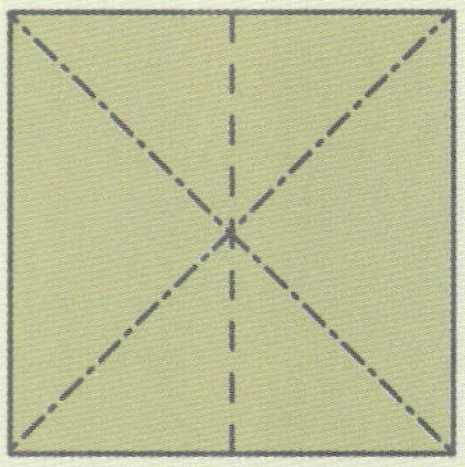

Sometimes, the two different types of fold lines are used together to show you how a combination of creases made in different directions through the paper (some backward, some forward) can be used to collapse the paper into a different shape.

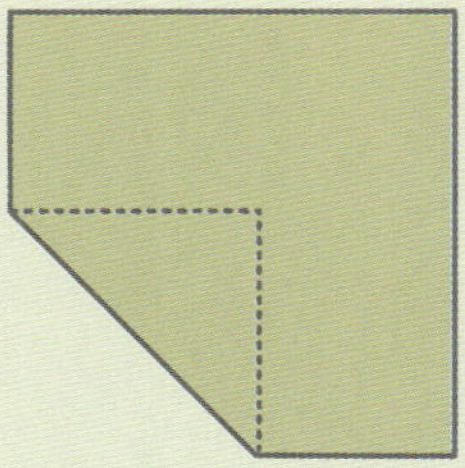

Dotted lines are also occasionally used to show hidden edges or fold lines: imaginary lines that are used to help situate a fold or that indicate lines to cut along. Sometimes, they are also used to show how the paper will be positioned after you have made the fold. This illustration shows what the result of following the folding instruction above would look like.

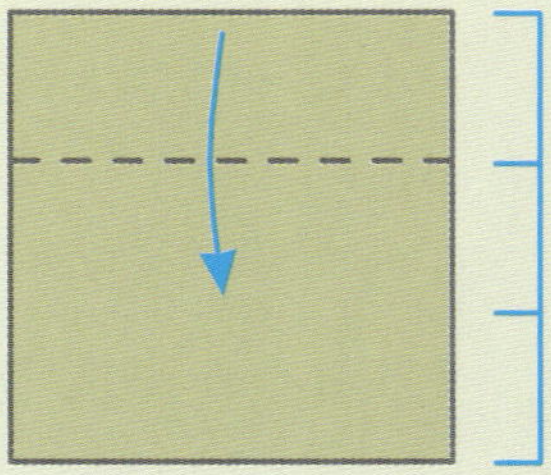

This type of symbol shows that the edge of the paper should be imagined as being divided into equal sections. This can help you situate your fold correctly. In this case, you would fold the top edge downward to make a crease one-third of the way down the paper. It is normally OK for this division to be approximate instead of precise.

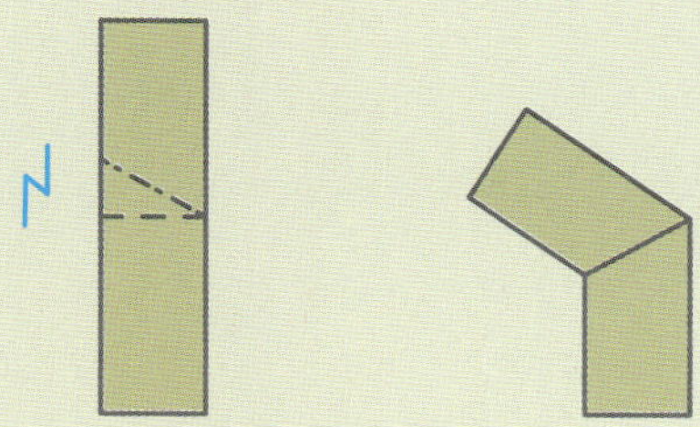

This type of symbol tells you to pleat the paper in a zigzag shape. The dashed fold line should be made toward you, and the dashed-and-dotted fold line should be made away from you.

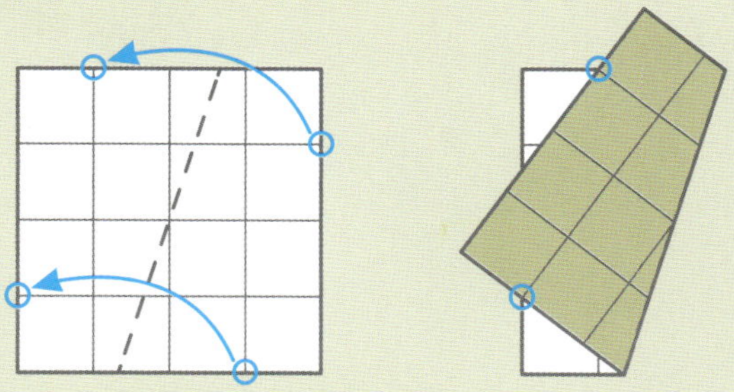

Circles are used to mark particular areas in the instruction or tell you where a specific fold should be placed.

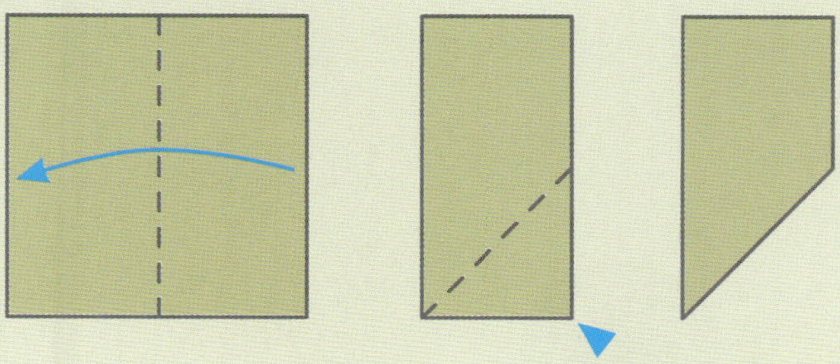

A "reverse fold" is when you need to turn a corner or a point inside out. After folding a corner or point, a push arrow symbol will tell you where to reverse the fold and turn the corner or point inside out.

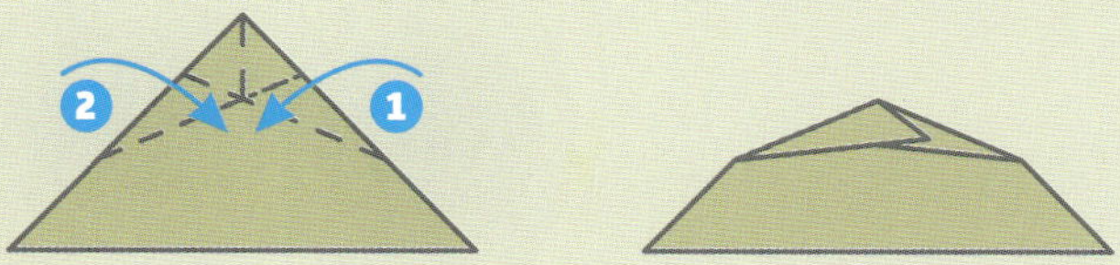

Sometimes, you will need to fold a small corner to blunt or round out an edge. Follow the different types of fold lines to create the shape. In this example, you would fold the right side down first, and then fold the left side down and flatten it to the right.

Helpful Tips:

- When folding, make sure the edges and corners are aligned before creasing the paper.
- You can use any square piece of paper to practice before using the paper templates.
- As you progress through the steps, turn the shape over at times to make sure the design is aligned correctly. For example, if you are folding down a foot or arm, make sure it is positioned correctly on the opposite side before creasing the paper.
- Two copies of paper templates are provided for each character. Use the first copy to practice. Once you are comfortable with the steps, use the second copy to create your final Pokémon!
- Feel free to use a combination of tape and glue to assemble your Pokémon—just be sure to align the shapes before adding tape or glue!

INTERMEDIATE

Pikachu

Mighty Pikachu can generate powerful electricity in the electric sacs on its cheeks. Get charged up before you start to fold Pikachu, and you'll be finished in a flash of lightning!

TYPE: Electric **HEIGHT:** 1'4" / .4 m **WEIGHT:** 13.2 lbs. / 6 kg

ADVANCED

How To Make Pikachu

Pikachu is folded from four pieces of paper: three large triangles that become its body and feet, head, and tail; and one small square that becomes its arms. You can find the templates on pages 57, 61, and 89. Carefully cut out each of the pieces.

Folding the Body & Feet

Make sure to start with the triangle template arranged so the asterisk is at the top.

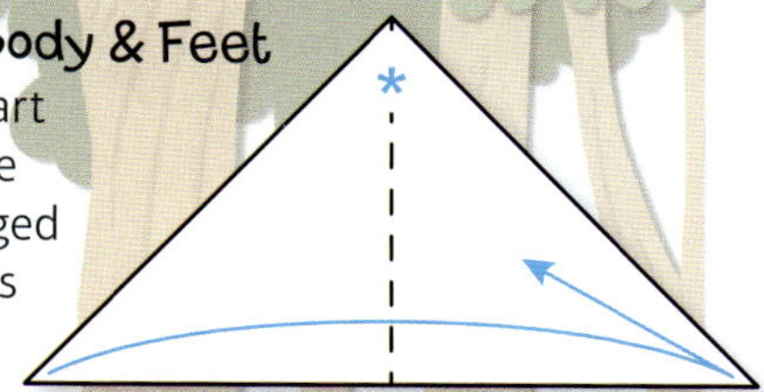

1 Fold in half sideways, then unfold.

2 Fold the left and right edges into the centerline.

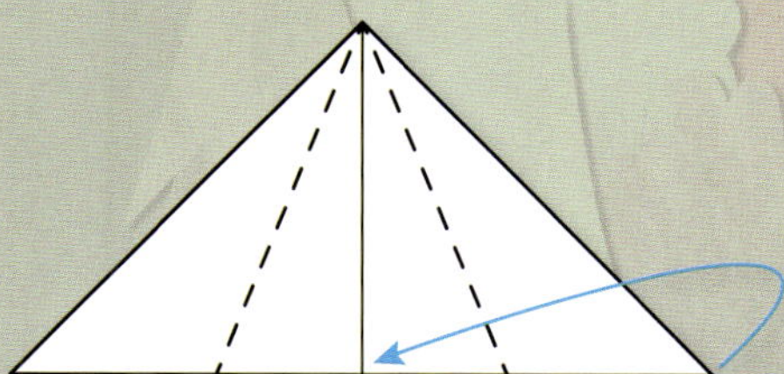

3 Fold up the bottom-left corner.

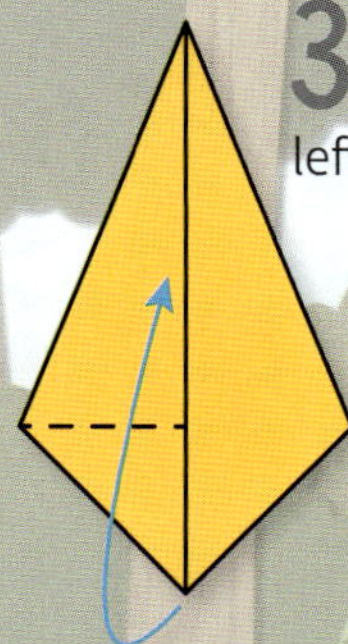

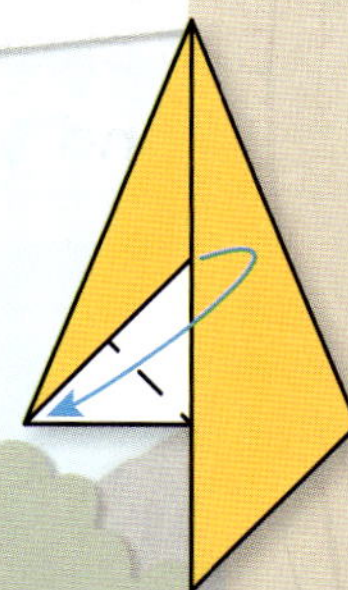

4 Fold the corner back down to the bottom-left corner.

5 Fold the flap down, then unfold.

6 Reverse fold the flap inside out.

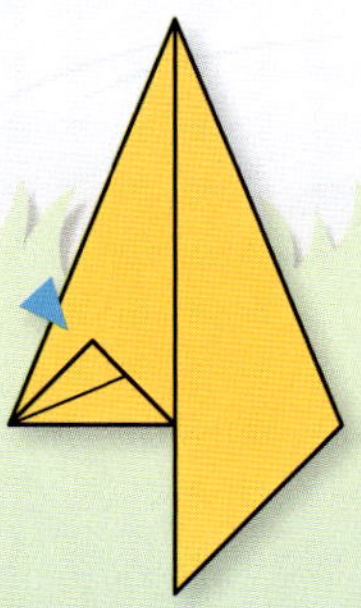

7 Slide the top of the flap down counterclockwise—showing the layer behind just slightly—and flatten.

8 Fold in the tip of the flap (left foot).

9 Repeat Steps 3–8 on the right side.

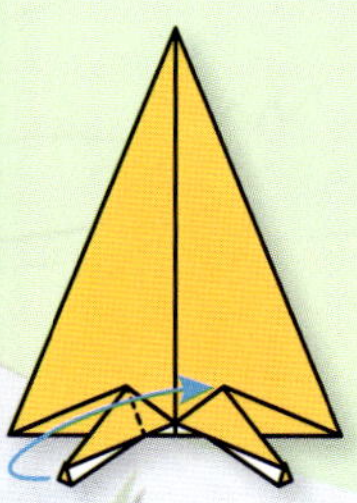

10 Fold the left foot up along the crease.

11 Fold the left foot back down at an angle (turn over to check the foot placement).

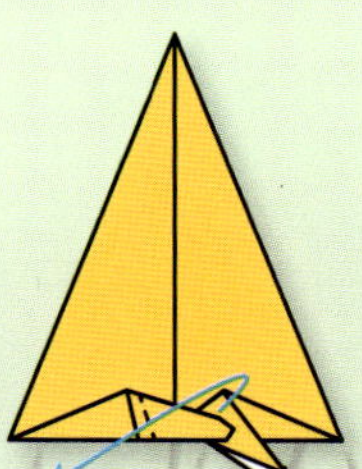

12 Repeat Steps 10–11 on the right foot.

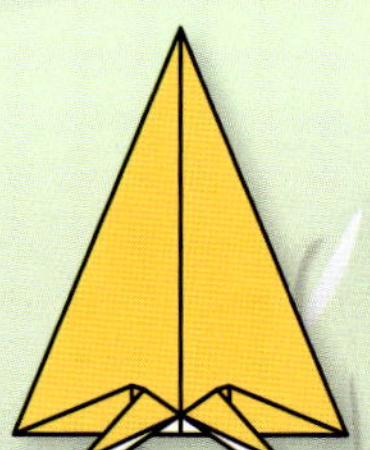

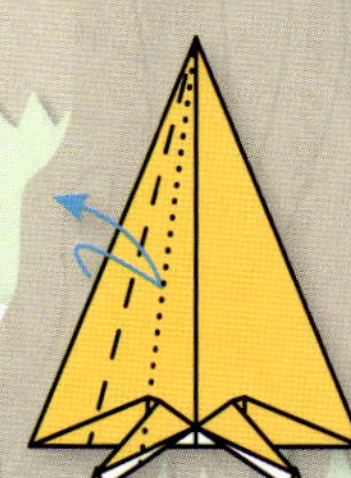

13 Fold in the left edge along the top corner of the foot, then unfold.

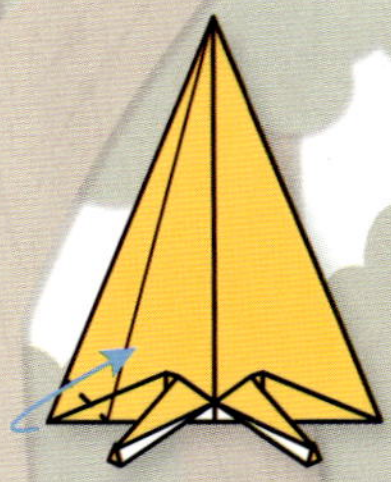

14 Fold the bottom-left corner in along the edge of the crease.

15 Fold the left edge in along the crease.

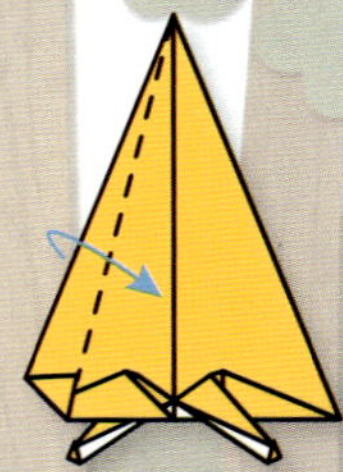

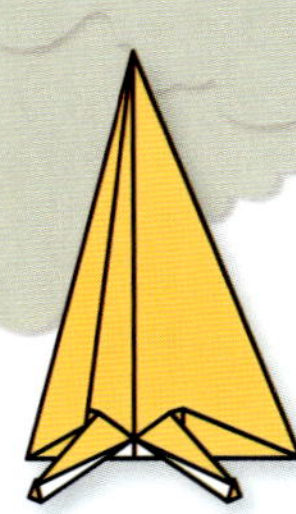

16 Repeat steps 13–15 on the right side.

17 Fold the top corner down (as shown). Turn the paper over.

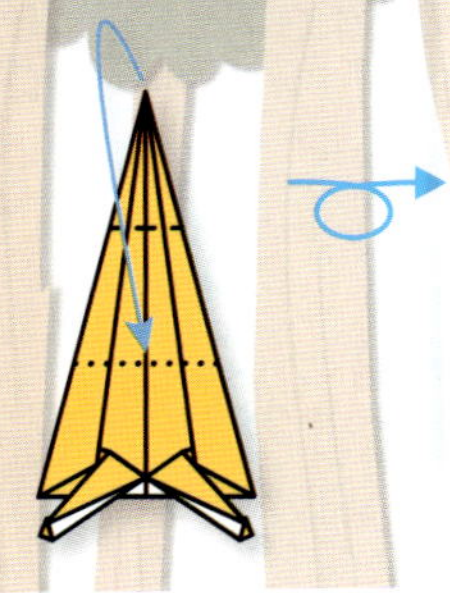

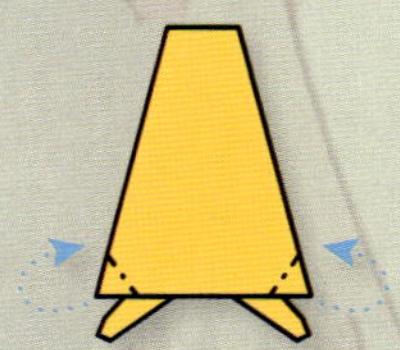

18 Fold the bottom corners back to round the body (will be thick).

19 Pikachu's body and feet are complete.

Folding the Head

Make sure to start with the triangle template arranged so the asterisk is at the top.

20 Fold in half sideways, then unfold.

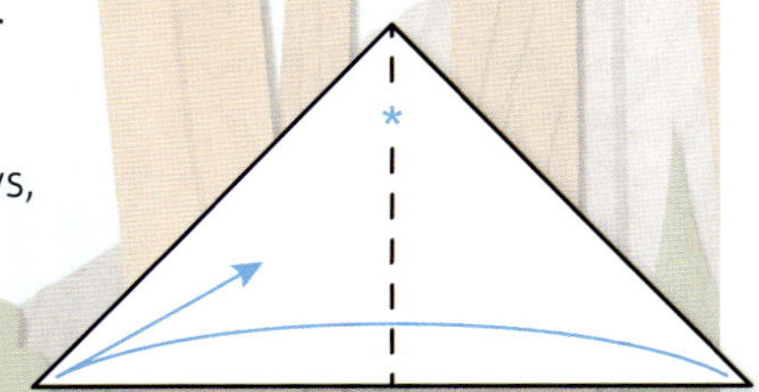

21 Fold the bottom corners up to the top corner.

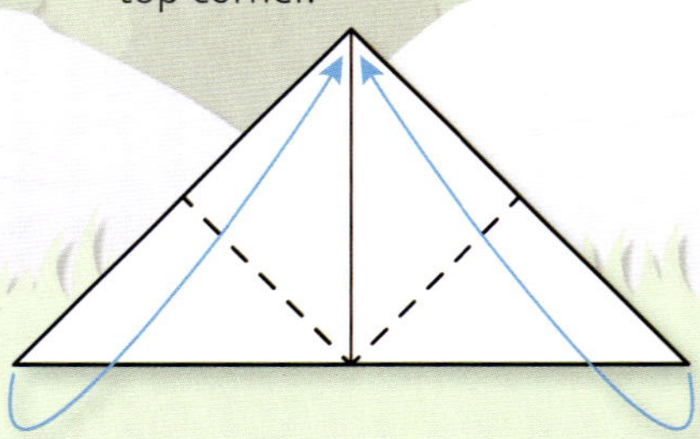

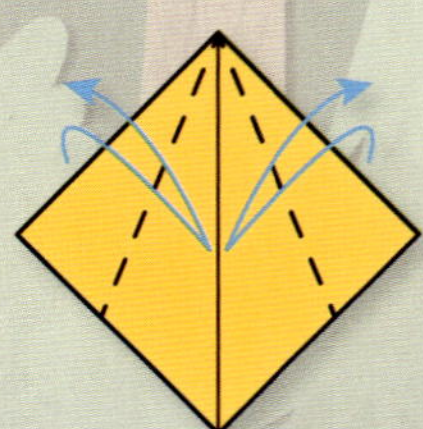

22 Fold the right and left corners to the centerline, then unfold.

23 Reverse fold the left and right corners inside out.

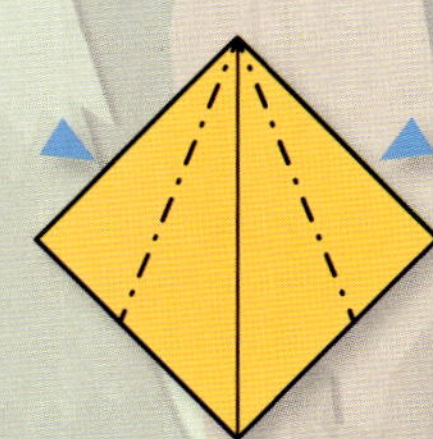

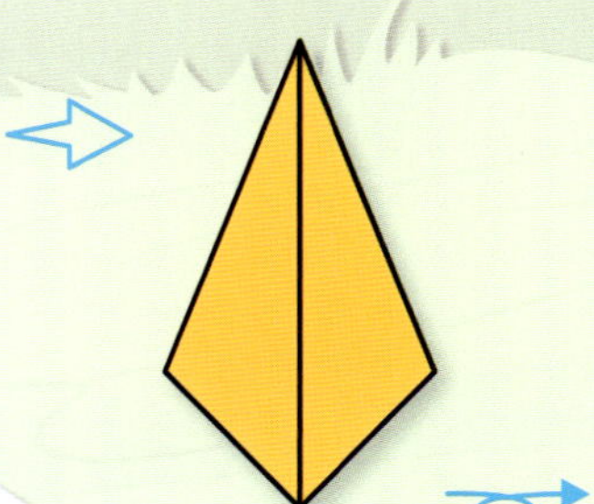

24 The result should look like this, then turn the paper over.

25 Fold the top layer down, then unfold. Turn the paper over.

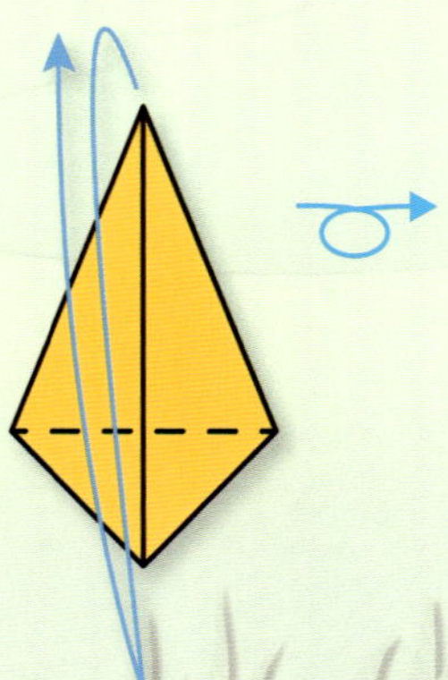

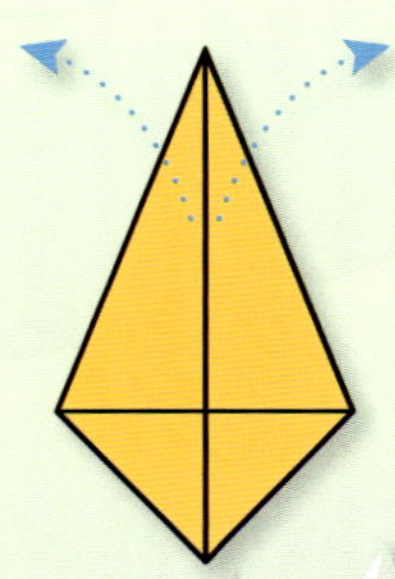

26 Unfold everything.

27 Fold the top corner down.

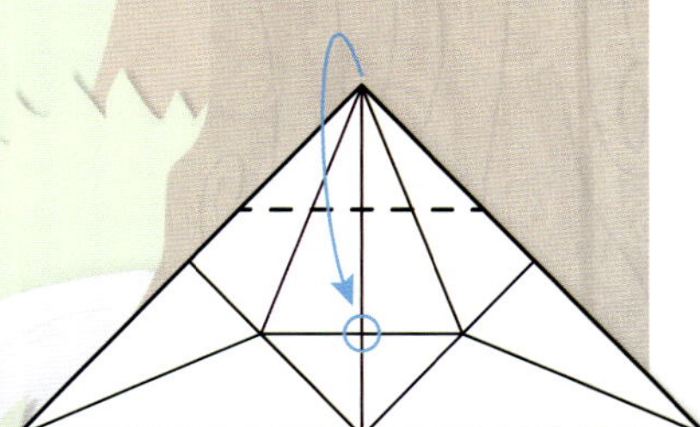

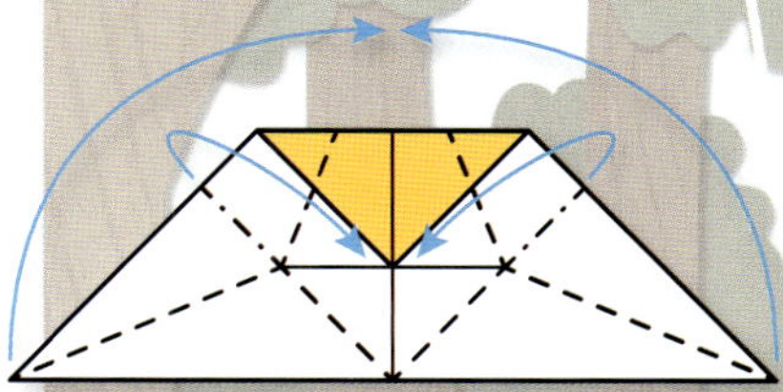

28 Refold to look like Step 26 again.

29 Fold the bottom corner up about halfway.

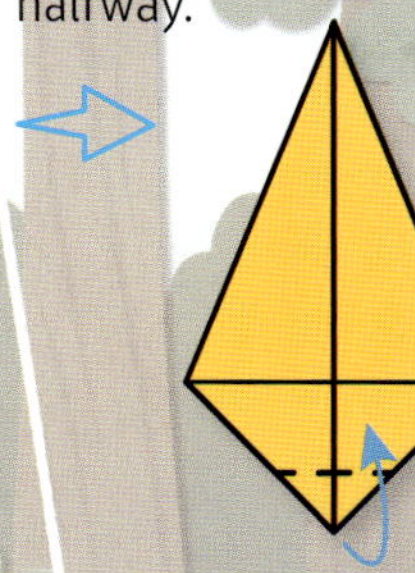

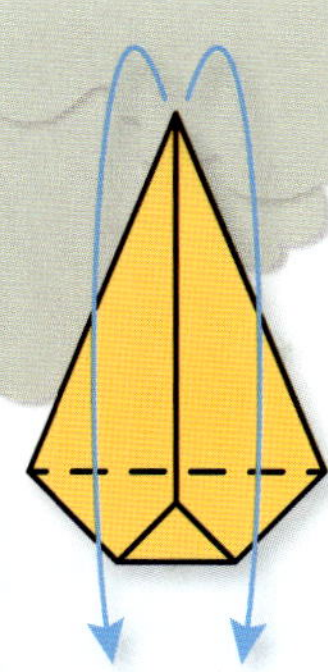

30 Fold the two long flaps down.

31 One at a time, fold the top corners down along the top edges of the flaps, then unfold.

32 Fold in the left edge, and then fold down the right edge.

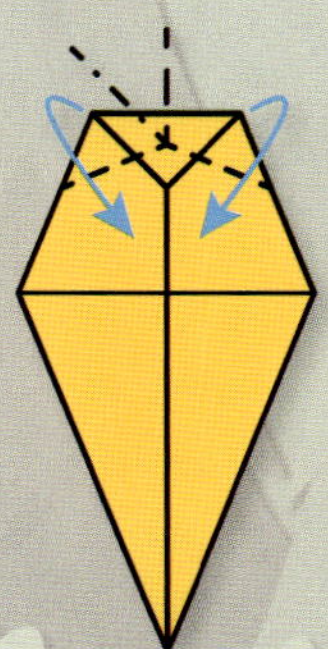

33 Fold the right flap up.

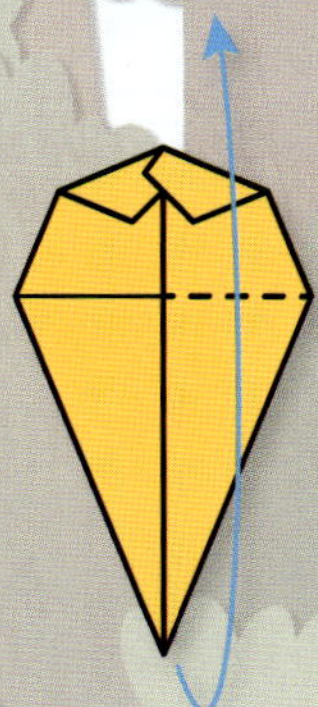

34 Fold the flap back down.

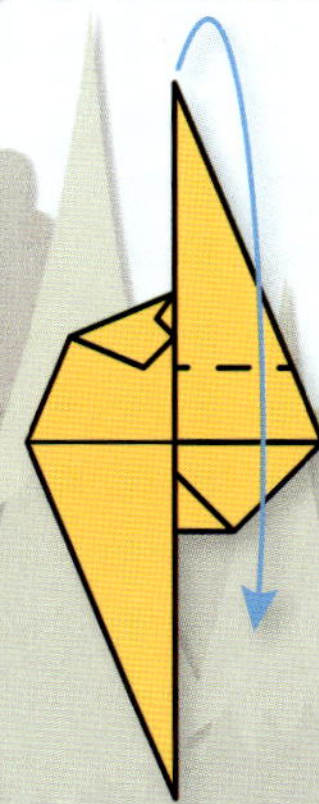

35 Fold the right corner in.

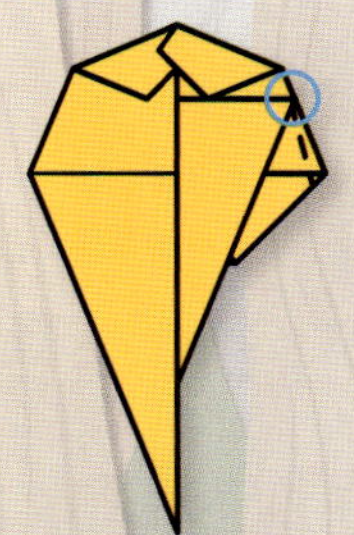

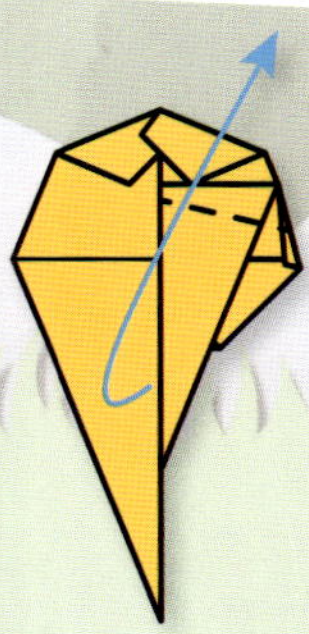

36 Fold the flap up again to the right (turn over to check the ear placement).

37 Reverse fold the right corner inside out.

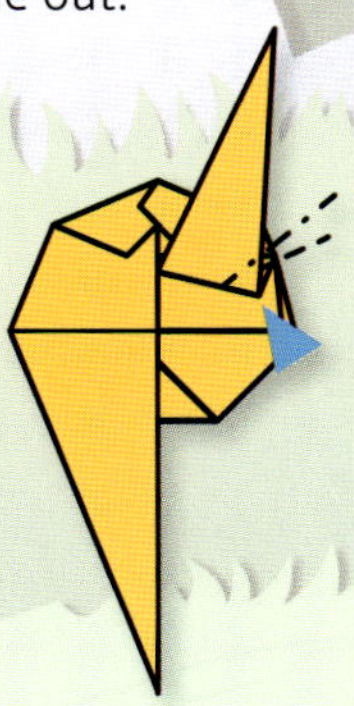

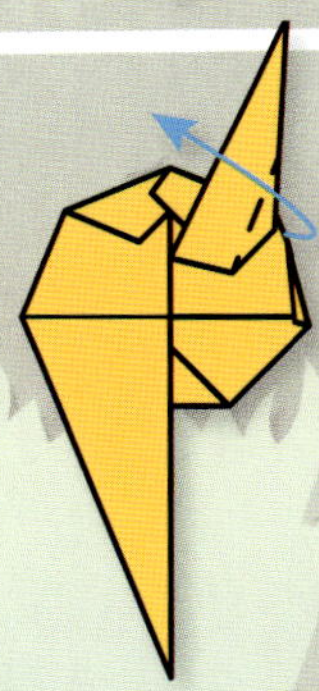

38 Fold the right edge of the flap in (turn over to check the ear shape).

39 Fold the left edge of the flap in—just a little (see next step).

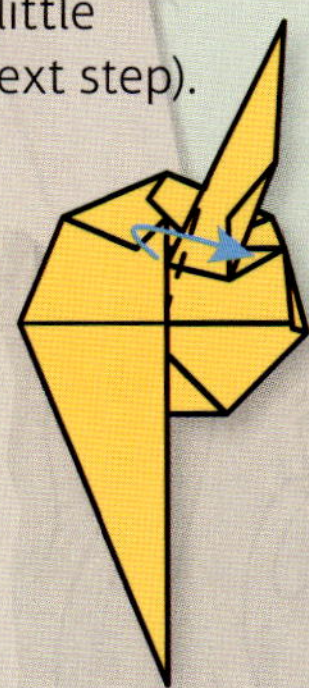

40 Fold the left flap up.

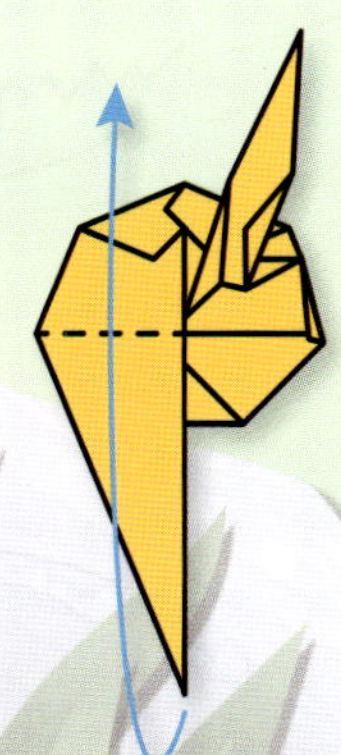

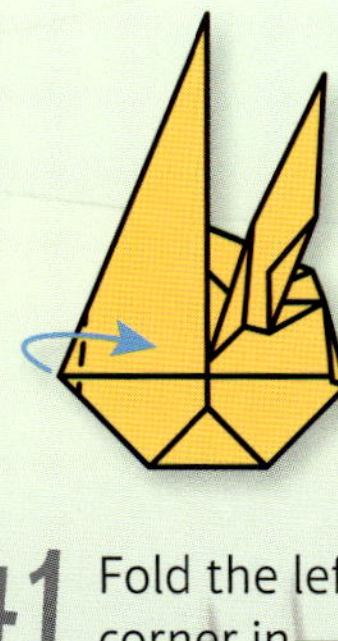

41 Fold the left corner in—even with the right side.

42 Fold the right edge of the flap to the left side.

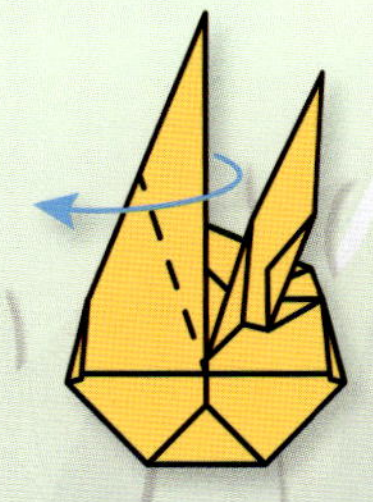

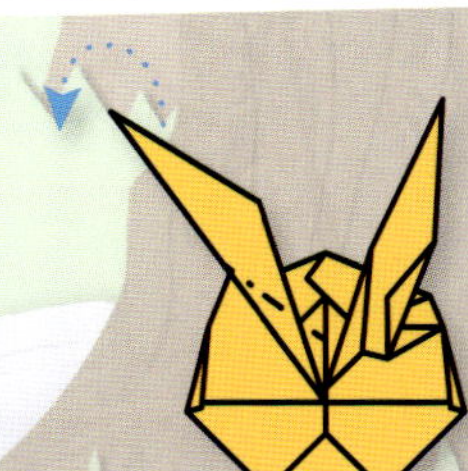

43 Turn the left ear inside and fold behind itself (turn over to check the ear placement).

44 Fold the tips of the ears to round. Turn the paper over.

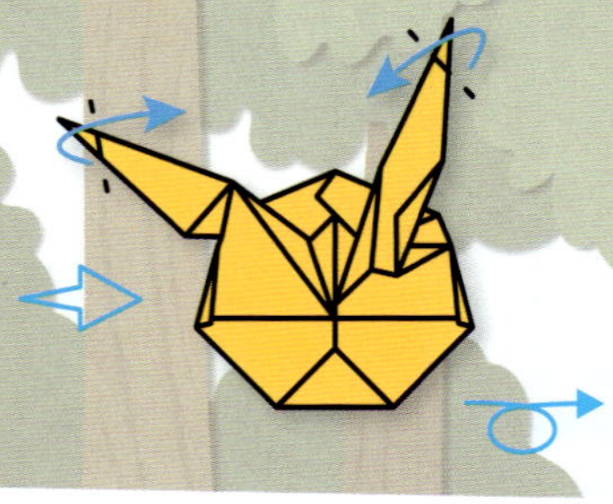

45 Narrow the right ear by folding the sides back a little.

46 Round the top of the head by folding back the corners a little.

47 Pikachu's head is complete.

Folding the Arms

Make sure to start with the small square template arranged so the asterisk is at the top.

48 Fold the bottom corner up to the top corner.

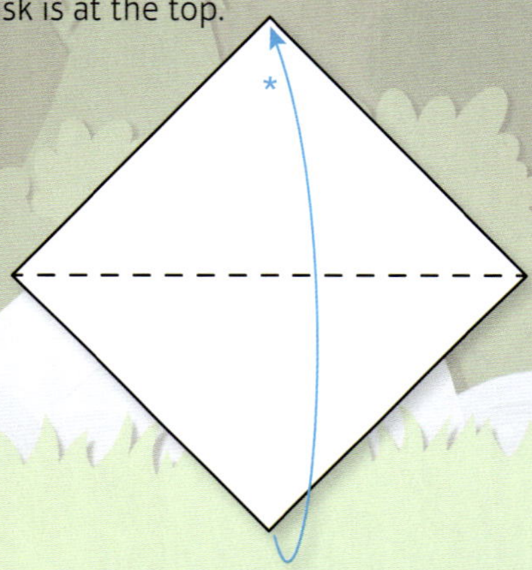

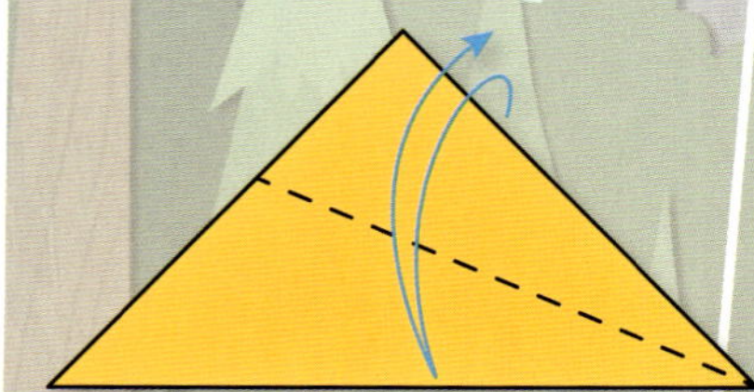

49 Fold the top-right edge down to the bottom edge, then unfold.

50 Fold the top-left edge down to the bottom edge, then unfold.

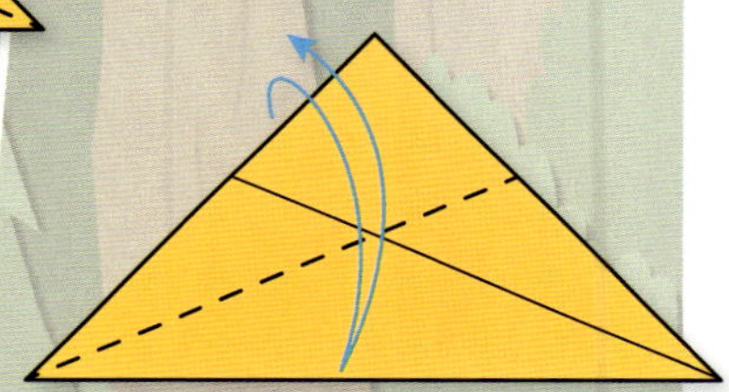

51 Fold the bottom edge up to the creases (marked with circles).

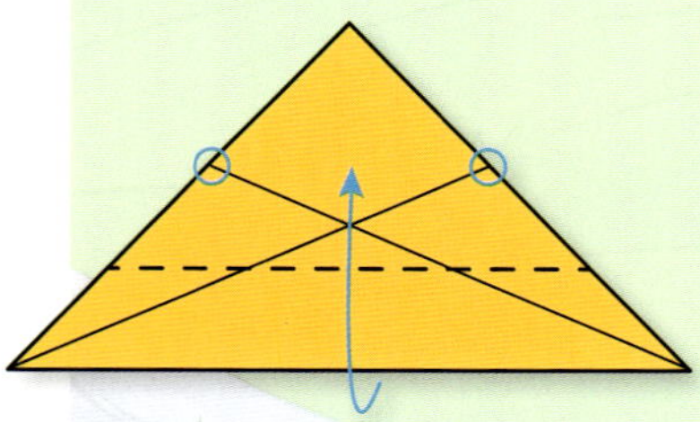

52 The result should look like this, then unfold.

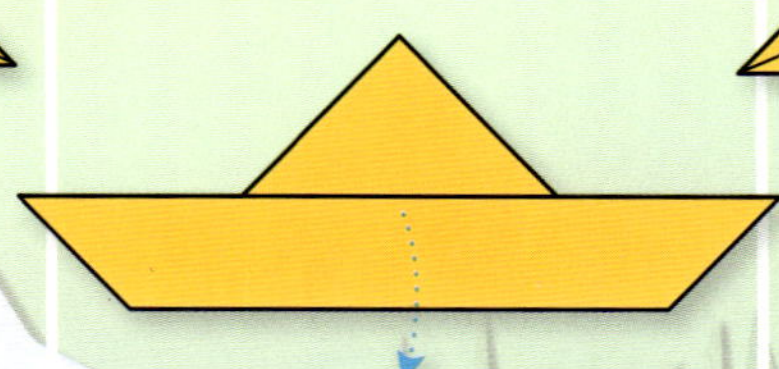

53 Fold the left edge down to the horizontal crease.

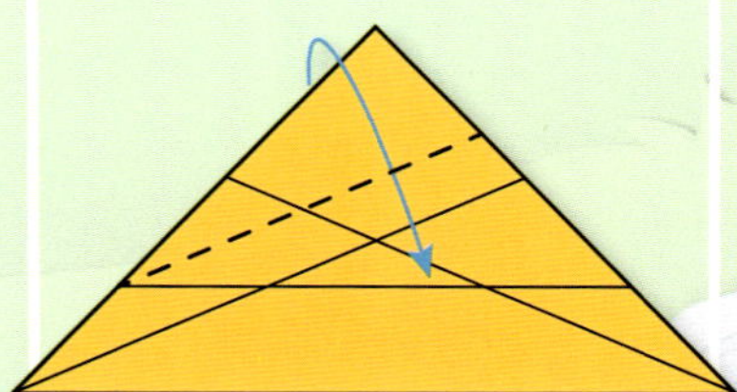

54 Fold the bottom edge up along the crease.

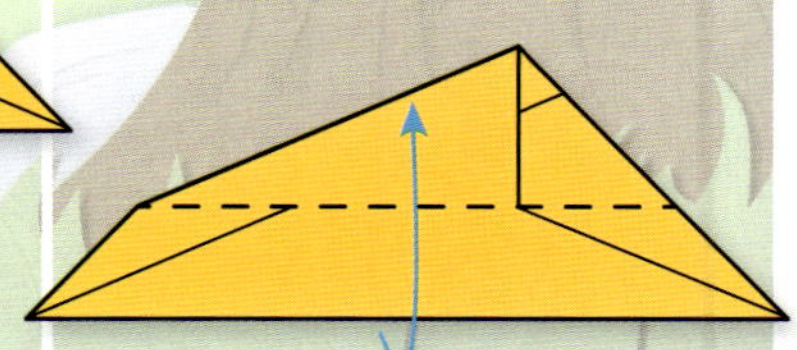

55 Fold the left corner down at a 45-degree angle (as shown), then unfold. Turn the paper over.

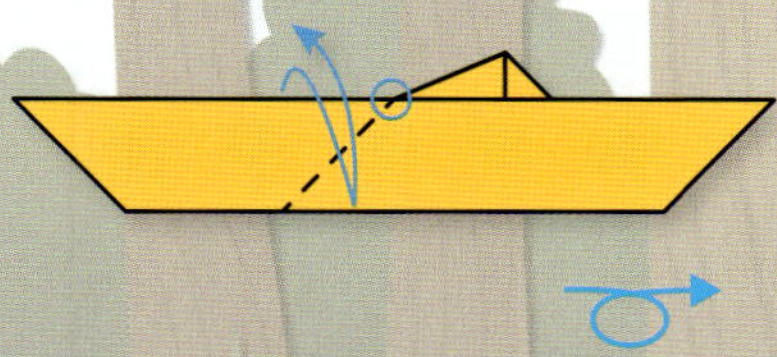

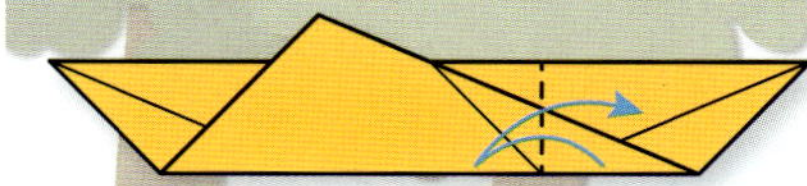

56 Fold the right corner over, then unfold.

57 Fold the right corner over, between the two creases.

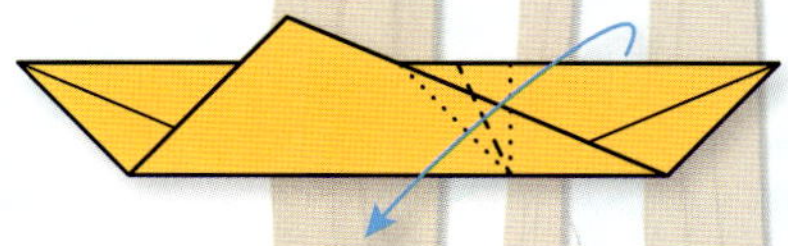

58 Fold the flap back (as shown).

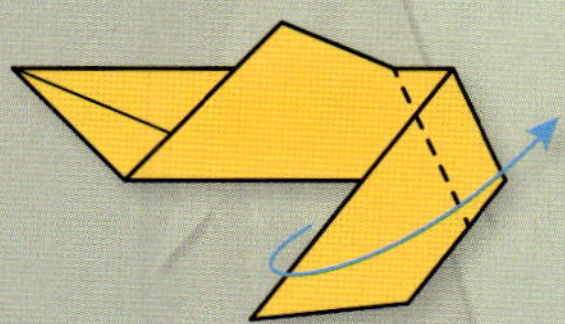

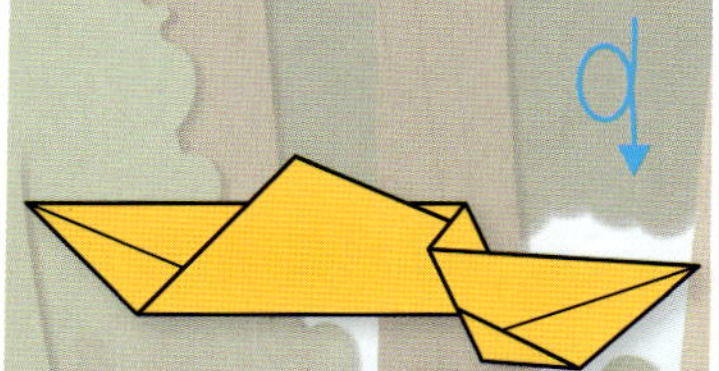

59 Turn over vertically.

60 Fold the left corner down (as shown), then unfold.

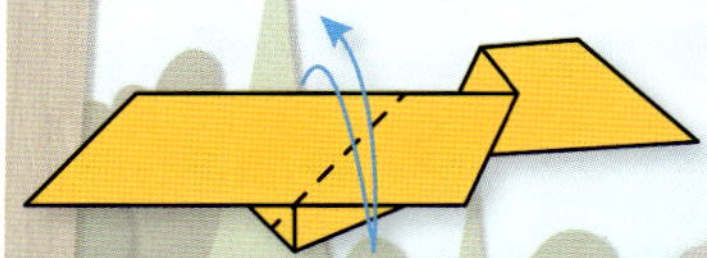

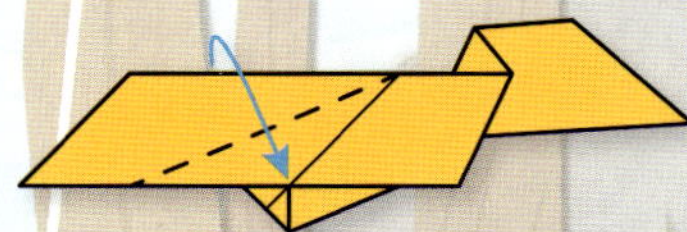

61 Fold the top edge down along the crease.

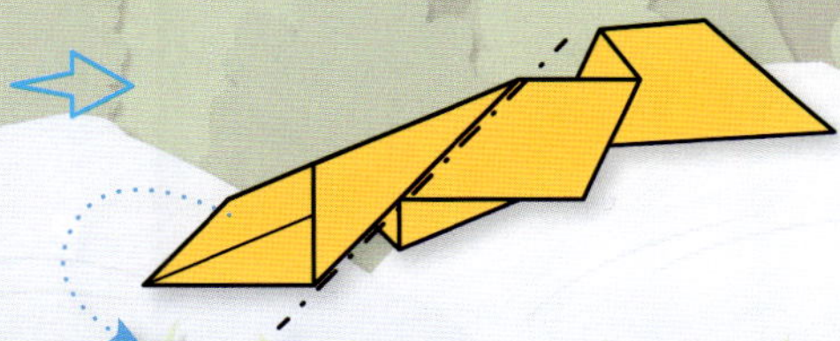

62 Pinch the left side and gently twist the inner layer down along the dotted fold line.

63 Fold the bottom corner up.

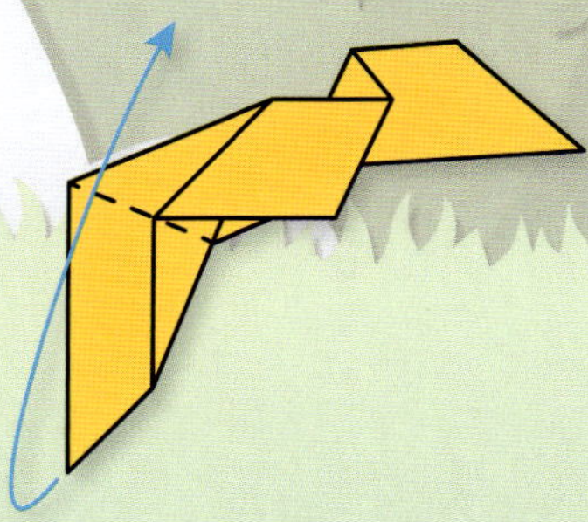

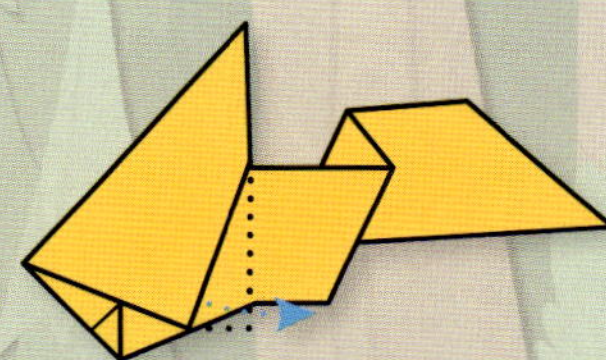

64 Gently pull out a portion of the hidden corner from behind the flap to round out the arm.

65 Fold the top corner of the flap back behind the edge.

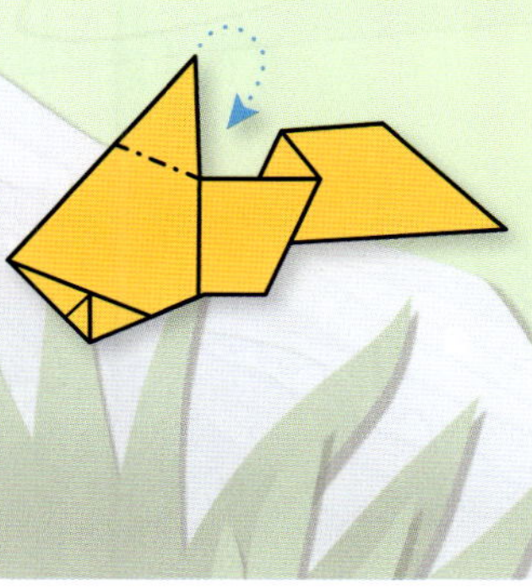

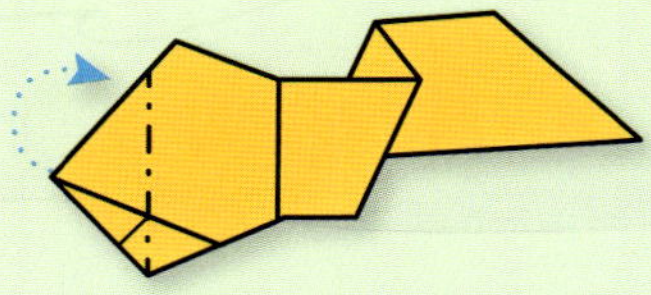

66 Fold the left corner of the flap back behind the edge.

67 Fold the corners back to shape.

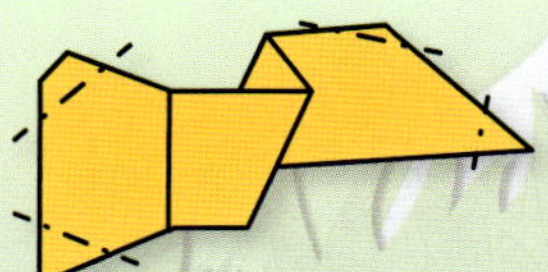

68 Pikachu's arms are complete.

Folding the Tail

Make sure to start with the triangle template arranged so the asterisk is at the top.

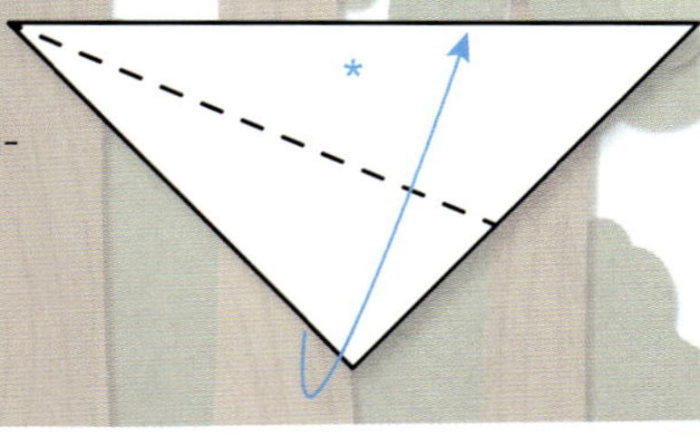

69 Fold the bottom-left edge up to the top edge.

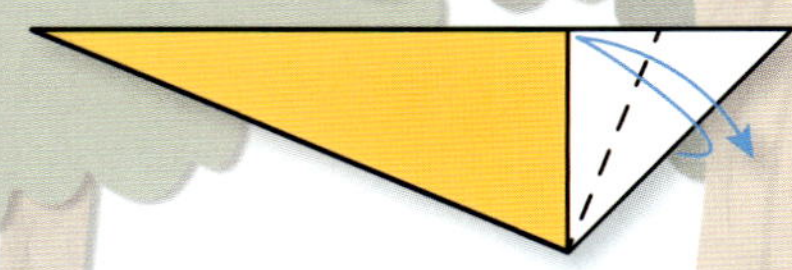

70 Fold the right corner in, then unfold.

71 Fold the right corner in along the edge.

72 Fold the right corner in again.

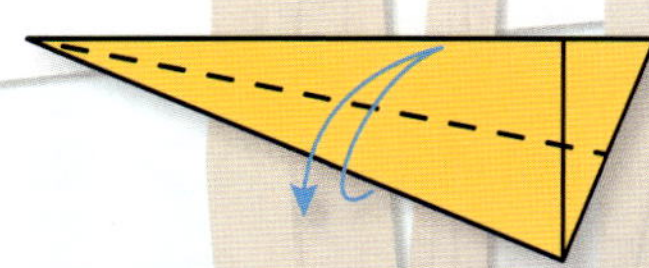

73 Fold the top edge down to the bottom edge, then unfold.

74 Fold the left corner in about one-third of the way along the crease.

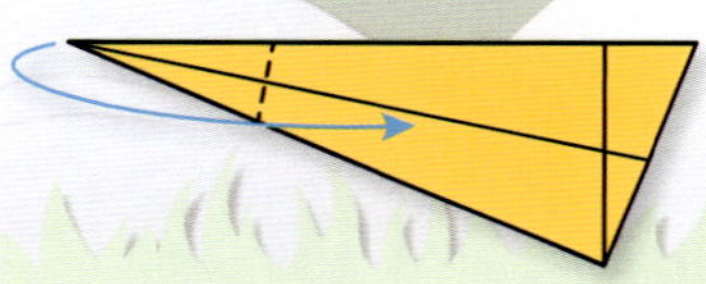

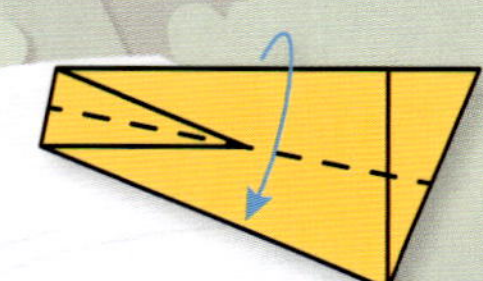

75 Fold the top edge down to the bottom edge.

76 Fold the right edge over along the top edge, a little more than halfway.

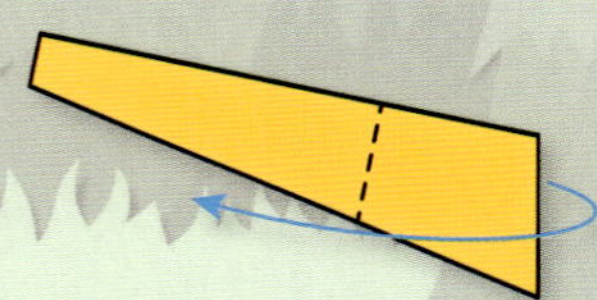

77 Fold the bottom-right corner up to the top edge, then unfold.

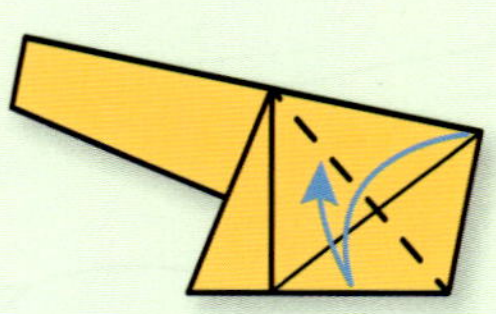

78 Fold the top-right corner down to the bottom edge, then unfold.

79 Pinch the top and bottom of the flap together as you fold up to the right.

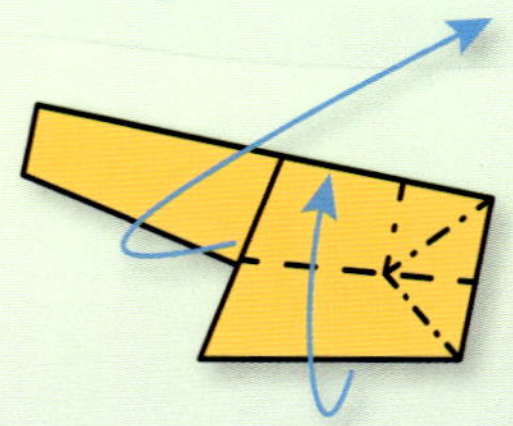

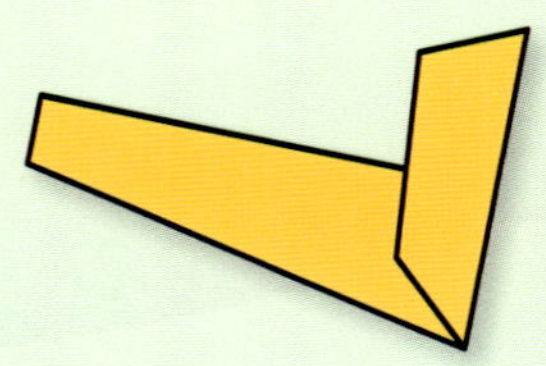

80 Rotate the paper counterclockwise.

81 Gently pull out some of the hidden layer from behind the bottom edge.

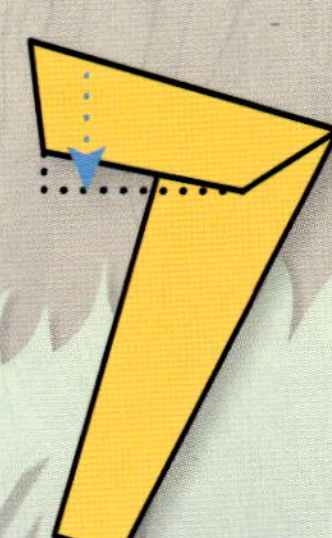

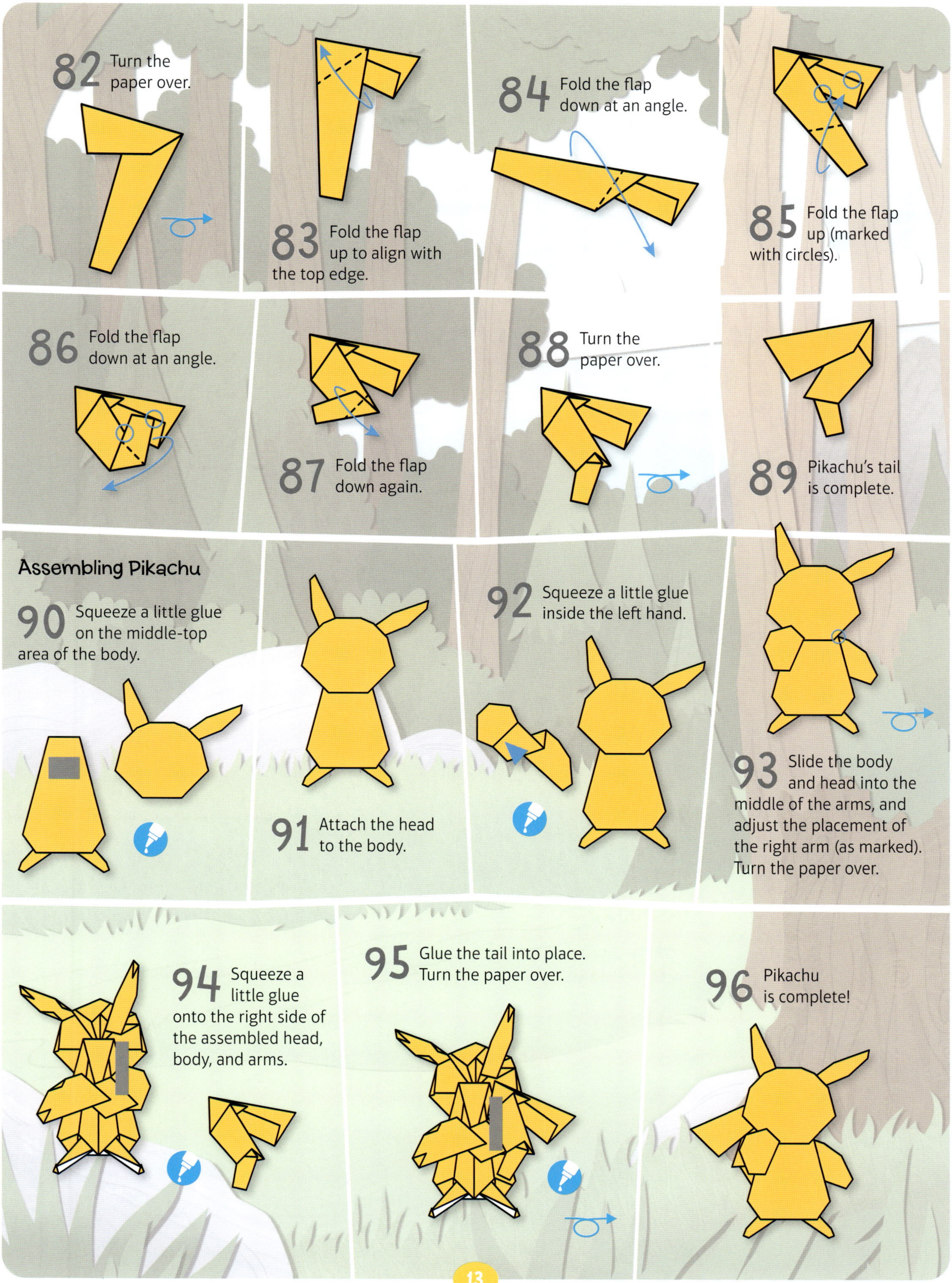
82 Turn the paper over.
83 Fold the flap up to align with the top edge.
84 Fold the flap down at an angle.
85 Fold the flap up (marked with circles).
86 Fold the flap down at an angle.
87 Fold the flap down again.
88 Turn the paper over.
89 Pikachu's tail is complete.
Assembling Pikachu
90 Squeeze a little glue on the middle-top area of the body.
91 Attach the head to the body.
92 Squeeze a little glue inside the left hand.
93 Slide the body and head into the middle of the arms, and adjust the placement of the right arm (as marked). Turn the paper over.
94 Squeeze a little glue onto the right side of the assembled head, body, and arms.
95 Glue the tail into place. Turn the paper over.
96 Pikachu is complete!

Snorlax

Gentle Snorlax loves nothing more than napping—except for filling its large belly with food. It spends most of its day eating and sleeping the hours away. Can you fold Snorlax into shape before it falls asleep?

TYPE: Normal **HEIGHT:** 6'11" / 2.1 m **WEIGHT:** 1014.1 lbs. / 460 kg

INTERMEDIATE

How To Make Snorlax

Snorlax is folded from four pieces of paper: three large squares that become its belly, feet, and arms; and one medium square that becomes its head. You can find the templates on pages 61, 65, and 69. Carefully cut out each of the pieces.

Folding the Head

Make sure to start with the small square template arranged so the asterisk is at the top.

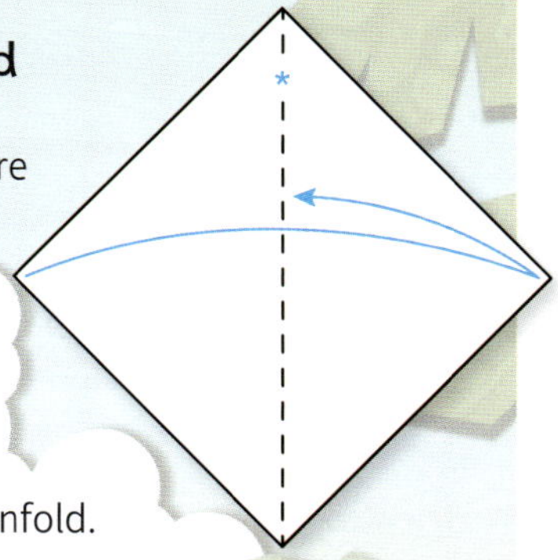

1 Fold in half sideways, then unfold.

2 Fold the left and right corners into the centerline.

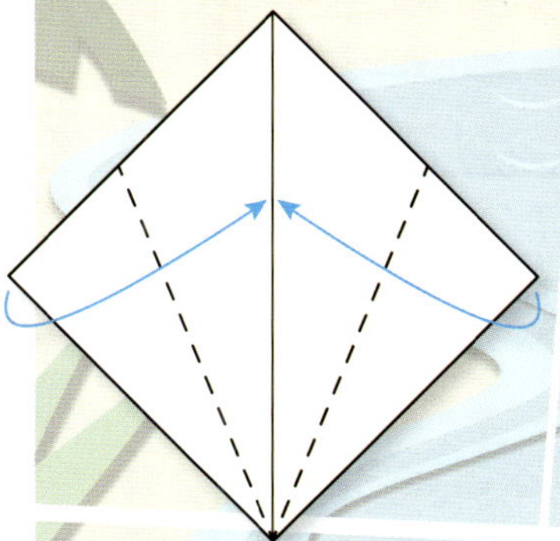

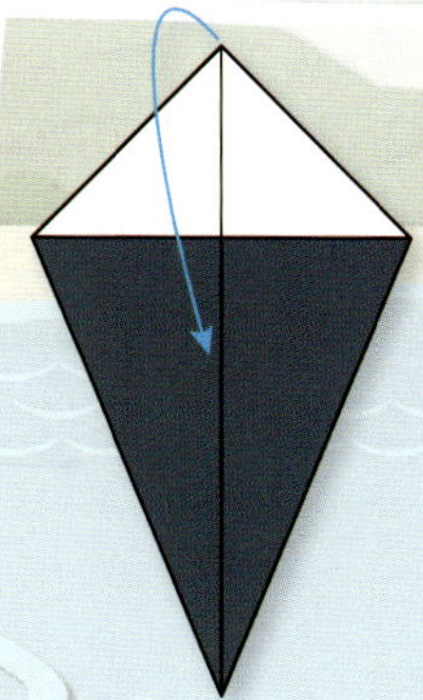

3 Fold the top corner down.

4 Fold the corner back up to the top edge.

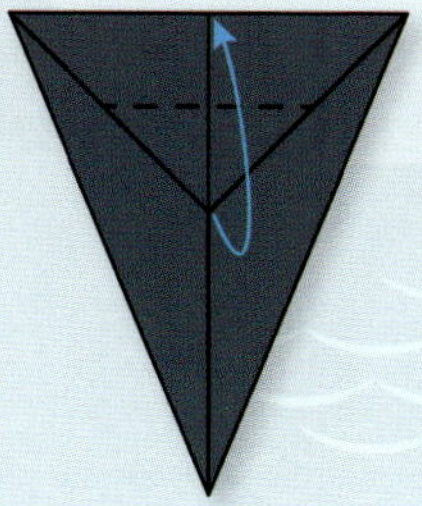

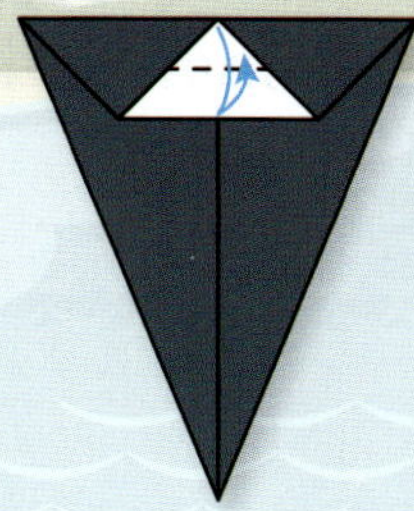

5 Fold the top corner down, then unfold.

6 Fold the top corner down to the crease.

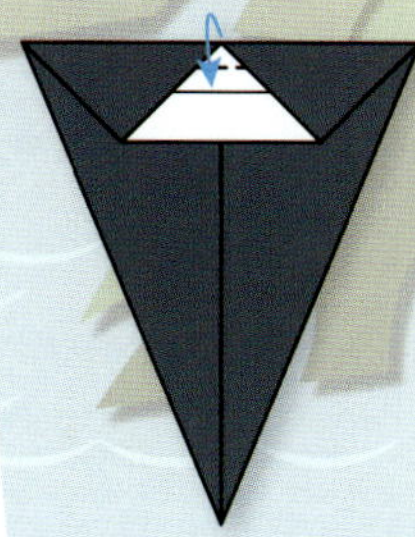

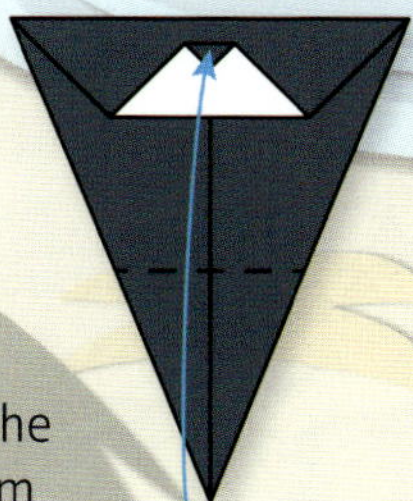

7 Fold the bottom corner up to the top of the small triangle.

8 Fold the top corners in to align with the corners of the small triangle (marked with circles).

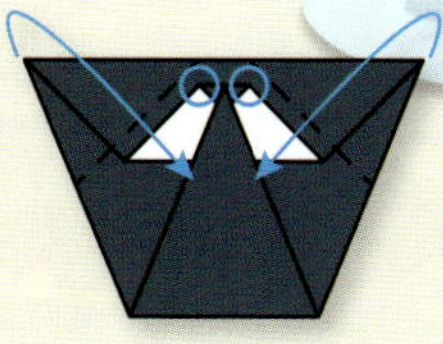

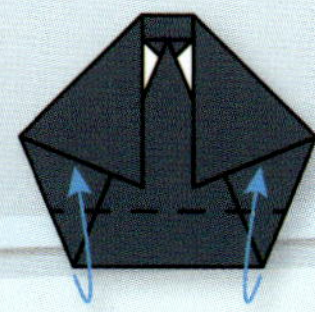

9 Fold the bottom edge up to lie along the edges (see next step).

10 The result should look like this (see image). Then unfold the bottom edge.

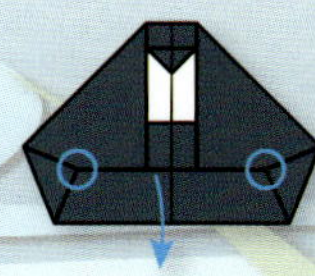

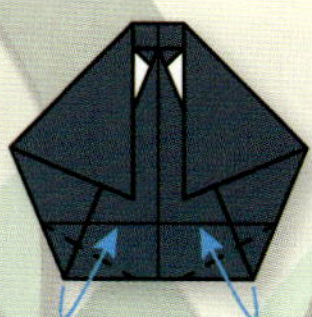

11 Fold the bottom corners into the crease.

12 Unfold the top flaps.

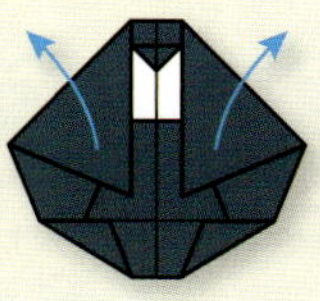

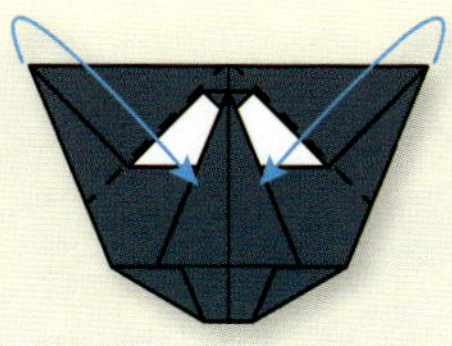

13 Fold the top corners into the centerline.

14 Fold the flaps out (as marked). Turn over to position the ears correctly.

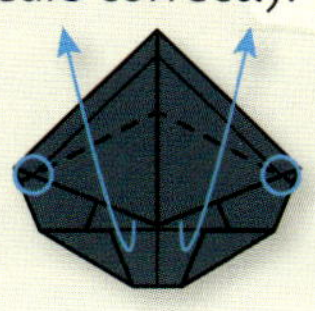

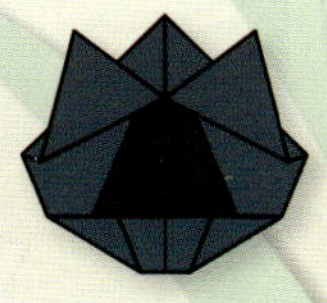

15 Tuck the shaded area under the flap beneath it.

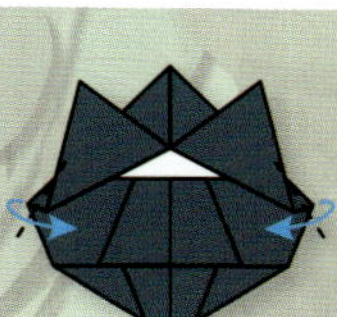

16 Fold the left and right corners in slightly.

17 To round the head, fold the right side of the top corner down first, and then flatten the left side down to the right (paper will be thick).

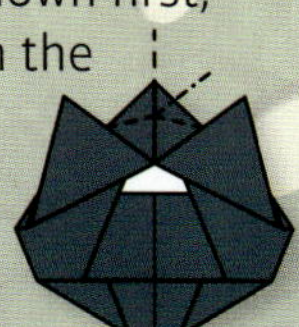

18 Turn the paper over.

19 Snorlax's head is complete!

Folding the Belly

Make sure to start with the large square template arranged so the asterisk is at the top.

20 Fold in half sideways, then unfold.

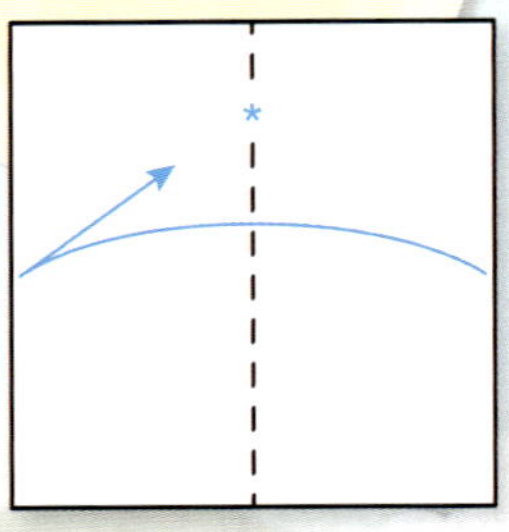

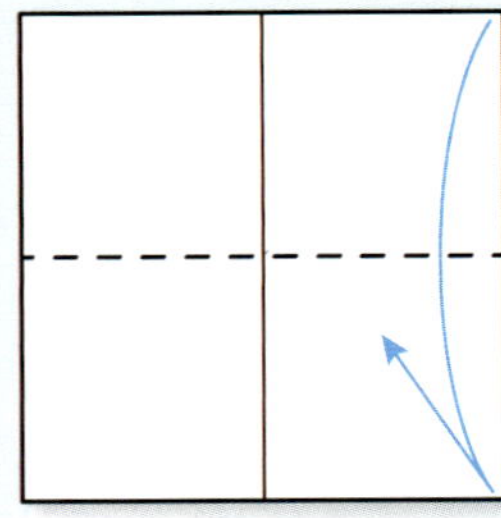

21 Fold in half from top to bottom, then unfold.

22 Fold the left and right edges into the centerline, then unfold.

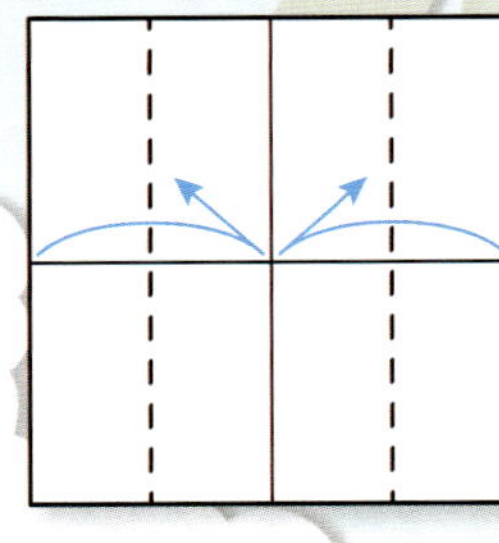

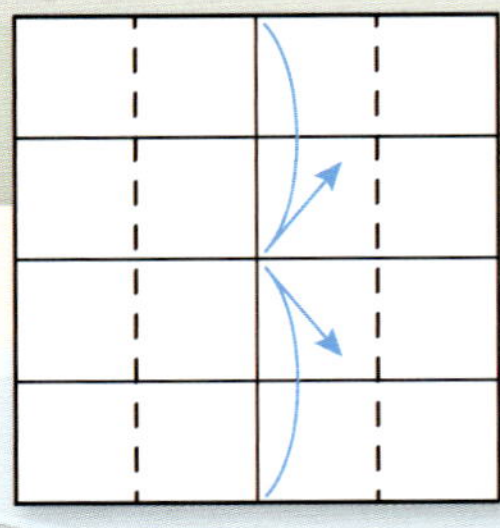

23 Fold the top and bottom edges into the centerline, then unfold.

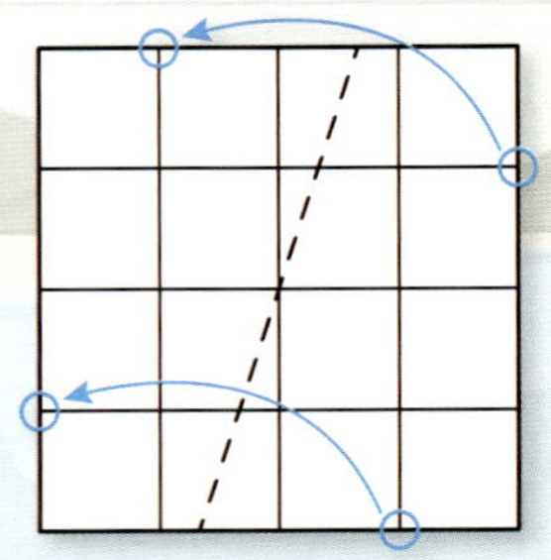

24 Fold the right edge over to the left—matching the circles as marked.

25 The result should look like this, then unfold.

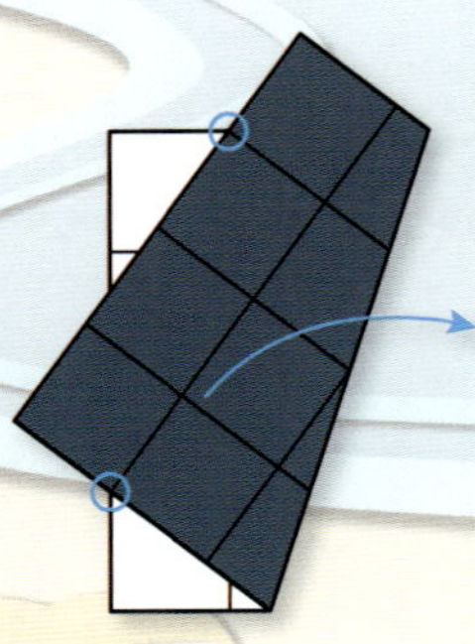

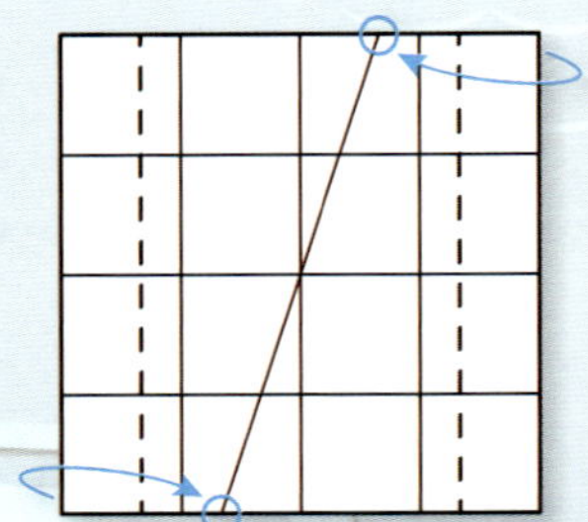

26 Fold the left and right edges into the crease.

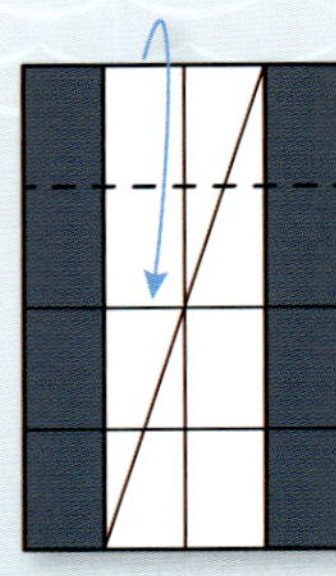

27 Fold the top edge down to the centerline.

28 Fold the top edge down to the bottom of the flap, then unfold.

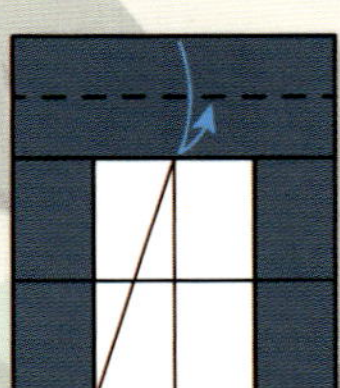

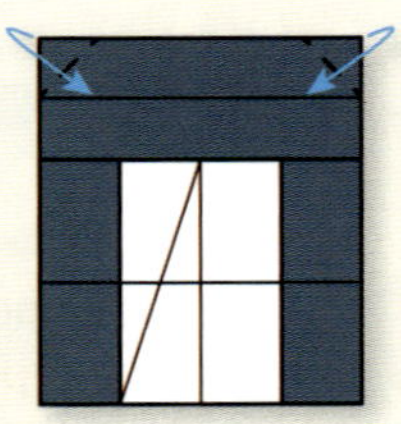

29 Fold the top corners to the crease.

30 Fold the bottom edge up to the crease.

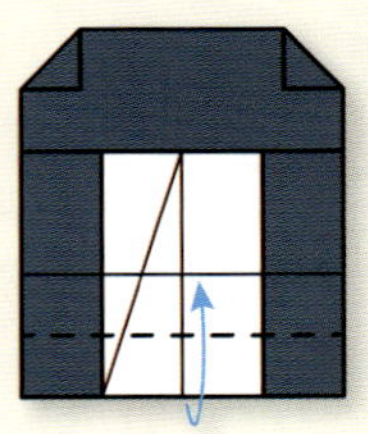

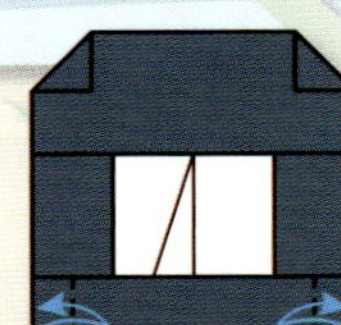

31 Fold the bottom corners in to create a crease (as shown), then unfold.

32 Fold the bottom corners through the crease (as shown).

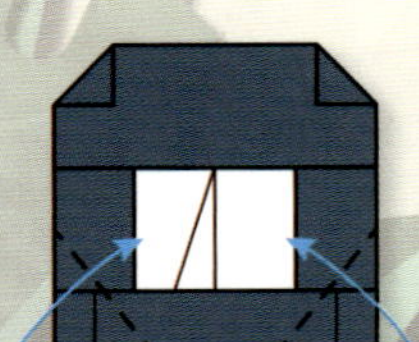

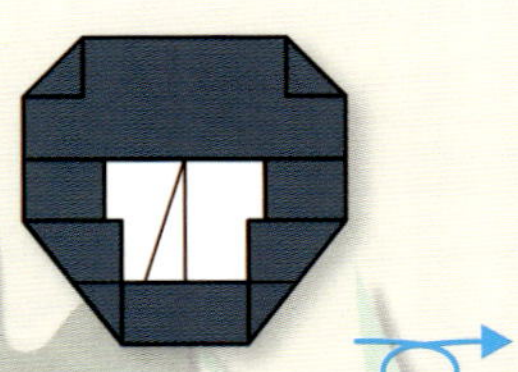

33 Turn the paper over.

34 Snorlax's belly is complete!

Folding the Arms

Make sure to start with the large square template arranged so the asterisk is at the top.

35 Fold in half along both diagonal lines, then unfold.

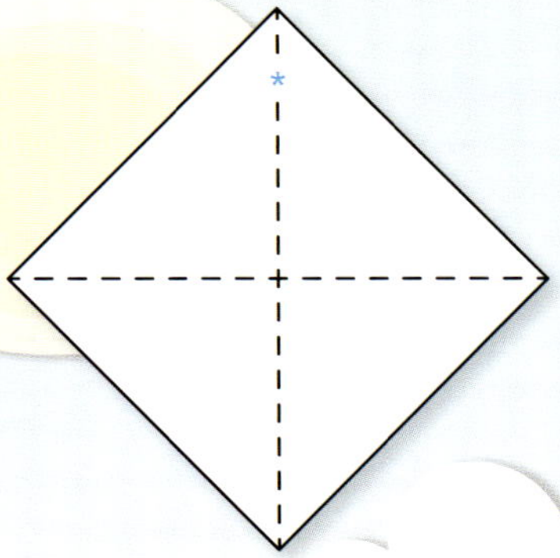

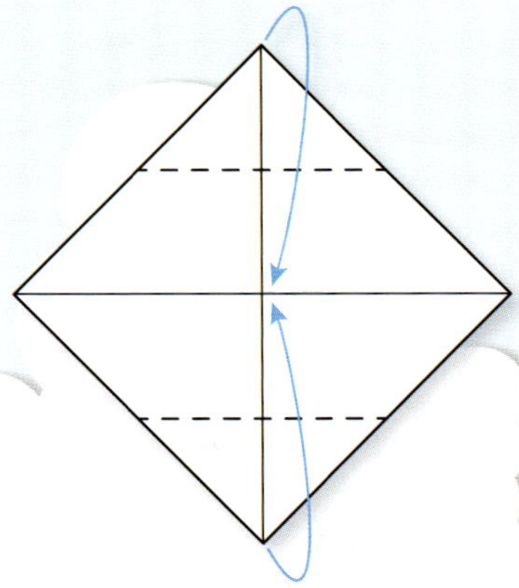

36 Fold the top and bottom corners into the center.

37 Fold the top and bottom edges into the center, then unfold.

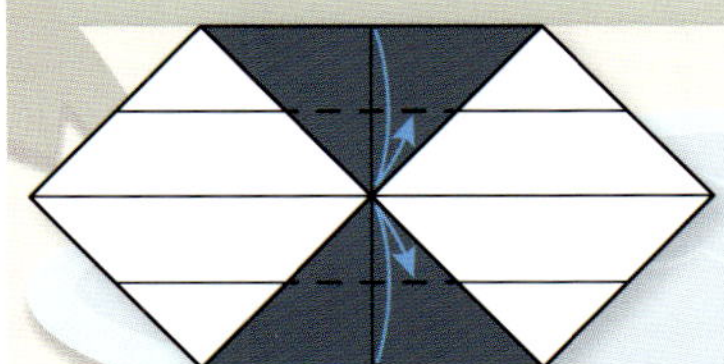

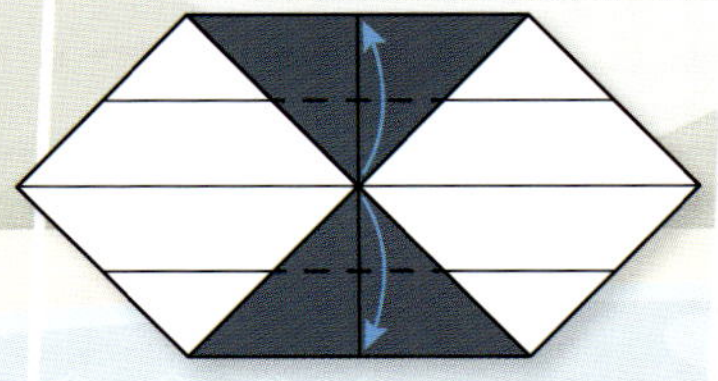

38 Fold the corners out to the edges.

39 Fold the bottom corners in (marked with circles).

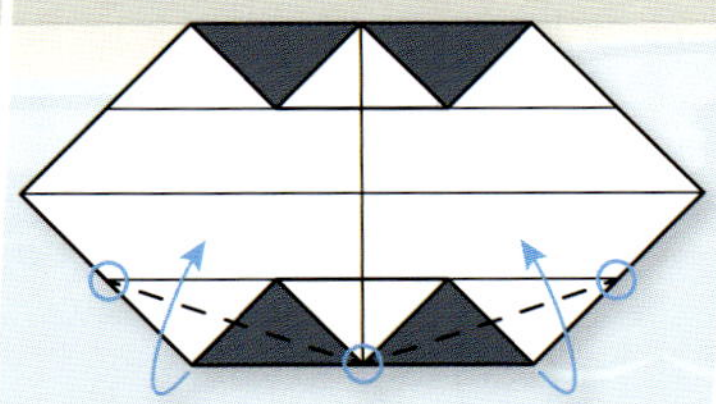

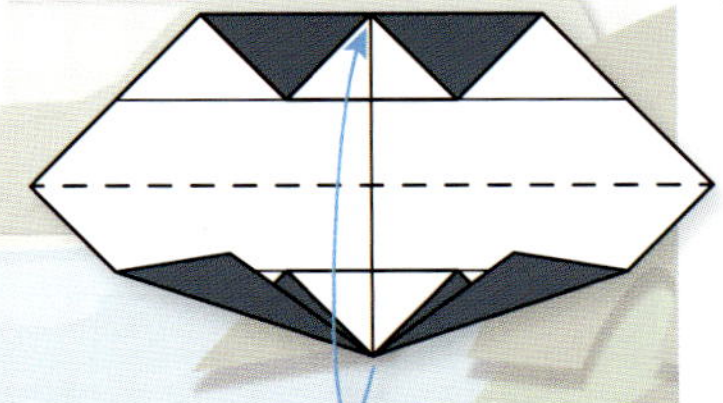

40 Fold the bottom edge up to the top edge.

41 Fold the right corner in.

42 Open the corner and flatten into a square.

43 Fold the left corner in, then unfold.

44 Fold the corner to the crease.

45 Fold the top-right corner down along the edge.

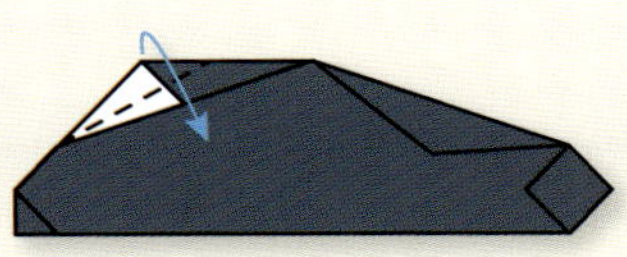

46 Fold the left corner down (as shown).

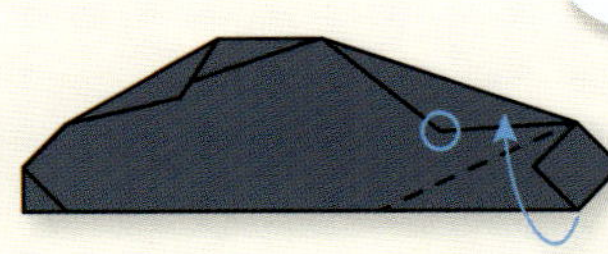

47 Fold the bottom-right corner up to cover the corner of the flap above (as marked).

48 Turn the paper over.

49 Fold the left corner in along the bottom edge (as shown).

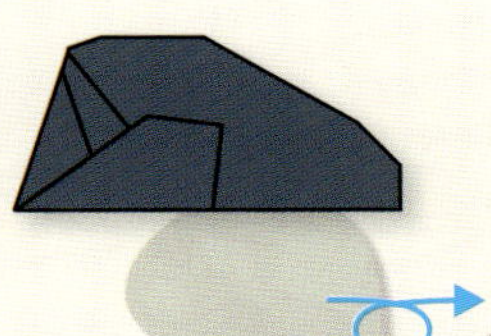

50 Turn the paper over.

51 Fold the flap forward along the dotted line (as shown).

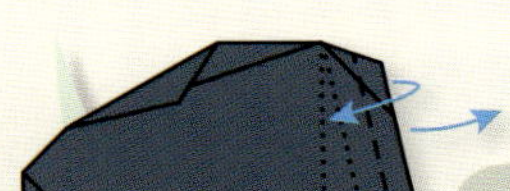

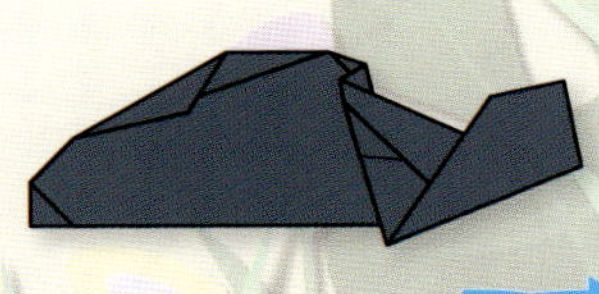

52 Turn the paper over.

53 Fold the right corner to the left along the centerline.

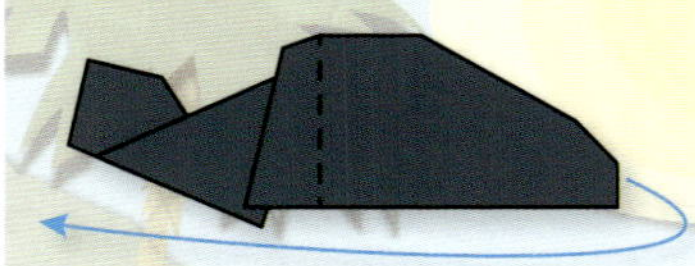

54 Fold the flap to the right along the edge behind.

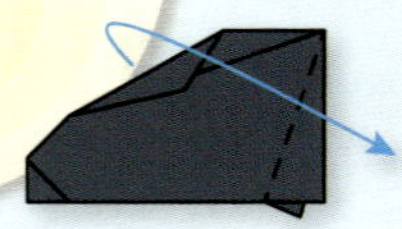

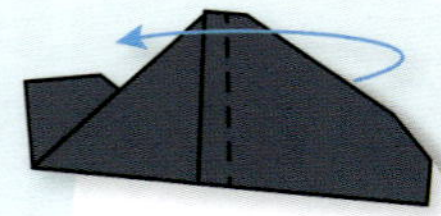

55 Fold the flap to the left along the first edge beneath (from Step 53), creating an accordion.

56 Fold the accordion open along the middle layer.

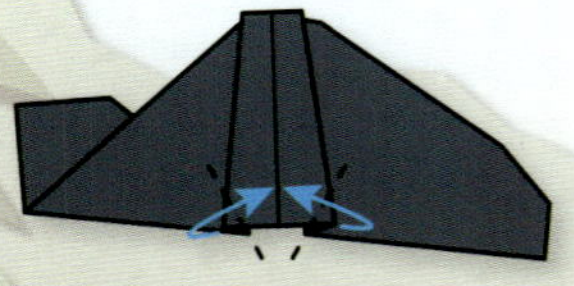

57 Fold the bottom center corners in, then unfold.

58 Reverse fold the corners inside out.

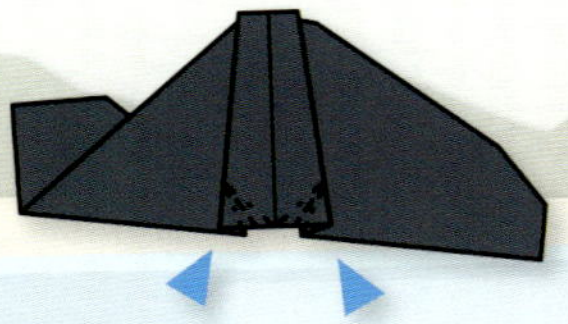

59 The result should look like this, then turn the paper over.

60 Unfold the bottom-right flap.

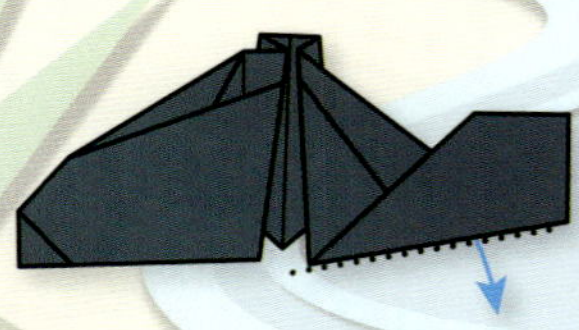

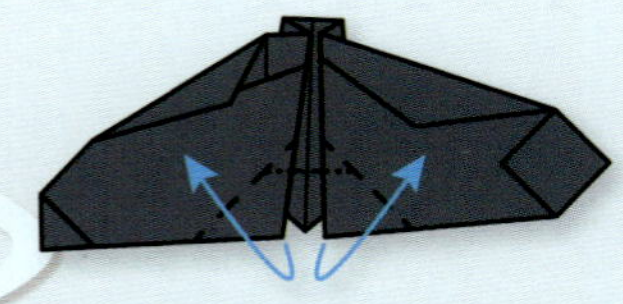

61 Fold the bottom-center corners outward (the center will pop up).

62 After folding open both corners, gently flatten on each side to create the square shape below.

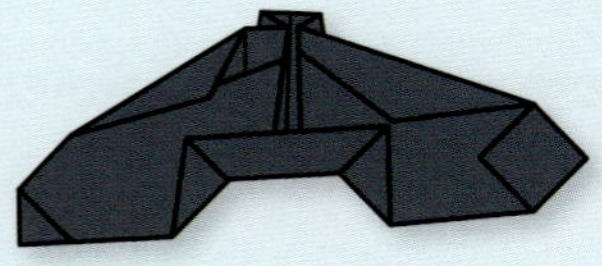

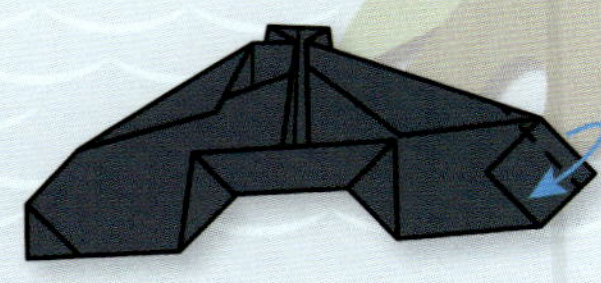

63 Fold the top right edge in.

64 Fold the right edge in. Turn the paper over.

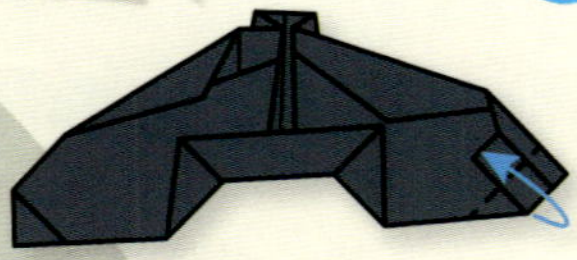

65 Fold the corners back slightly to round them.

66 Snorlax's arms are complete!

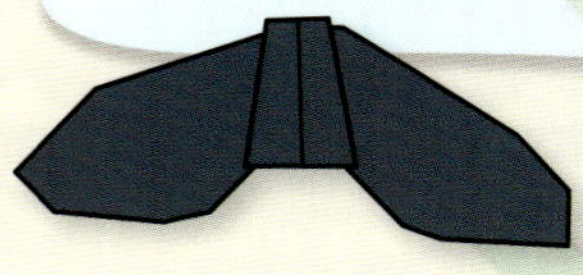

Folding the Feet

Make sure to start with the large square template arranged so the asterisk is at the top.

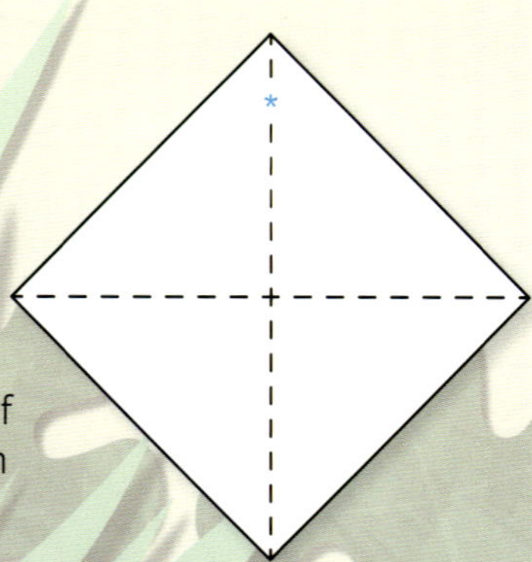

67 Fold in half along both diagonal lines, then unfold.

68 Fold the top and bottom corners into the center.

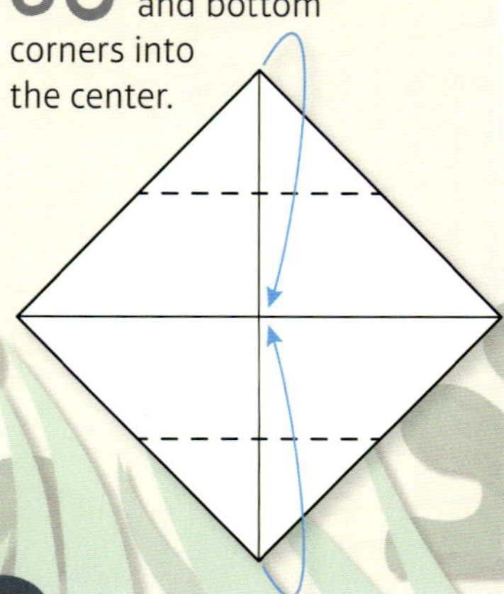

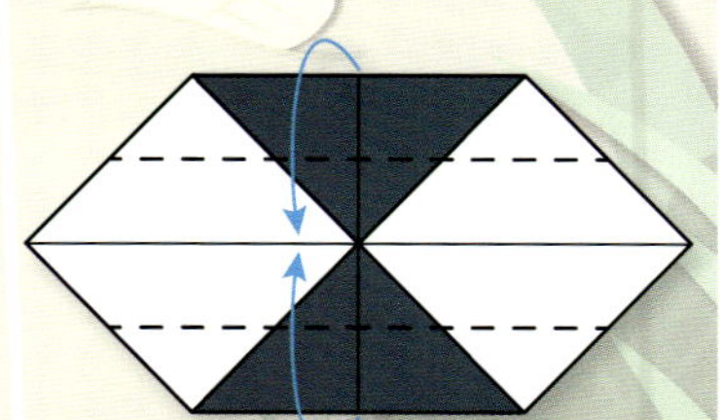

69 Fold the top and bottom edges into the center.

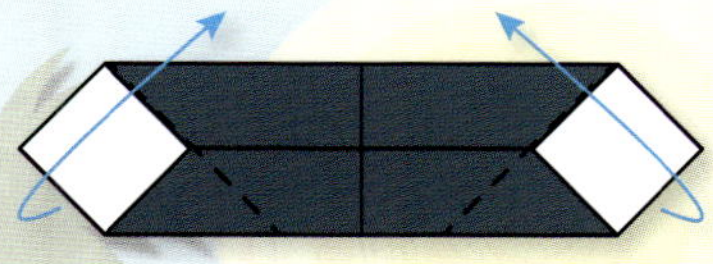

70 Fold the bottom-left and bottom-right edges up.

71 Turn the paper over.

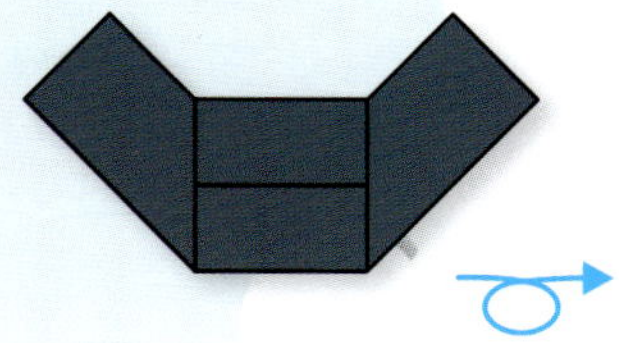

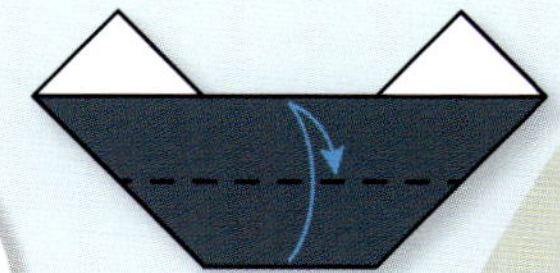

72 Fold the bottom edge up to the top edge, then unfold.

73 Fold the top corners down.

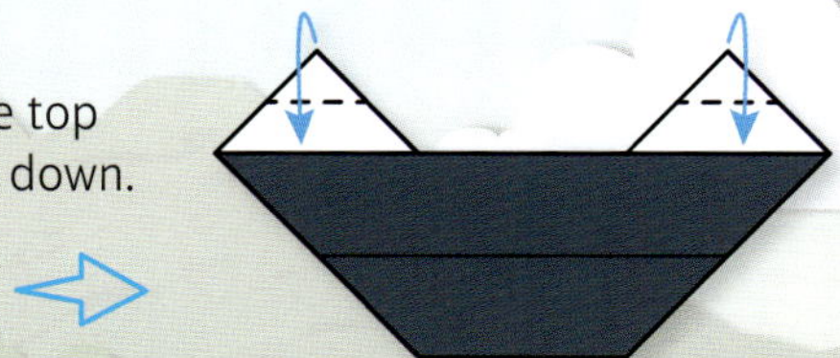

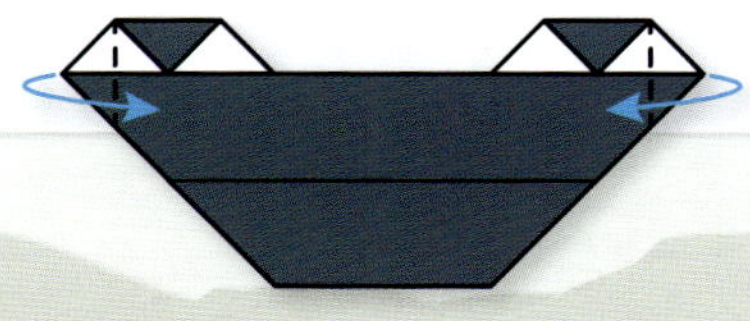

74 Fold the corners in.

75 Fold the top corners down.

76 Turn the paper over.

77 Snorlax's feet are complete.

Assembling Snorlax

78 Squeeze a little glue on the top-middle area of the arms.

79 Attach the head to the arms (as shown), careful to align the belly lines.

80 Squeeze a little glue on the middle area of the feet.

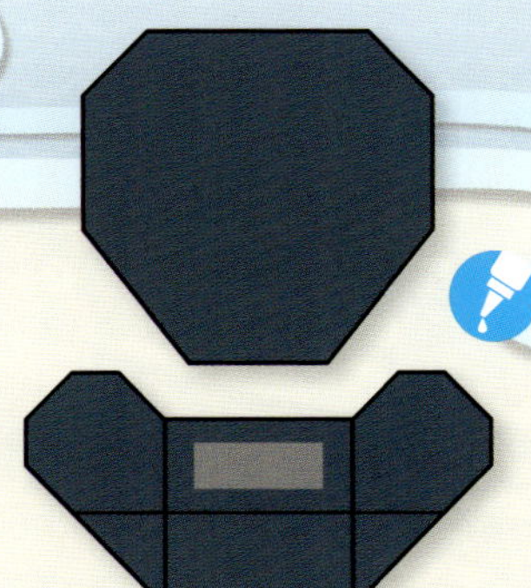

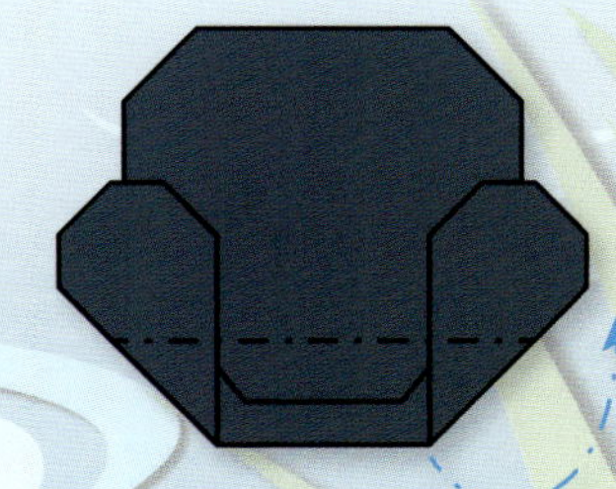

81 Slide the belly between the feet. Align and glue the feet in place. Fold the bottom edge to the back, along the crease.

82 Turn the paper over.

83 Squeeze a little glue on the middle area of the head and arms.

84 Attach the head and arms to the belly (as shown), careful to align the belly lines.

85 Snorlax is complete!

Larvitar

Born underground, Larvitar feeds on soil. Its green, rocky skin and spike on the top of its head can make for some tricky folds—but also a great choice for origami.

TYPE: Rock / Ground **HEIGHT:** 2' / .6 m **WEIGHT:** 158.7 lbs. / 72 kg

ADVANCED

How To Make Larvitar

Larvitar is folded from two pieces of paper: one large square and one small square. The large square becomes its body and right foot, and the small square becomes its tail and left foot. You can find the templates on pages 73 and 85. Carefully cut out each of the pieces.

Folding the Body & Right Foot

Make sure to start with the large square template face-up—with the eye at the top.

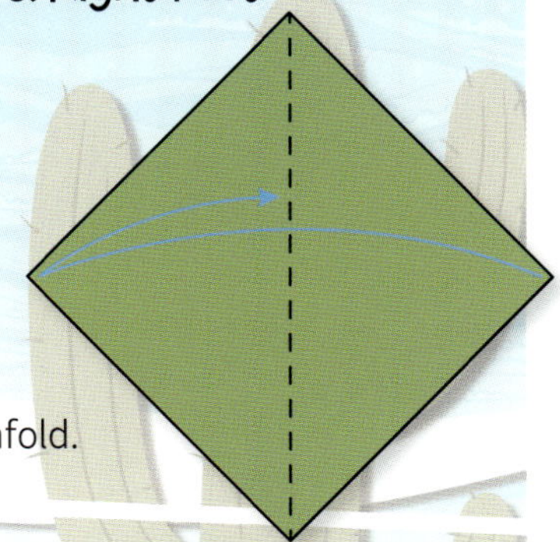

1 Fold in half sideways, then unfold.

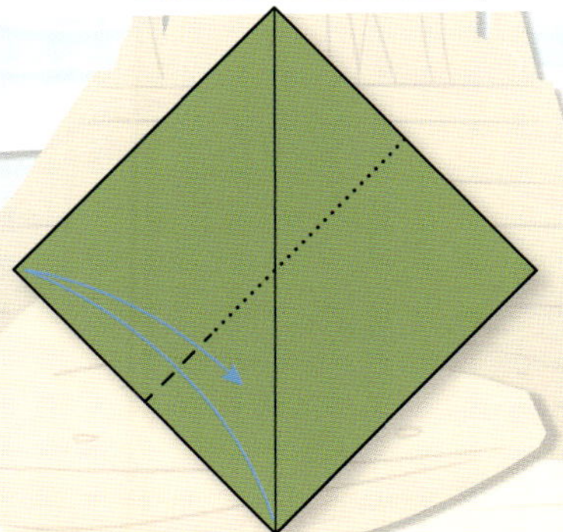

2 Fold the top-left edge down to bottom-right edge. Create a reference point by making a crease at the bottom edge, then unfold.

3 Crease at the one-fourth mark.

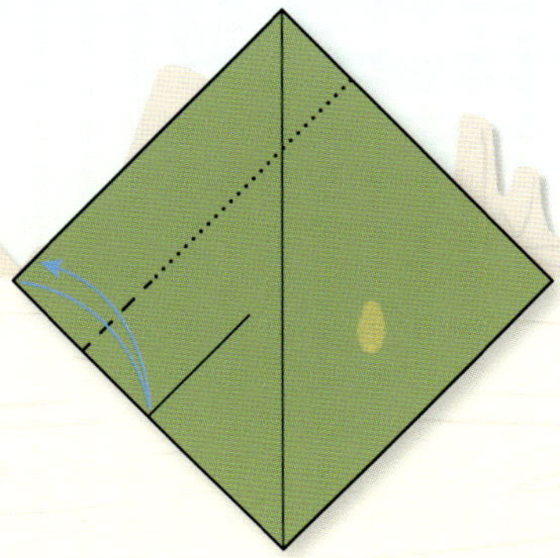

4 Crease at the one-eighth mark.

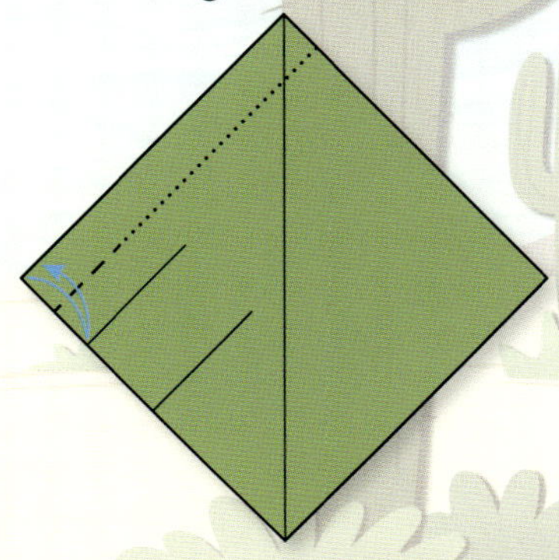

5 Fold at the three-fourths mark and crease to the centerline.

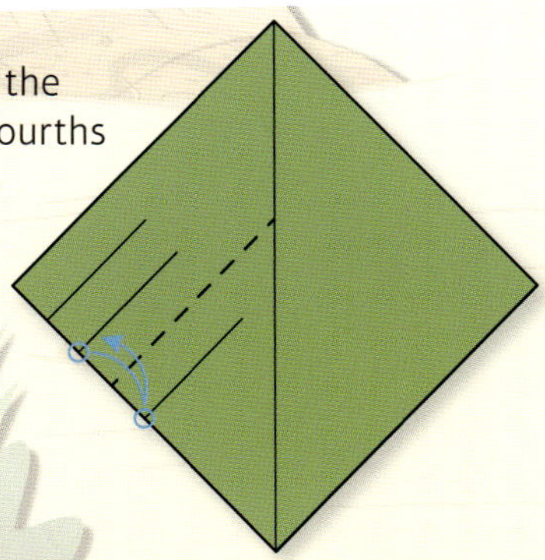

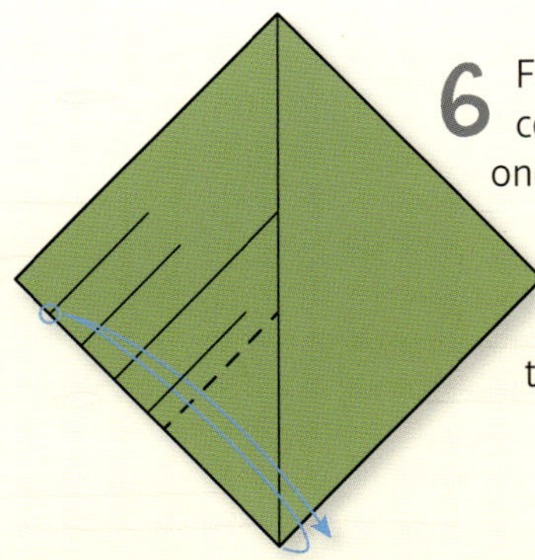

6 Fold the bottom corner to the one-eighth mark and crease to the centerline, then unfold.

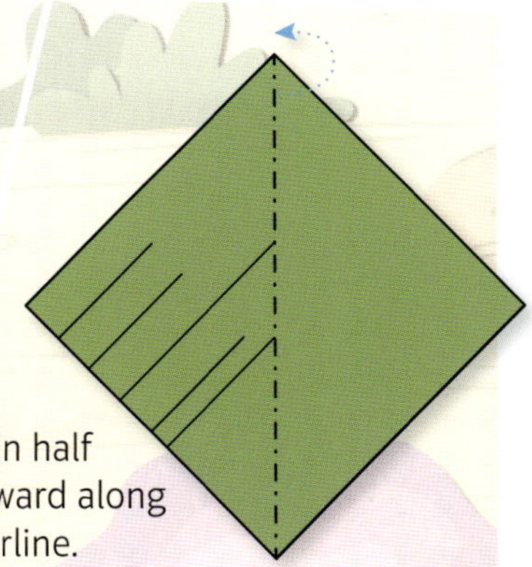

7 Fold in half backward along the centerline.

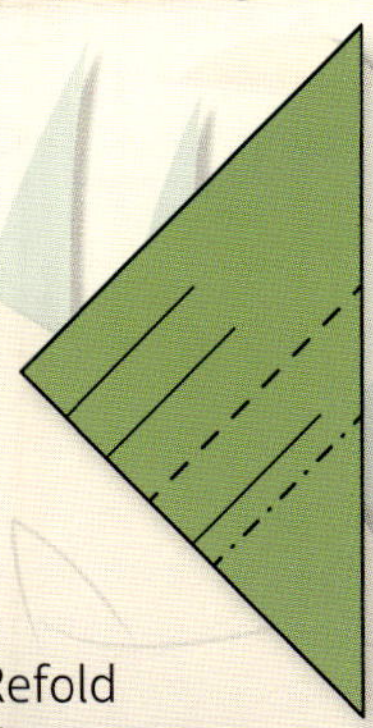

8 Refold the creases from Steps 5 and 6 through both layers of paper.

9 Reverse fold along the creases, so the triangle extends out from inside the shape.

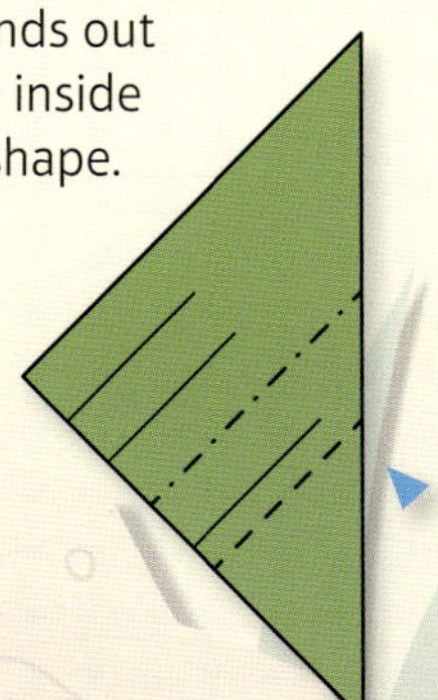

10 Turn the paper over.

11 Fold the top-right corner behind.

12 Fold the right corner down, then unfold.

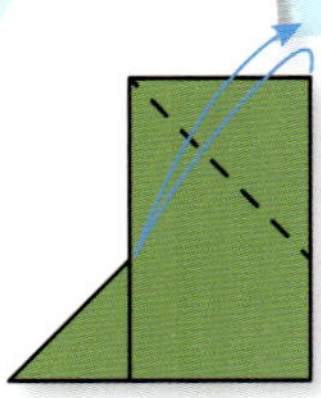

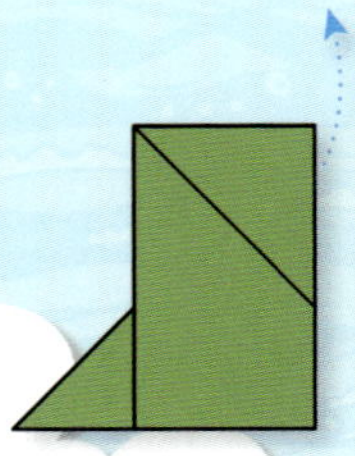

13 Unfold the flap.

14 Open the flap and flatten it into a square.

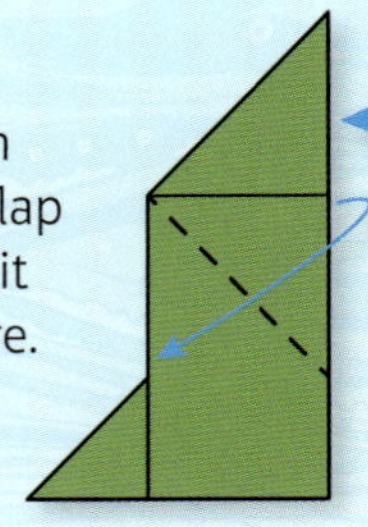

15 Fold the edges into the centerline, then unfold.

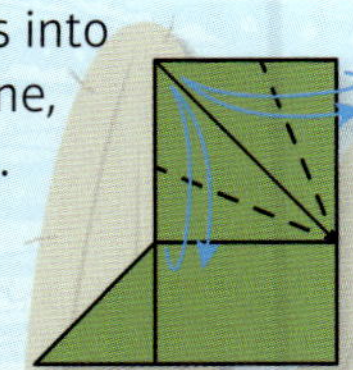

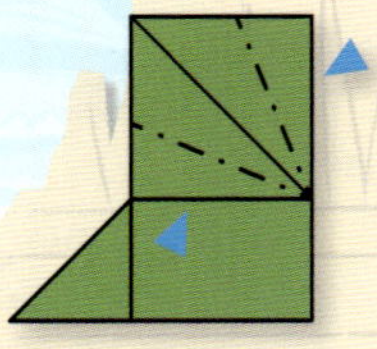

16 Reverse fold the corners inside the square.

17 Lift the flap as you fold it along the centerline, closing up the flap to the right.

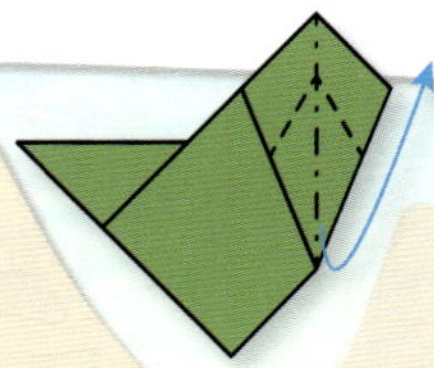

18 Rotate the paper so the spike points up.

19 Open up the back layers to the middle (as shown), and swing open the right layers to the front. Carefully flatten so the edges align.

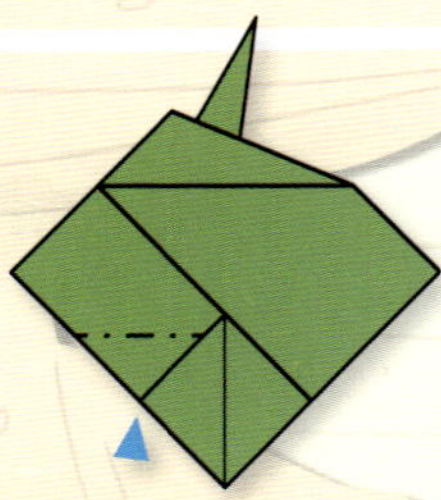

20 Fold the triangle up so the belly aligns underneath, and then reverse fold the triangle inside (as marked).

21 Fold the top-left flap in along the hinge.

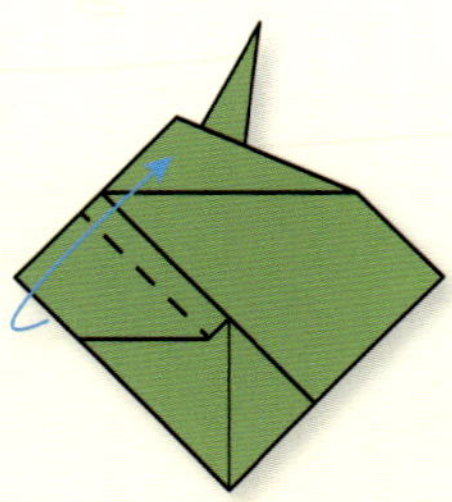

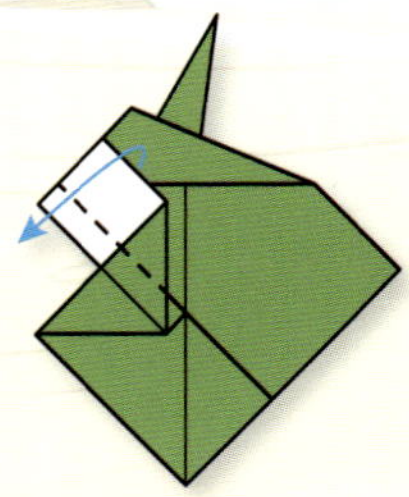

22 Fold the flap back down along the edge behind it, careful to align the belly.

23 Turn the paper over.

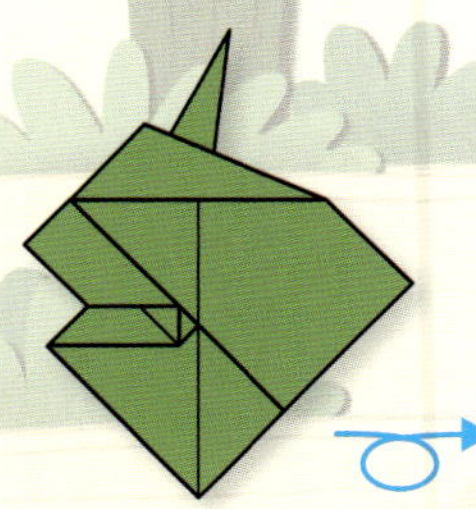

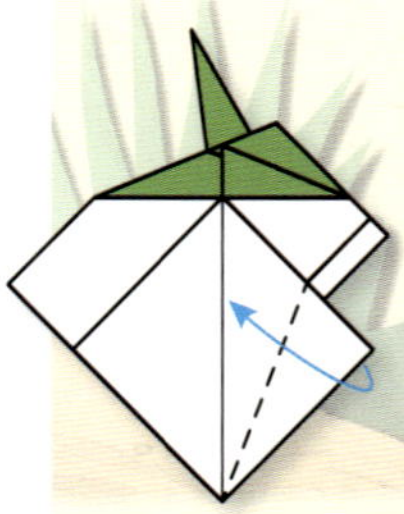

24 Fold the lower-right corner into the centerline.

25 Fold out the top corner of the flap along the edge above (turn over to check the belly is aligned).

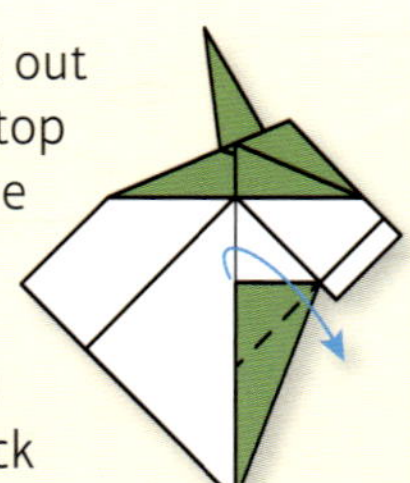

26 Gently pull out the layer of paper from behind the flap. Again, check the belly is aligned on the opposite side.

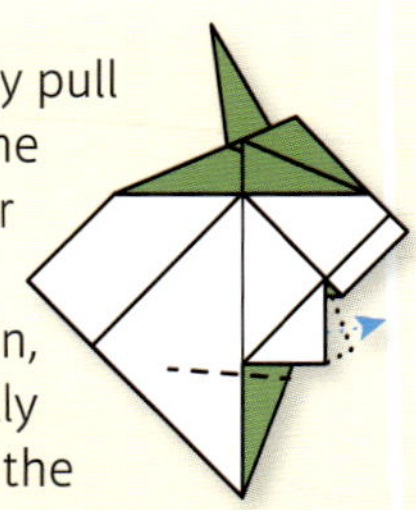

27 Fold the right corner in.

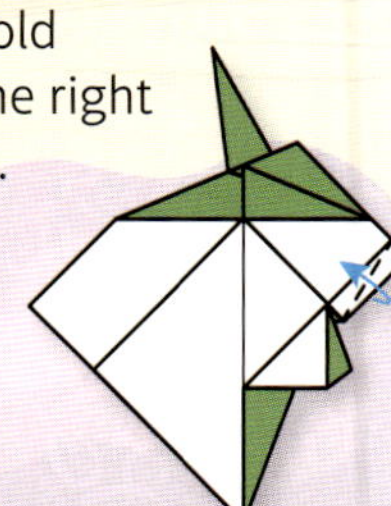

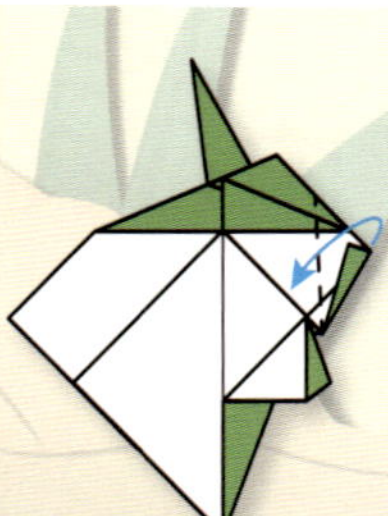

28 Fold the right corner in, along the folded edge.

29 Fold the corner in (as marked), leaving some space at the bottom-right corner (as marked).

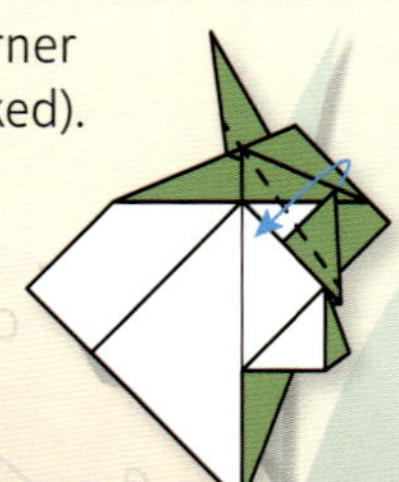

30 Fold up the flap (as shown). Check that the belly aligns on the opposite side.

31 Fold in the corner above to round the belly.

32 Fold the left edge into the centerline.

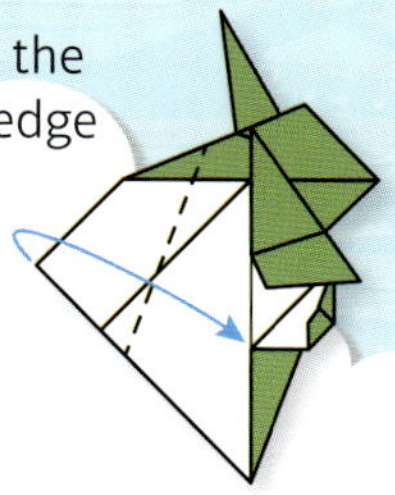

33 Fold the bottom-left corner in, then unfold.

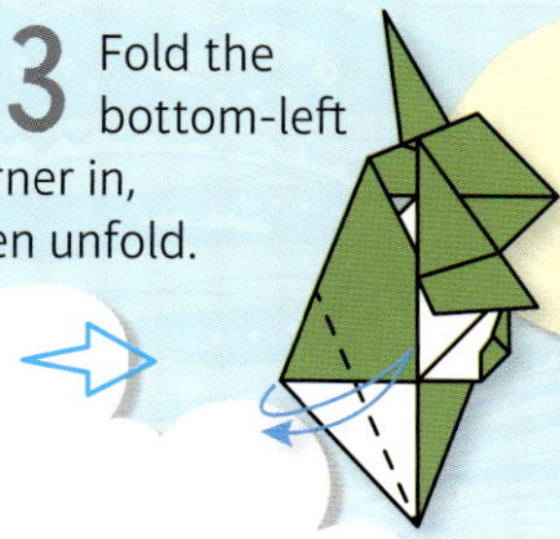

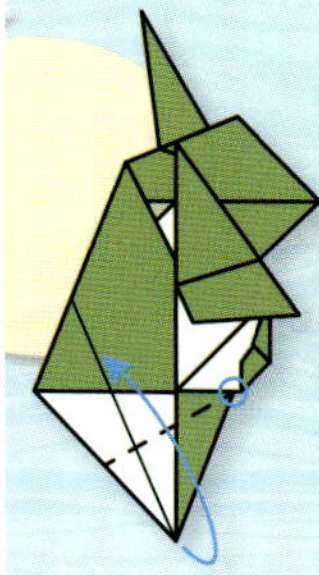

34 Fold the bottom corner in to lie on the crease.

35 Fold the flap down, parallel to the edge above.

36 Reverse fold the right corner inside slightly (as shown) and flatten.

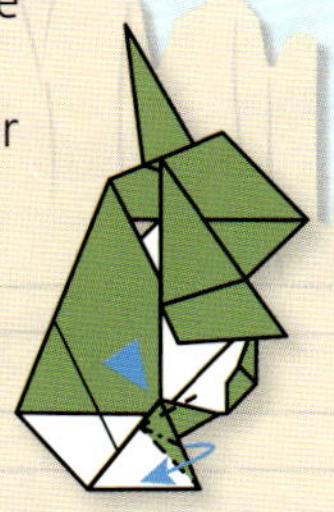

37 Fold the left corner in.

38 Fold the bottom-left corner in to make the foot.

39 Turn the paper over.

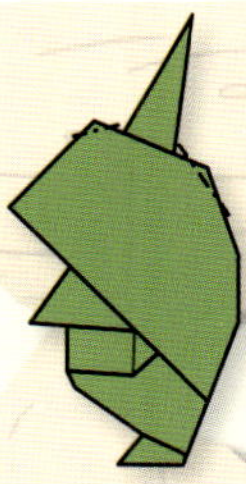

40 Fold the top-left and top-right corners back to round the head (will be thick).

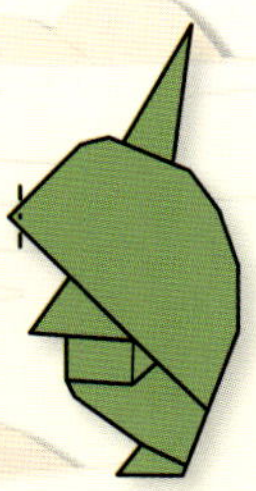

41 Fold the left corner back behind—to round the nose.

42 Reverse fold the tip of the horn.

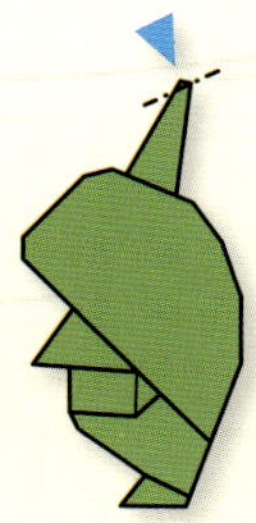

43 Reverse fold the tip again, so it slants.

44 Larvitar's body and right foot are complete.

Folding the Tail & Left Foot

Make sure to start with the small square template arranged so the asterisk is at the top.

45 Fold in half sideways, then unfold.

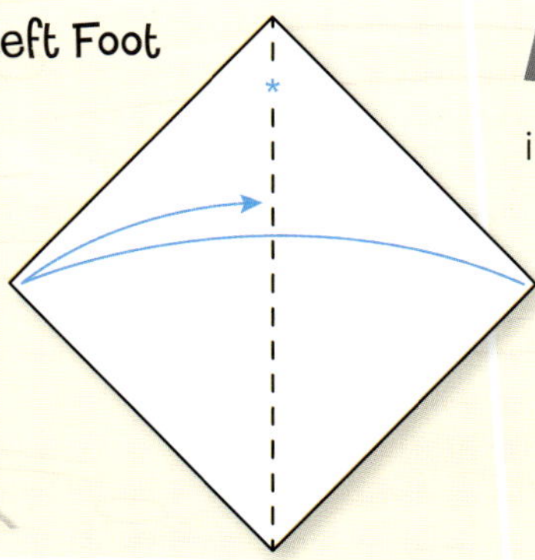

46 Fold left and right corners into the centerline.

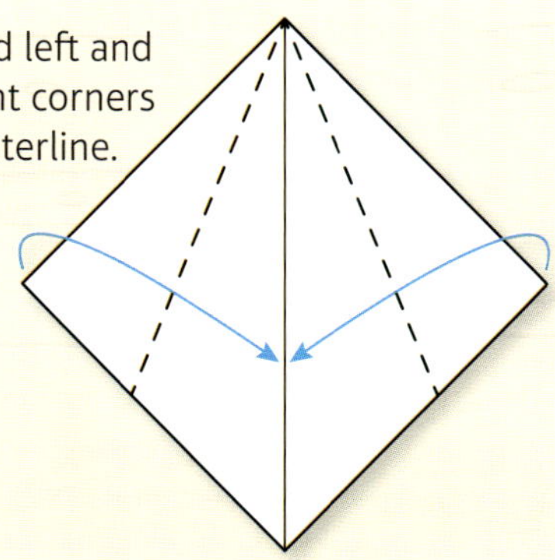

47 Turn the paper over.

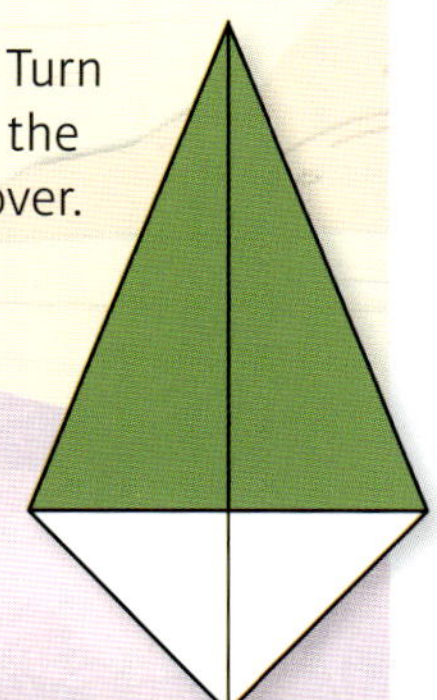

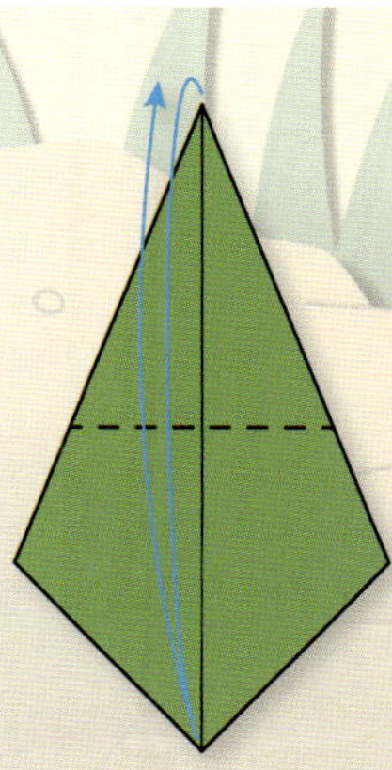

48 Fold the top corner down to the bottom corner, then unfold.

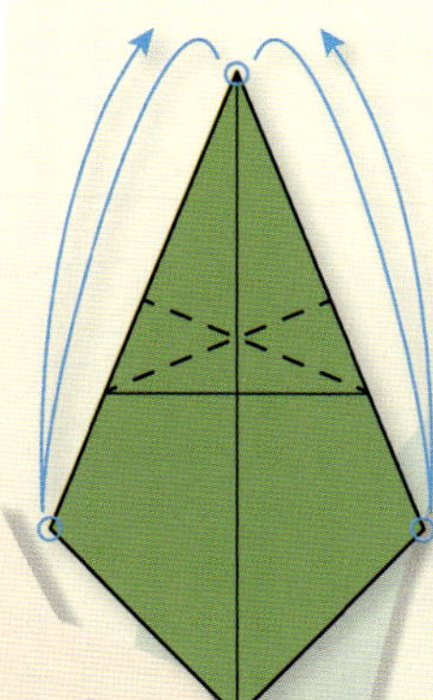

49 Fold the top corner down to the right and left corners, then unfold.

50 Turn the paper over.

51 Fold open the left flap, so the edge lies along the crease.

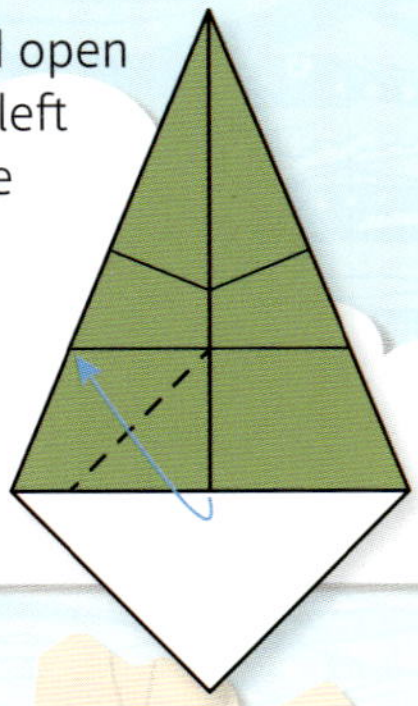

52 Fold the bottom-right edge up along the edge of the flap, then unfold.

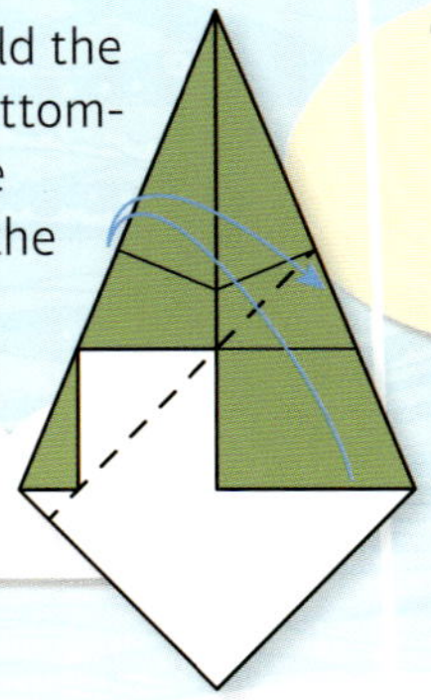

53 Fold open the right flap, so the edge lies along the crease.

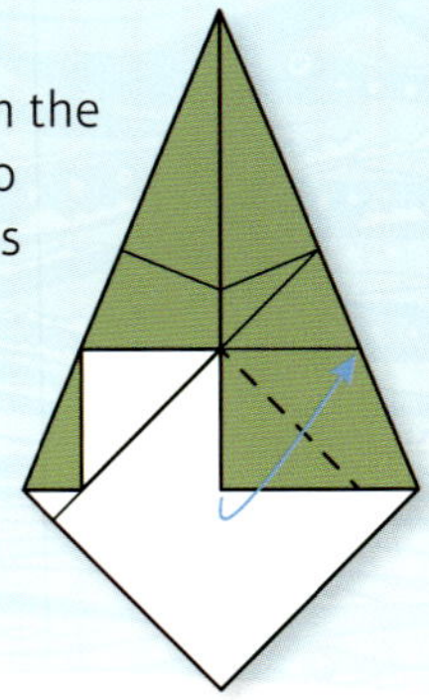

54 Fold the bottom-left edge up along the edge of the flap, then unfold.

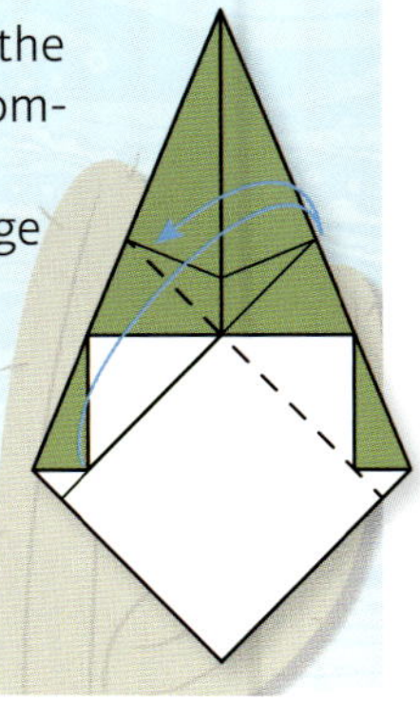

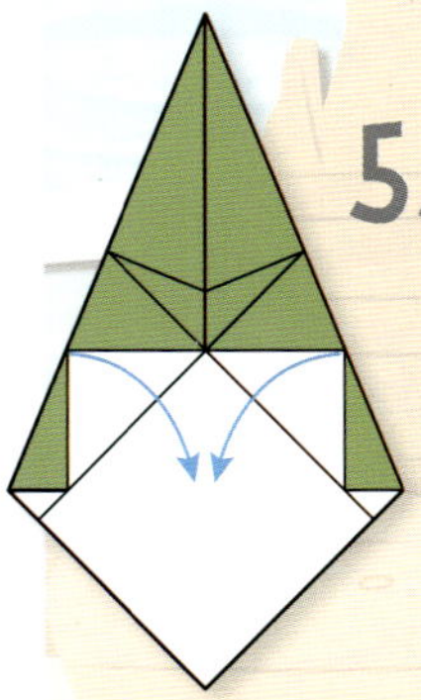

55 Unfold the flaps.

56 Using the existing creases, lift the sides while folding the top corner down to the bottom corner. Carefully flatten down the flap.

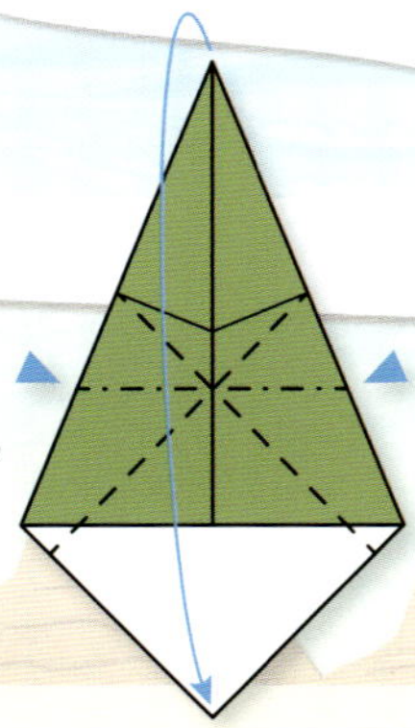

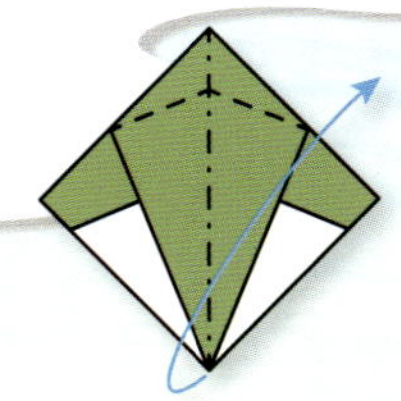

57 Squeeze the flap together and fold it up to the right.

58 Open the flap and flatten gently.

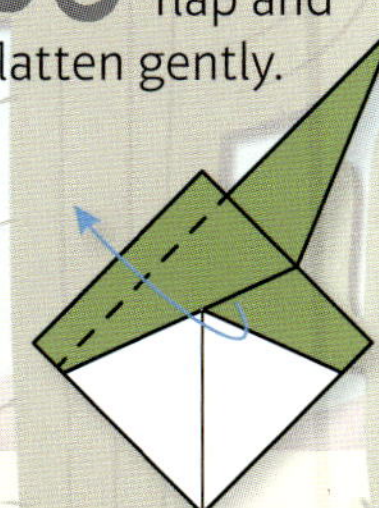

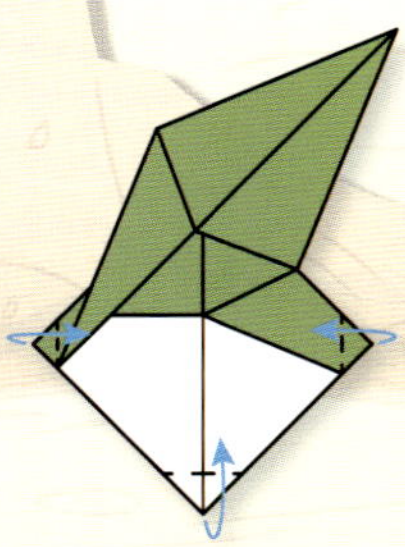

59 Fold the corners in.

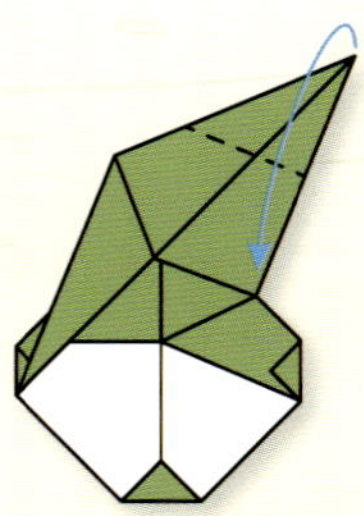

60 Fold the top corner down along the right edge.

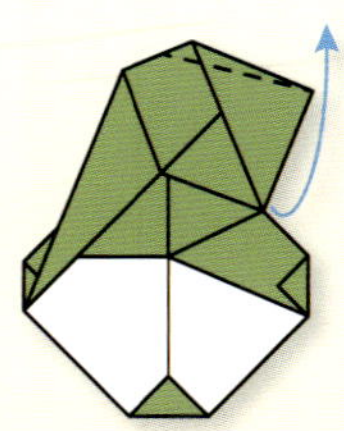

61 Fold the corner up again—making a pleat.

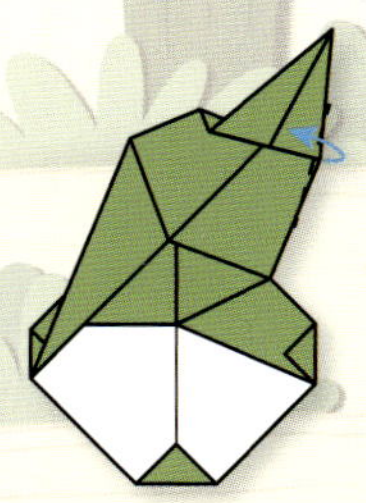

62 Fold the corner in a bit to round.

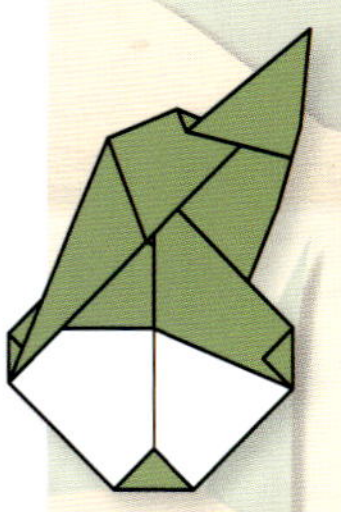

63 Turn the paper over.

64 Larvitar's tail and left foot are complete.

Assembling Larvitar

65 Squeeze a little glue on the tail (as shown).

66 Attach the body, so the left foot and tail are visible (as shown). Larvitar is complete!

Spheal

Spheal's rotund body means it rolls better than it walks. Spheal claps its fins when it's happy. Take your time as you fold its two small tusks and short, flat tail—and you'll be clapping with joy when you're done, too!

TYPE: Ice / Water **HEIGHT:** 2'7" / .8 m **WEIGHT:** 87.1 lbs. / 39.5 kg

BEGINNER

How To Make Spheal

Spheal is folded from two pieces of paper: one large square and one small triangle. The large square becomes its body and left leg; the small triangle becomes its tail and right leg. You can find the templates on pages 77 and 97. Carefully cut out each of the pieces.

Folding the Body

Make sure to start with the large square template; arrange it so the asterisk is at the top.

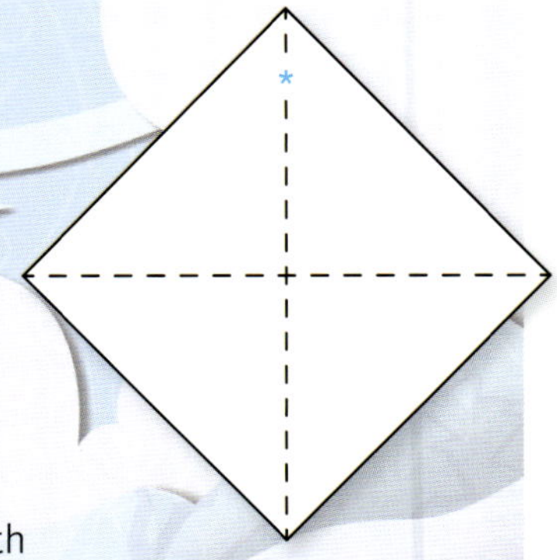

1 Fold in half along both diagonal lines, then unfold.

2 Fold the top and bottom edges into the center.

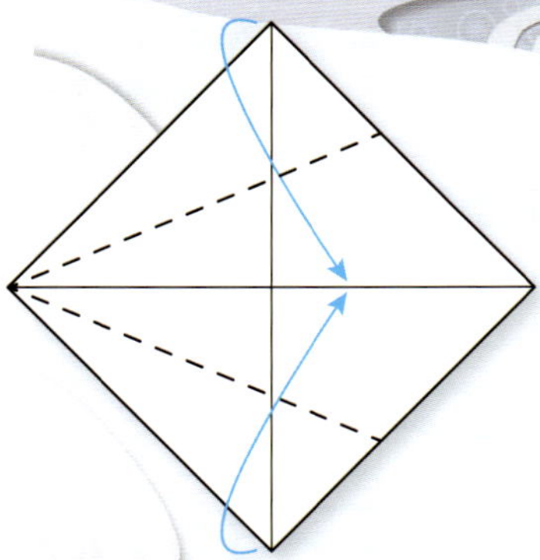

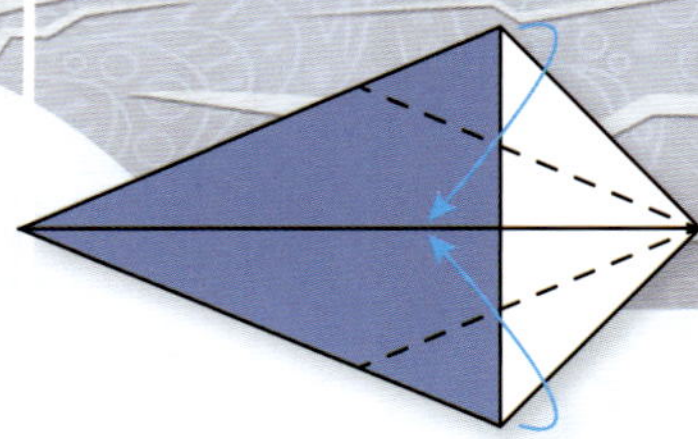

3 Fold the top and bottom corners into the center.

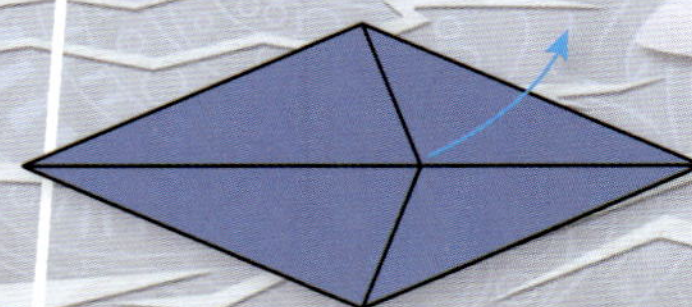

4 Unfold the top flap.

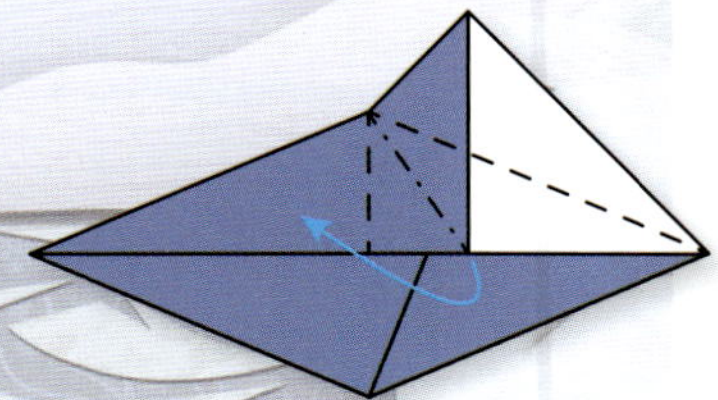

5 Using the existing creases, fold the top flap out to the left so it lays flat against the centerline.

6 Unfold the bottom flap.

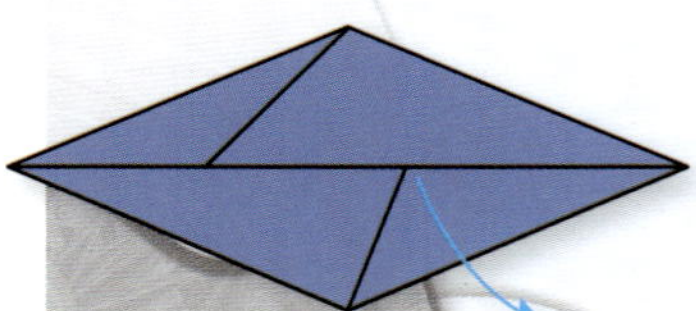

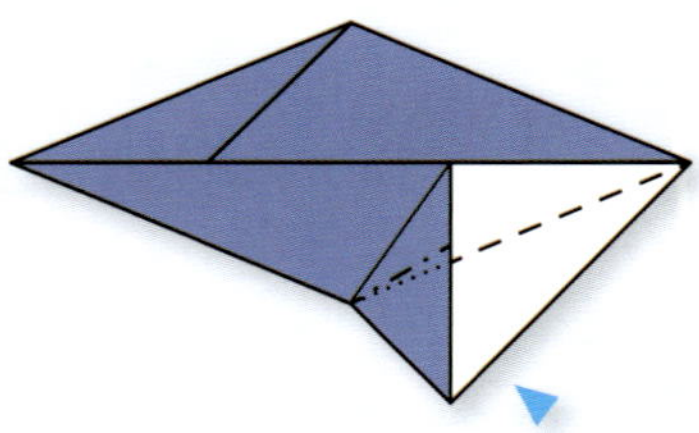

7 Using the existing creases, reverse fold the bottom flap inside so the right edge lays parallel to the centerline (see next step).

8 Using the creases, reverse fold the top flap inside (as shown).

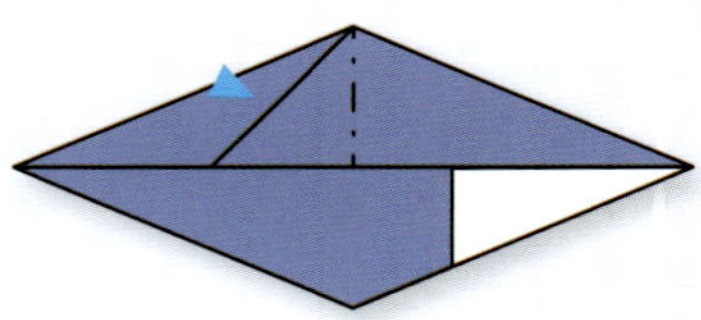

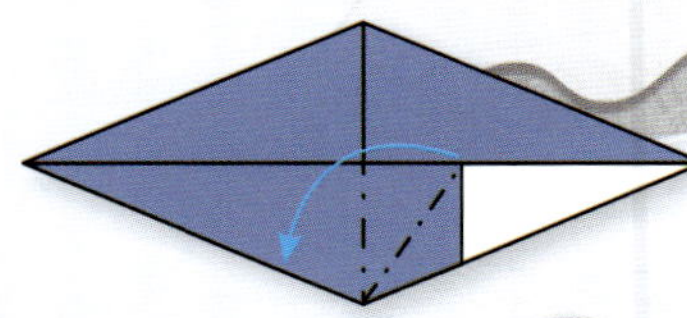

9 Just like in Step 5, using the existing creases, fold the bottom flap corner out to the left.

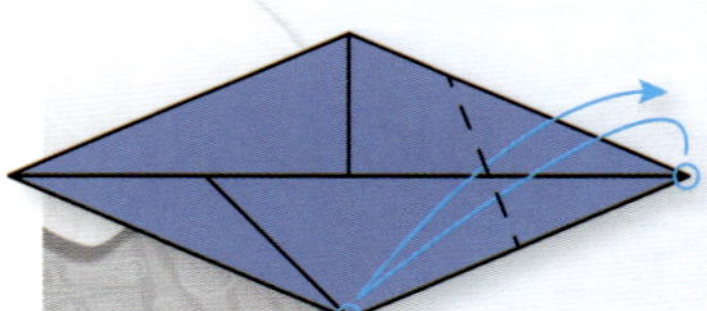

10 Fold the right corner to the bottom corner, then unfold.

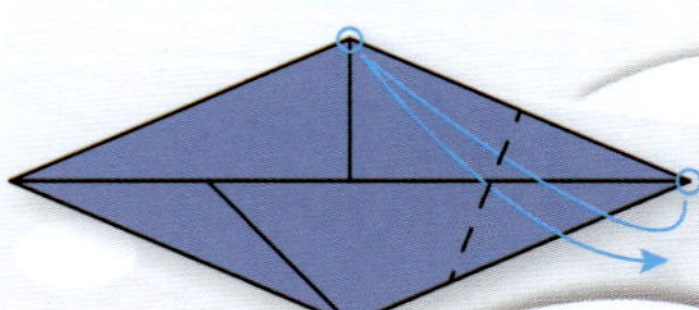

11 Fold the right corner to the top corner, then unfold.

12 Fold the upper flap up along the crease from Step 11—leaving a little space between its edge and the crease.

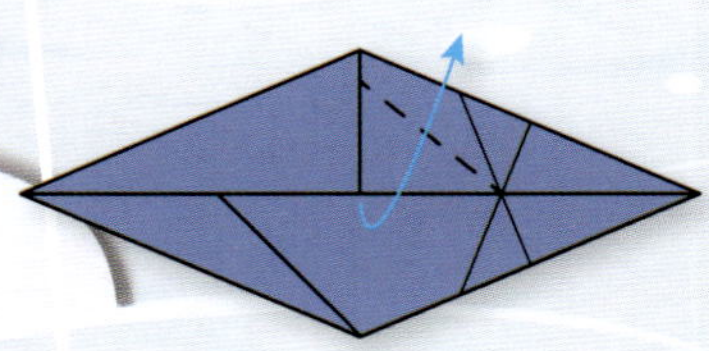

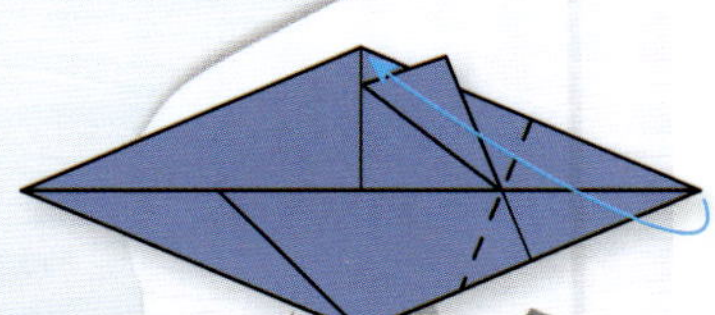

13 Fold the right corner up to the top corner using the crease from Step 11.

14 Fold the right corner in along the edge, then unfold.

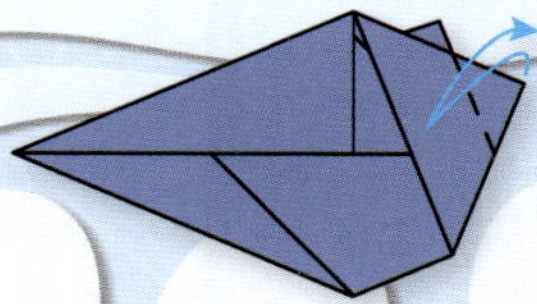

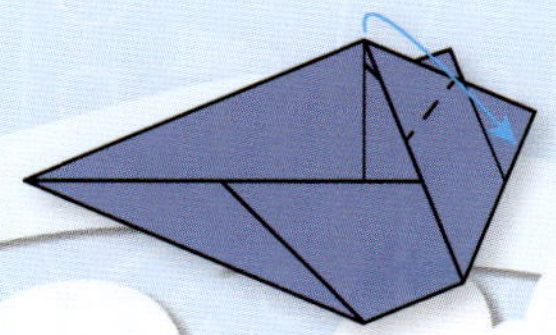

15 Fold the top corner down to the right edge, so the seam in the flap is parallel to the top right edge.

16 Fold the right corner along the crease and under the flap.

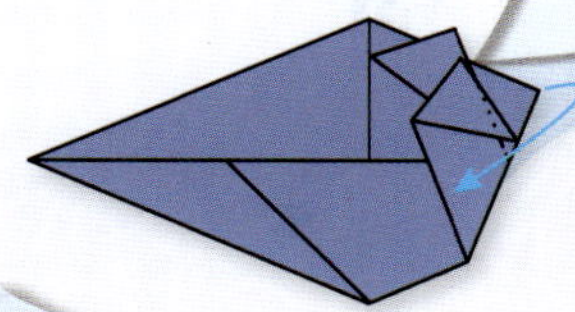

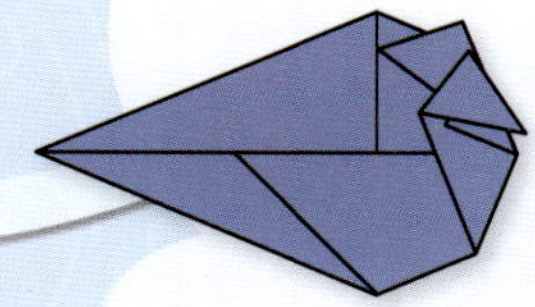

17 The result should look like this.

18 Reverse fold the bottom corner inside to the right so it is back to how it was in Step 8.

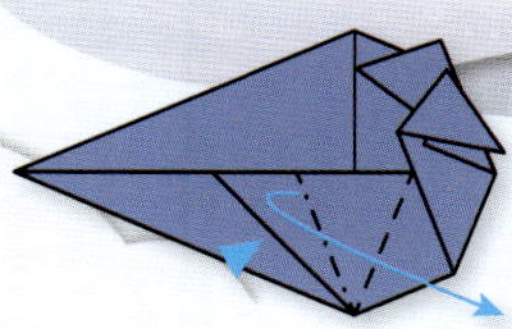

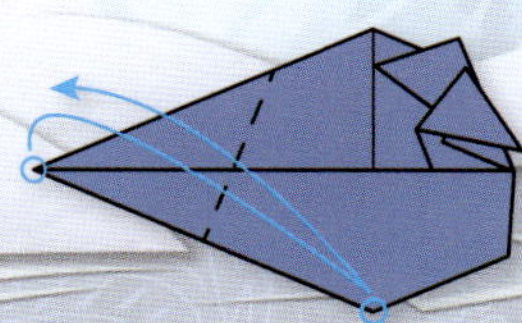

19 Fold the left corner to the bottom corner, then unfold.

20 Fold the left corner to the top corner, then unfold.

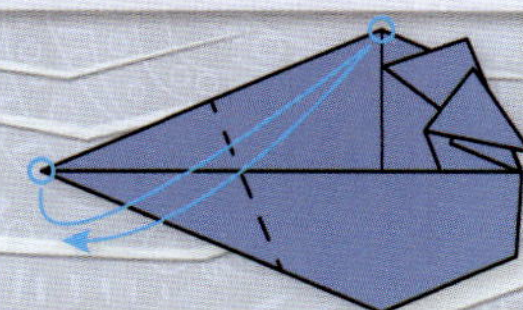

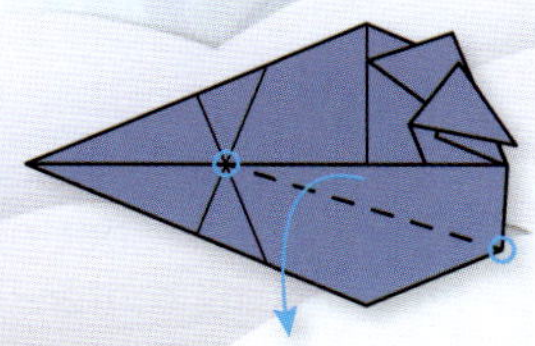

21 Fold the bottom flap down from the two markers.

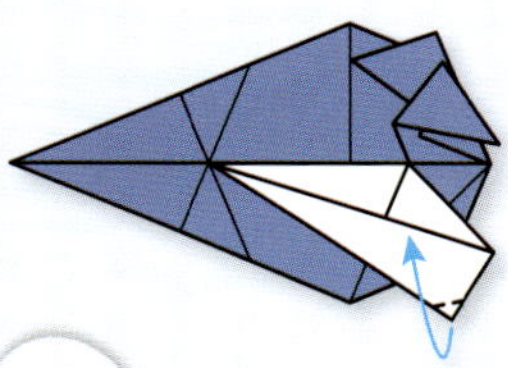

22 Fold up the right bottom tip.

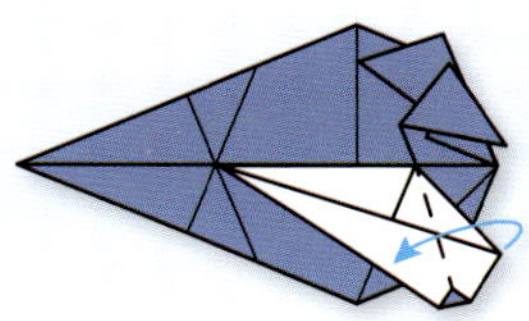

23 Fold the right corner of the flap along the crease.

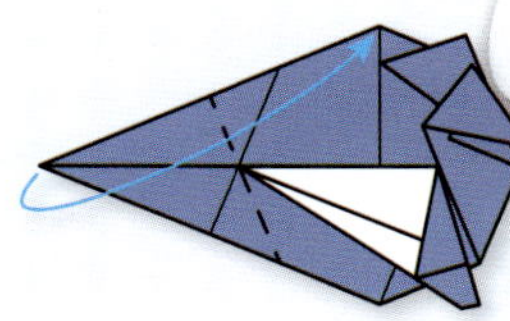

24 Fold the left corner to the top corner along the crease.

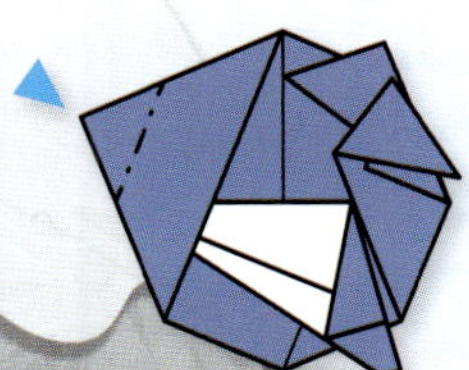

25 Fold in the left corner to create a crease, then reverse fold inside so the flap lies along the top edge.

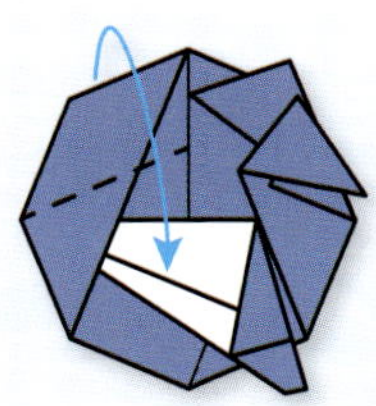

26 Fold the top layer down along the hinge.

27 Tuck the shaded area under the layer beneath (as shown).

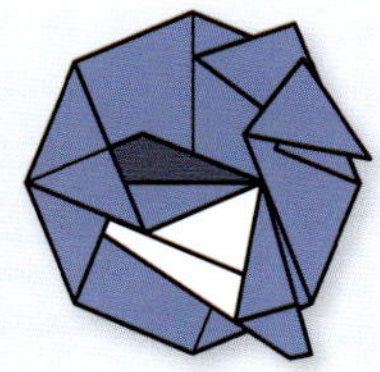

28 Turn the paper over.

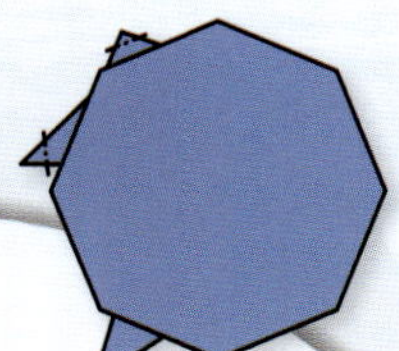

29 Fold the upper left two points back to round their edges.

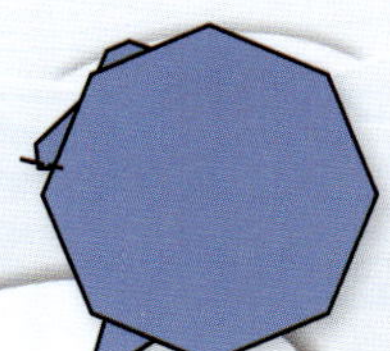

30 Fold the bottom edge of the lower-left tip to round the edge further.

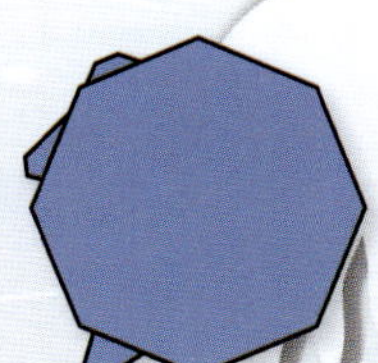

31 Spheal's body and left leg are complete.

Folding the Tail & Right Leg

Make sure to start with the small triangle template; arrange it so the asterisk is at the top.

32 Fold in half sideways, then unfold.

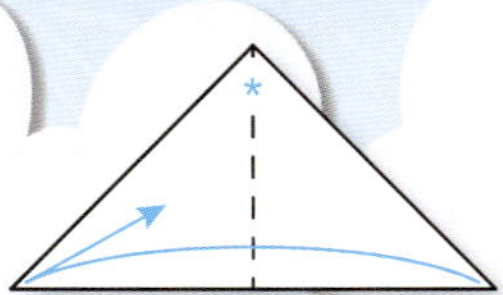

33 Fold the left edge down to the bottom edge, then unfold.

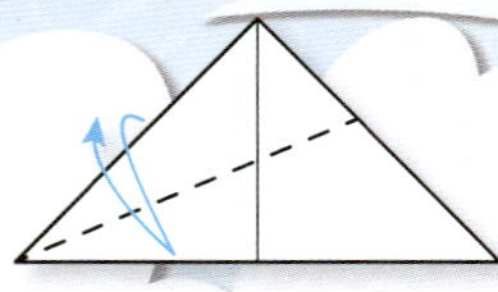

34 Fold the right edge down to the bottom edge, then unfold.

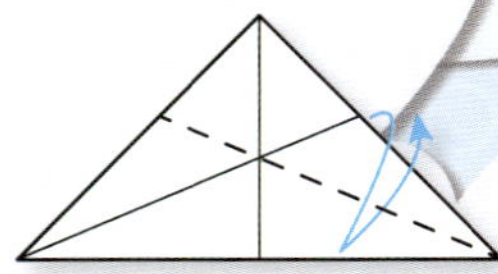

35 Fold the bottom edge toward the top, creasing where the folds meet.

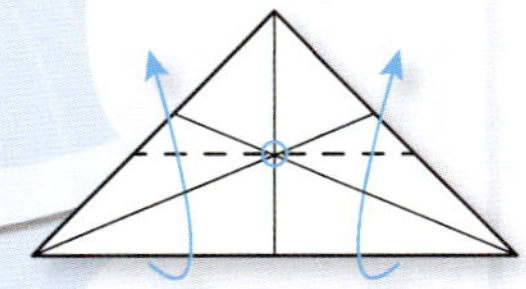

36 Fold the right corner down along the edge beneath.

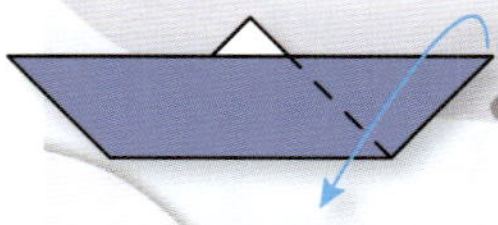

37 Fold the left edge of the flap up to the right edge.

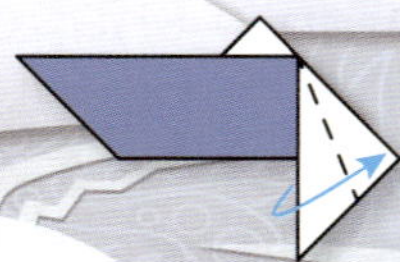

38 Turn the paper over.

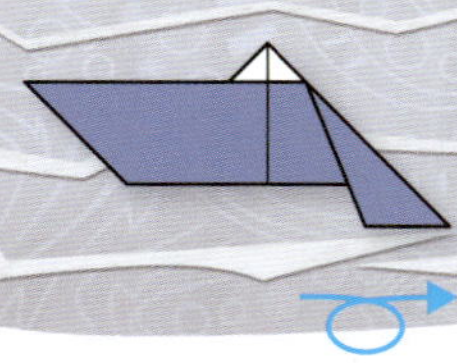

39 Fold the right corner up to the centerline.

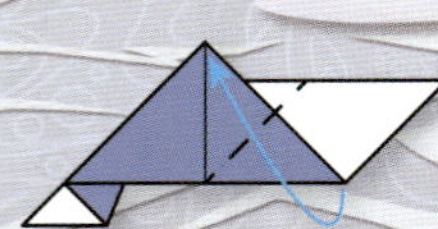

40 Turn over vertically.

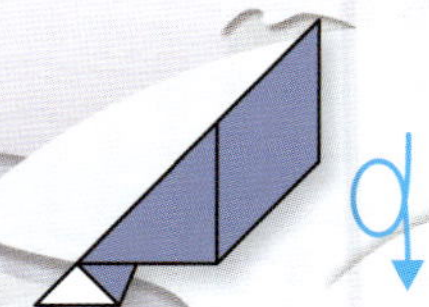

41 Fold the marked edge up to the edge just above it.

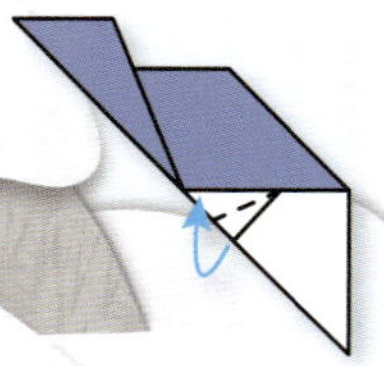

42 Tuck the bottom corner up under the flap (as shown).

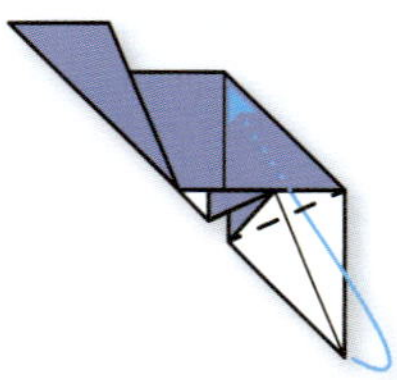

43 Fold the middle corner in to round.

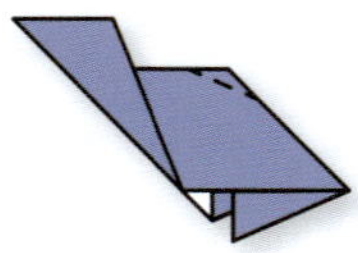

44 Fold the top left section to the right—matching the circles.

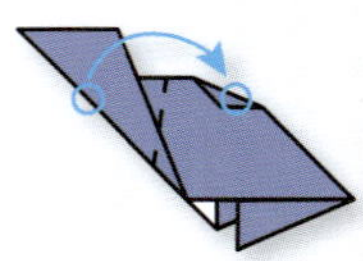

45 Fold the three corners in.

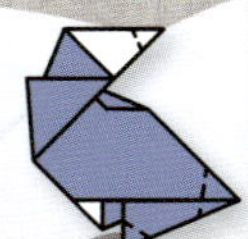

46 Turn over vertically.

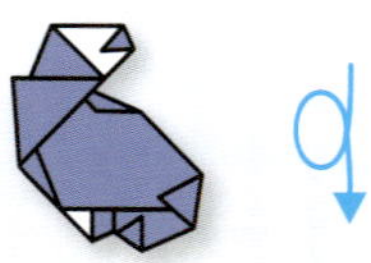

47 Spheal's tail and right leg are complete.

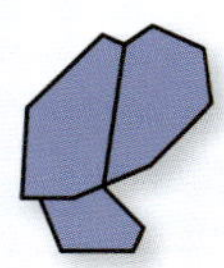

Assembling Spheal

48 Place some tape in the bottom-left corner (as marked).

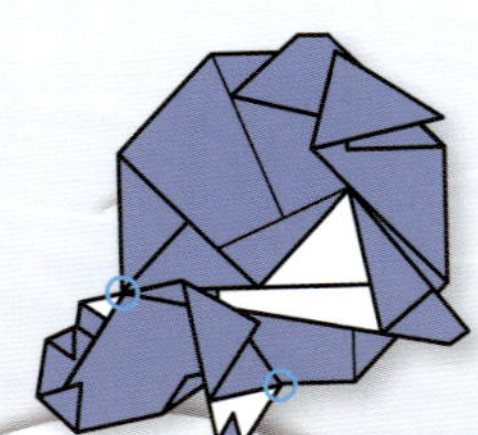

49 Attach the tail and right leg where marked.

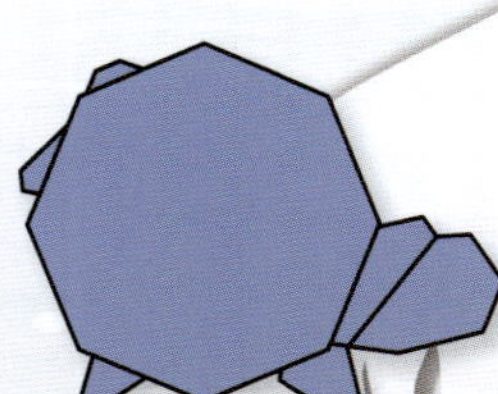

50 Spheal is complete!

Bidoof

Active and agile, Bidoof gnaws on rocks and logs to whittle down its front teeth. Nothing perturbs Bidoof with its nerves of steel. Don't let anyone or anything disturb you as you fold Bidoof into shape.

TYPE: Normal **HEIGHT:** 1'8" / .5 m **WEIGHT:** 44.1 lbs. / 20 kg

INTERMEDIATE

How To Make

Bidoof

Bidoof is folded from three pieces of paper: three large squares. One square becomes its feet and tail; one square becomes its body; and one square becomes its head. You can find the templates on pages 81, 85, and 89. Carefully cut out each of the pieces.

Folding the Feet & Tail

Make sure to start with the square template face-up—with the feet on the bottom.

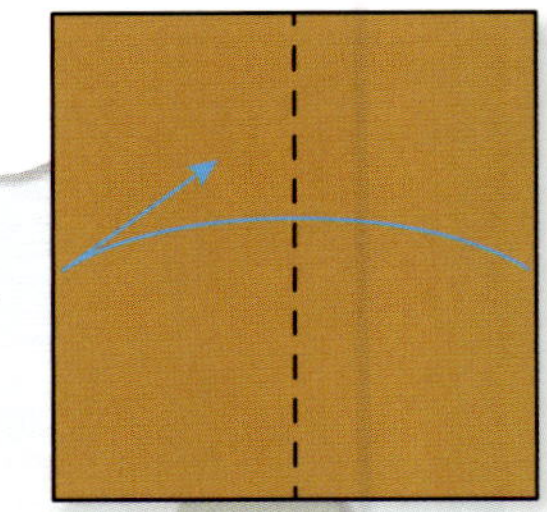

1 Fold in half sideways, then unfold.

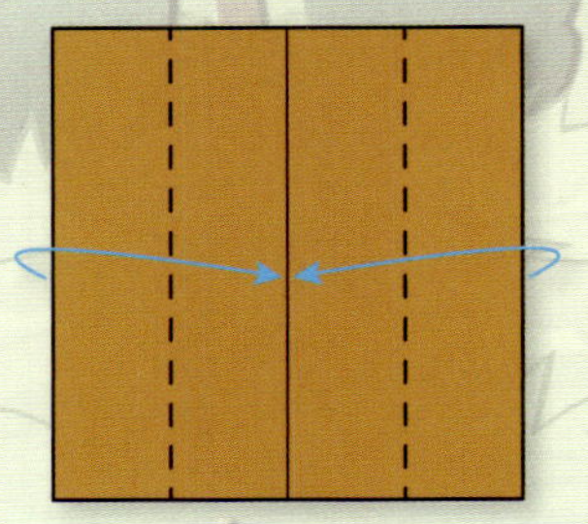

2 Fold the left and right edges to the center.

3 Fold out to the edges, then unfold.

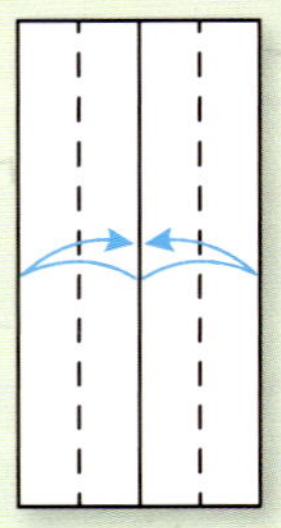

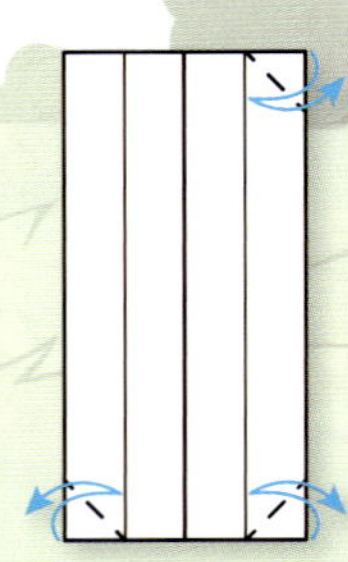

4 Fold three corners to the crease, then unfold (as shown).

5 Reverse fold the three corners inside out.

6 Fold the top layer out to the edges.

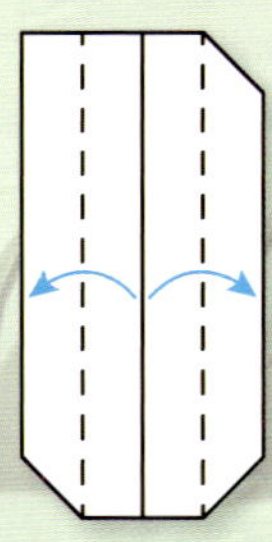

7 Fold the top-right corner down.

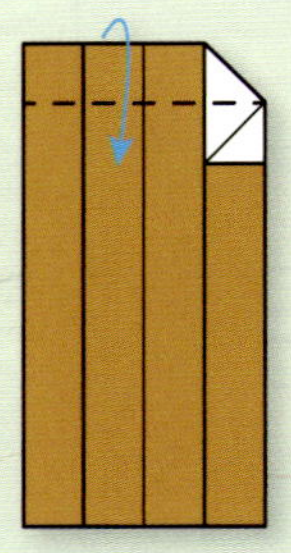

8 Fold the top edge down (as shown).

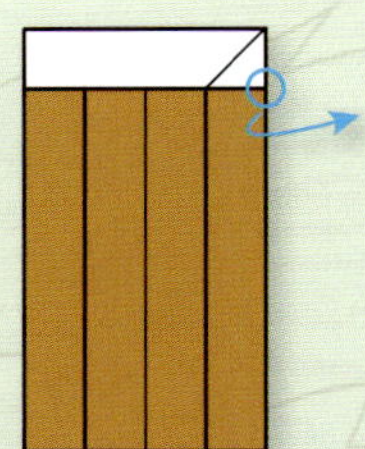

9 Pull the top-right corner flap (marked with a circle) out to the side.

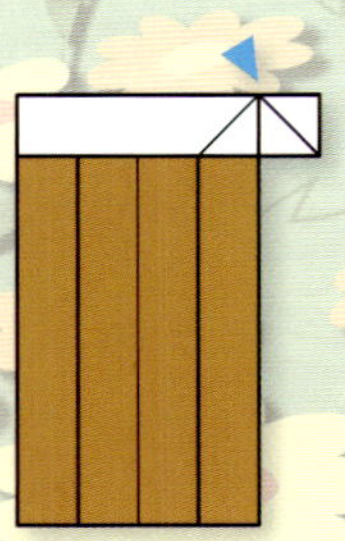

10 Flatten the open corner flap down.

11 Fold the bottom two corner flaps up.

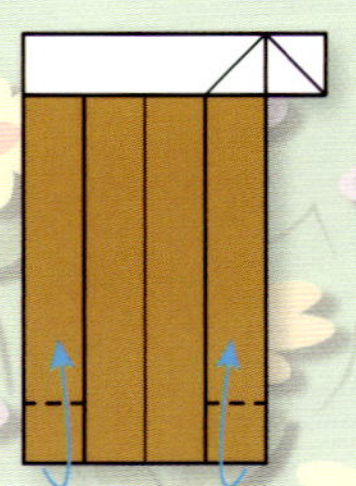

12 Fold the bottom edge up (as shown).

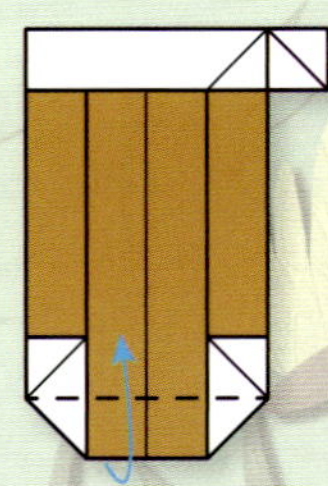

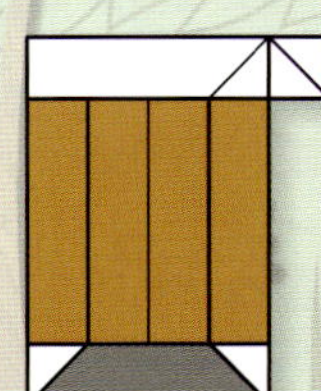

13 Tuck the shaded flap under the outside corners.

14 Fold the corner flaps down.

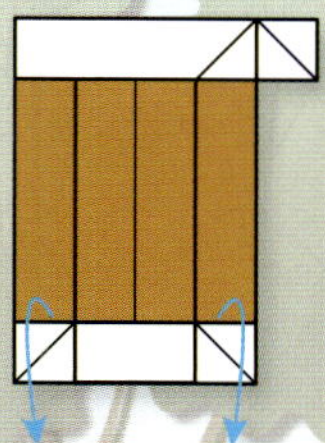

15 Turn the paper over.

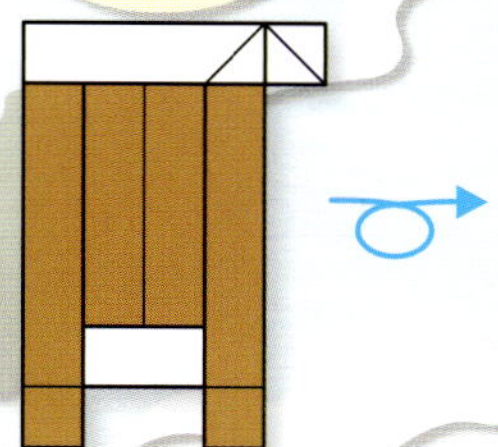

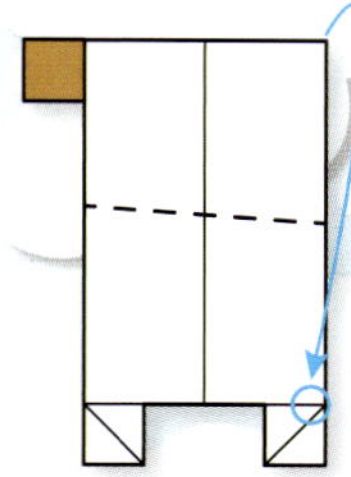

16 Fold the top edge down at an angle (marked with a circle).

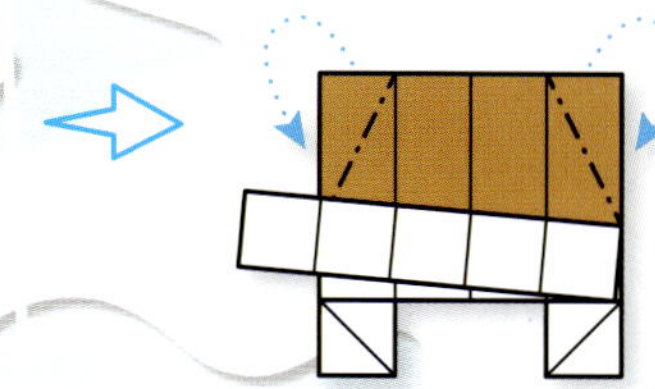

17 Fold the upper corners to the back.

18 Fold the edge from Step 16 up.

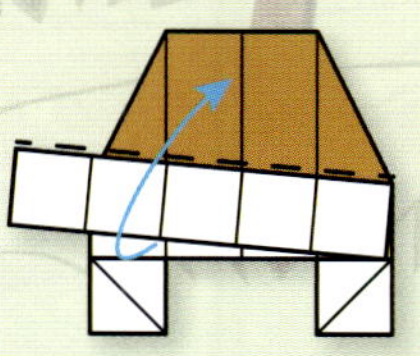

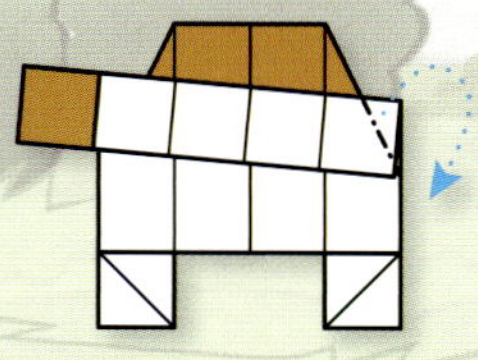

19 Fold the right corner to the back.

20 Fold in the left flap.

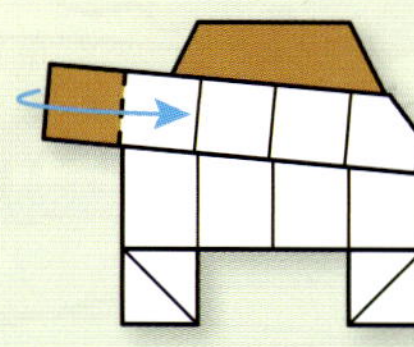

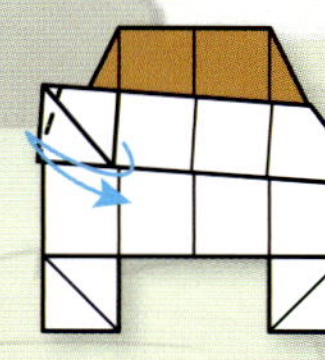

21 Fold the flap to the left, then unfold.

22 Fold in the top-right and bottom-right corners of the flap.

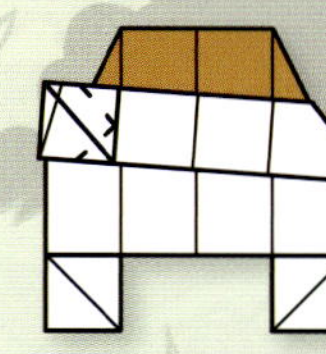

23 Fold in the right tip.

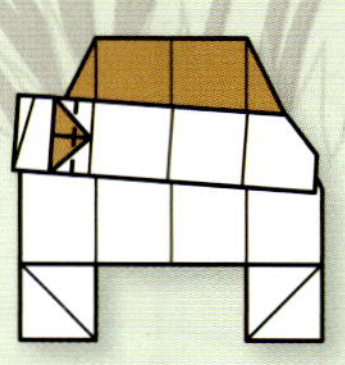

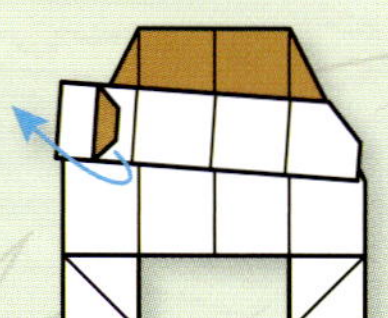

24 Fold out the flap along the crease.

25 Fold the two bottom squares up.

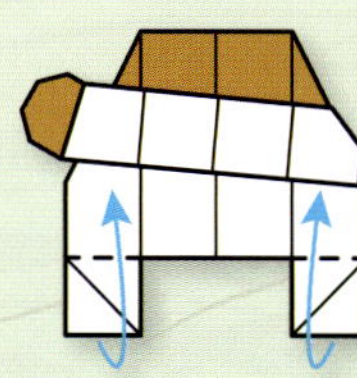

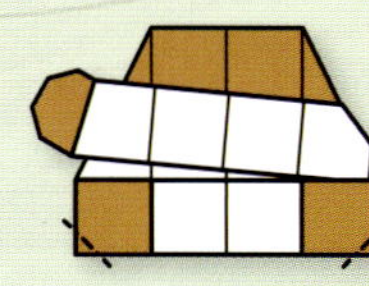

26 Fold the bottom corners back.

27 Bidoof's feet and tail are complete.

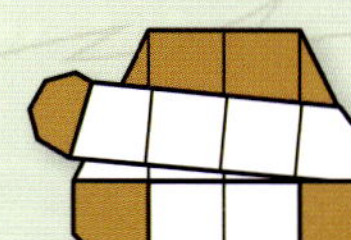

Folding the Body

Make sure to start with the square template arranged so the asterisk is at the top.

28 Fold in half sideways, then unfold.

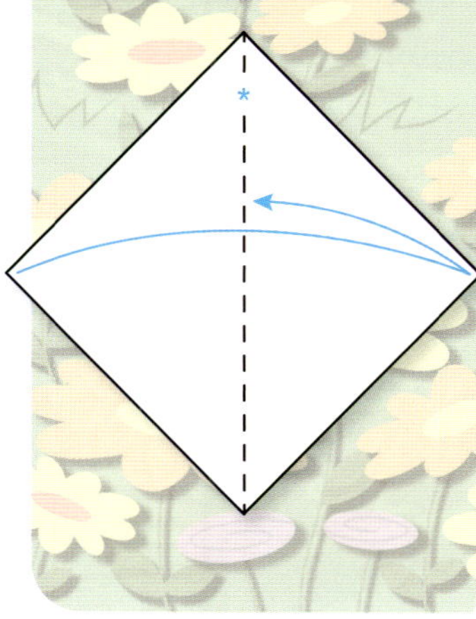

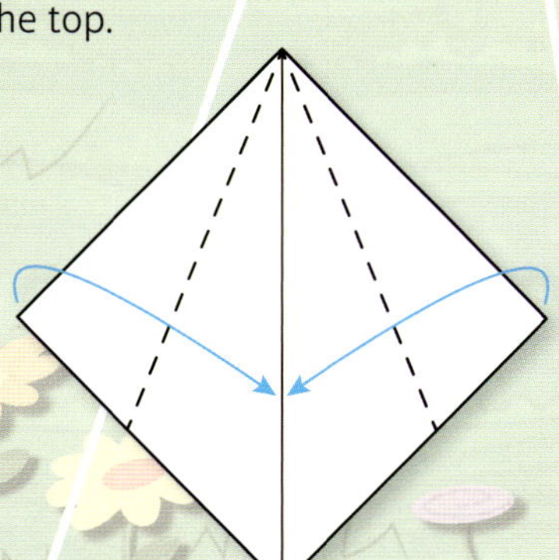

29 Fold the left and right edges to the centerline.

30 Fold the bottom corner up.

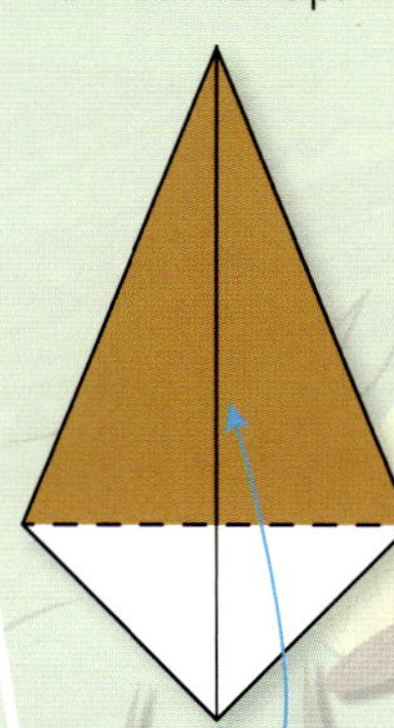

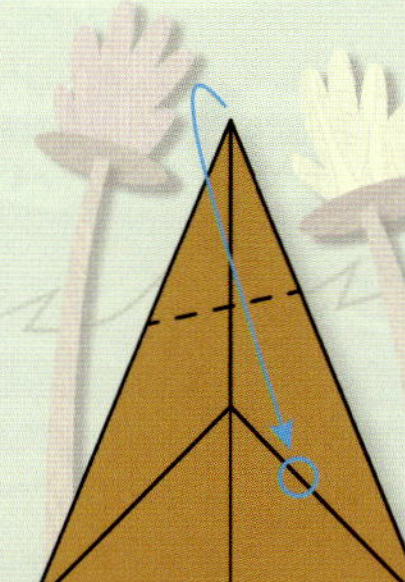

31 Fold the top corner down to the marker, along the edge of the bottom flap.

32 Create two reference points by making a crease at each of the two edges (as shown).

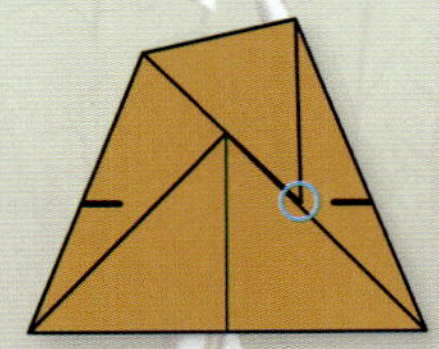

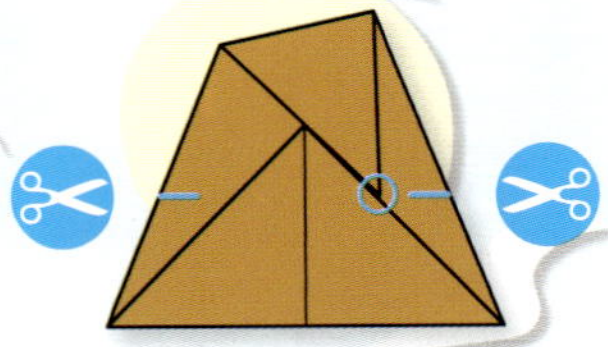

33 Make a cut at each reference point, cutting halfway across to the flap.

34 Fold in the top edges of the cuts.

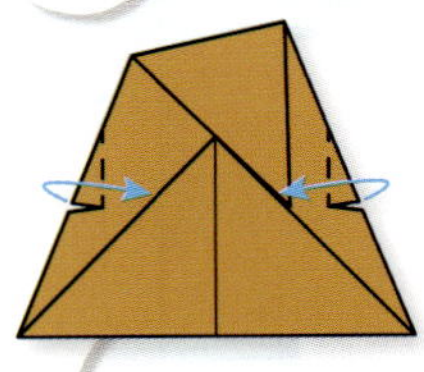

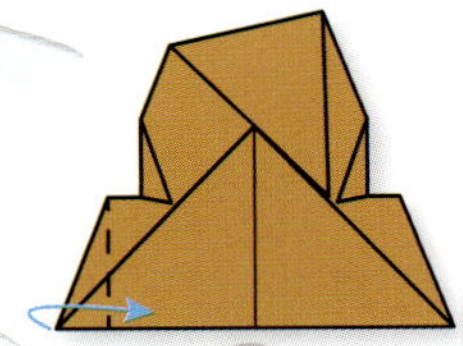

35 Fold in the bottom-left edge.

36 Fold in the top-left corner.

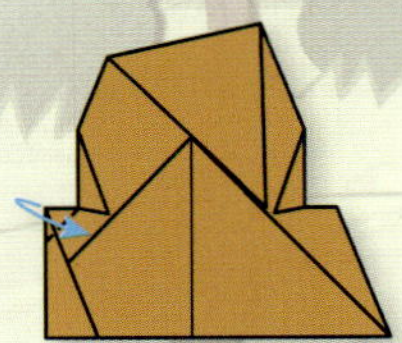

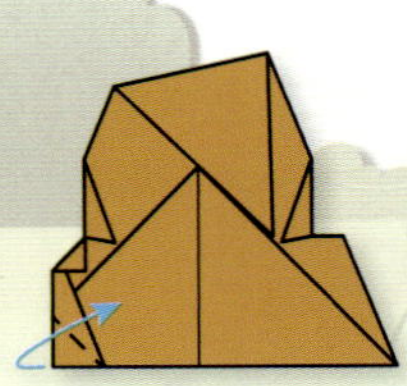

37 Fold in the bottom-left corner.

38 Fold in the bottom-right corner.

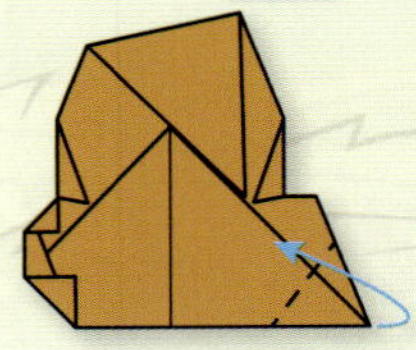

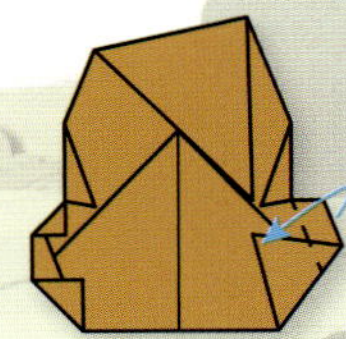

39 Fold in the right edge (as shown).

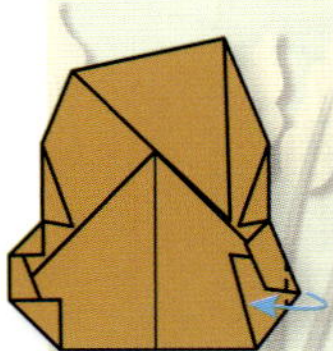

40 Fold in the bottom-right point.

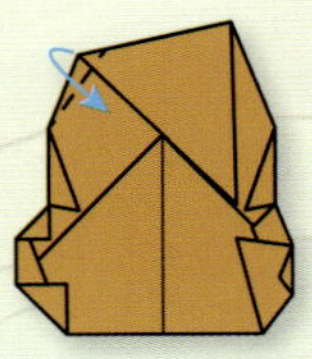

41 Fold in the top-left edge. Turn the paper over.

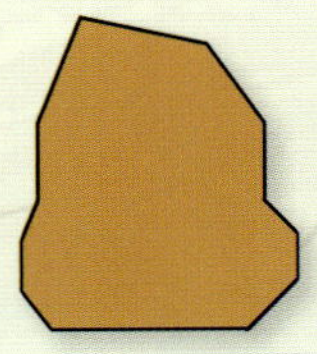

42 Bidoof's body is complete.

Folding the Head

Make sure to start with the square template face-up—with the head at the top.

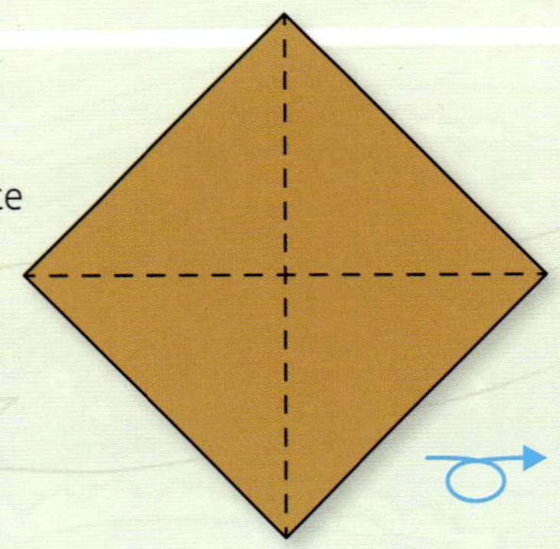

43 Fold in half along both diagonal lines, then unfold. Turn the paper over.

44 Fold in half along both edges, then unfold.

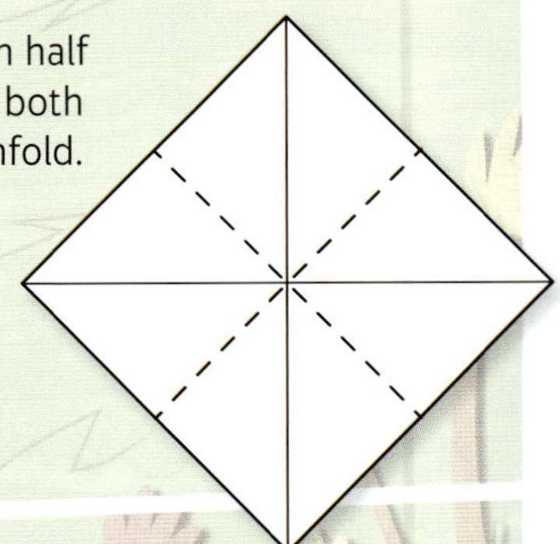

45 Fold the bottom corner up to the center.

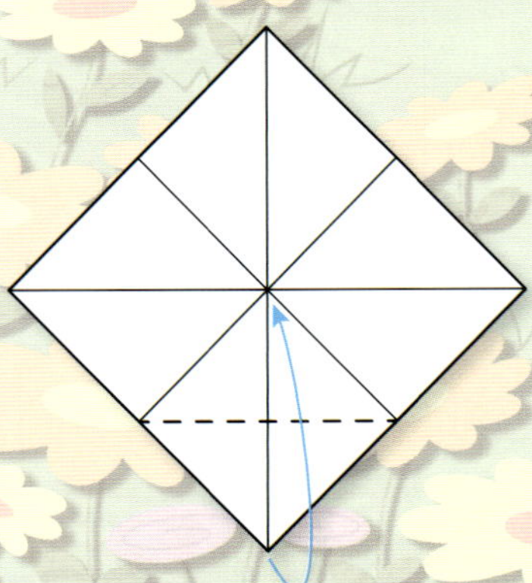

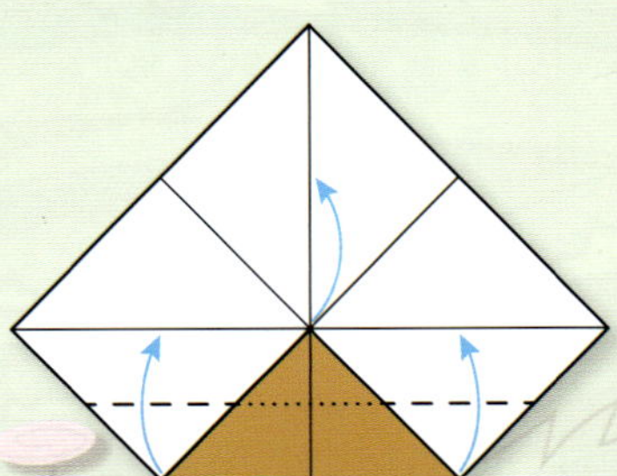

46 Slide the corner up so that the crease from Step 45 lines up with the centerline.

47 Fold the top corner down.

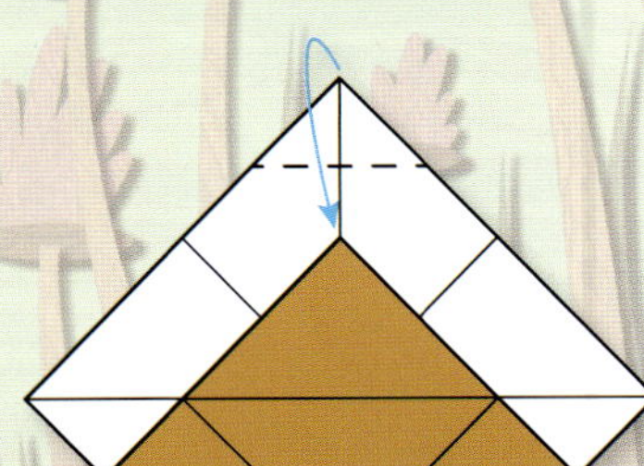

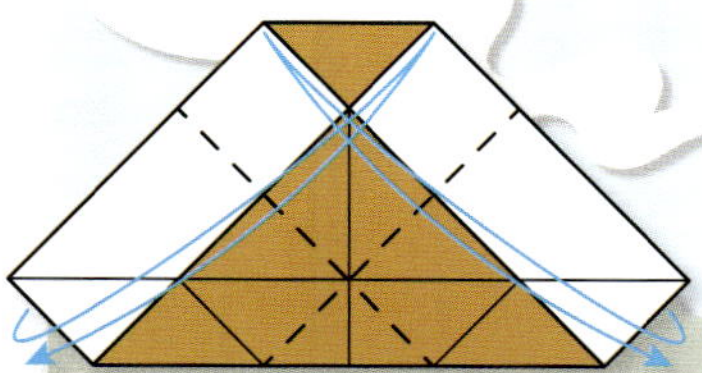

48 Fold along existing creases, then unfold (as shown).

49 Fold in the bottom corners (marked with circles).

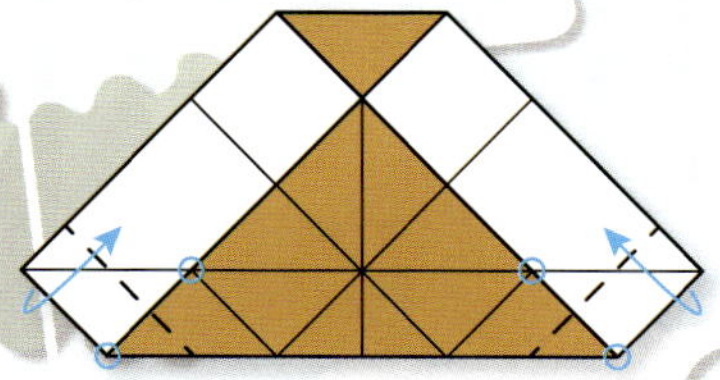

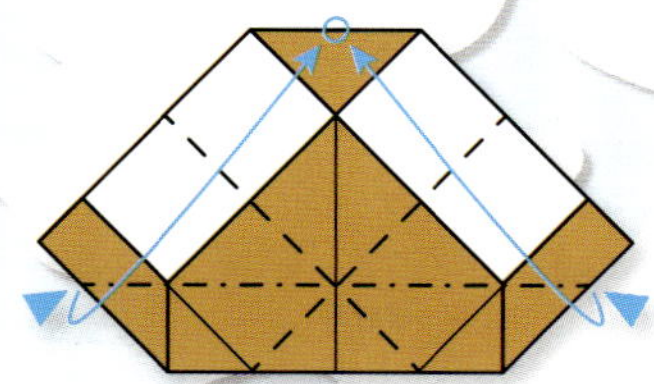

50 Push the two sides up from the bottom along the existing creases to meet at the centerline (marked with a circle).

51 The result should look like this. Turn the paper over.

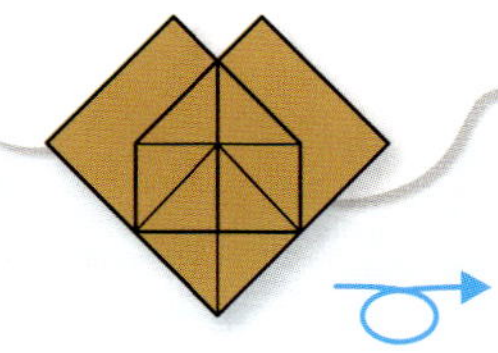

52 Fold the top layer of the upper-right corners back.

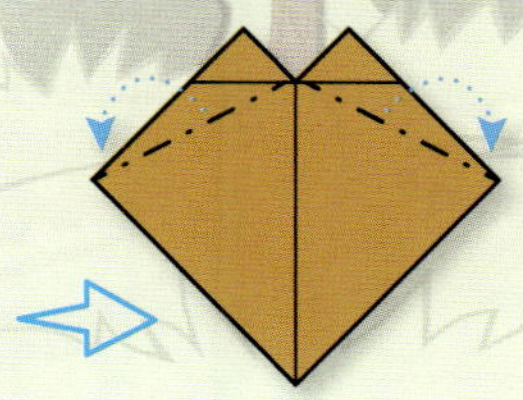

53 Turn the paper over.

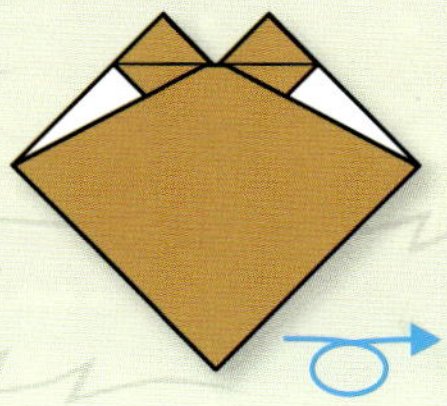

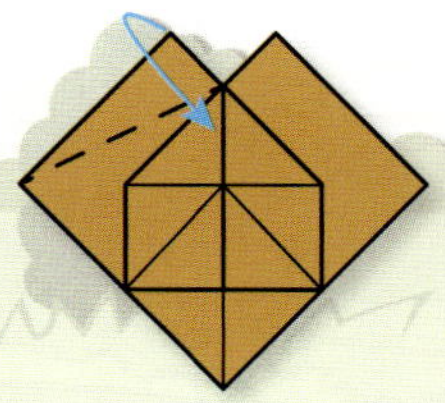

54 Fold the top-left flap down, as shown.

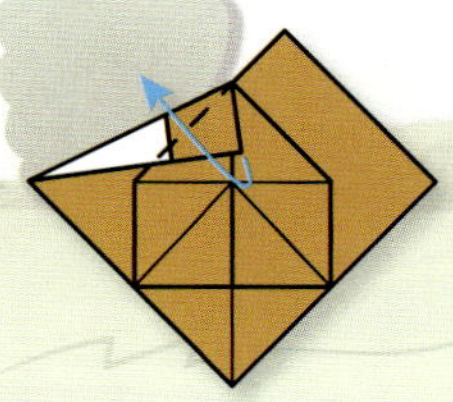

55 Fold the small left flap up and to the left.

56 Gently pull out the hidden layer behind the ear flap.

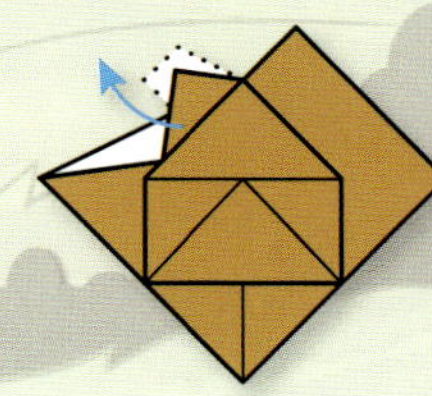

57 Repeat Steps 54–56 on the right side.

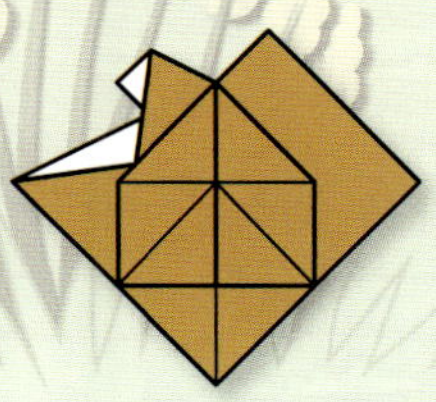

58 The result should look like this:

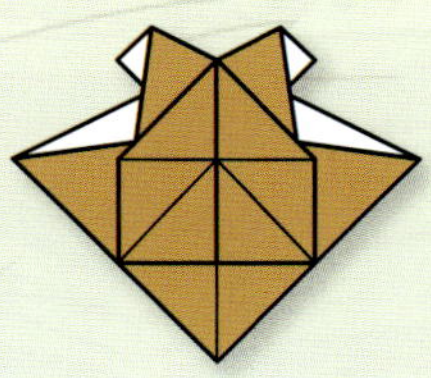

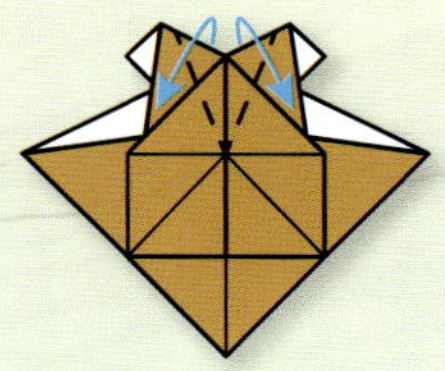

59 Fold the top flaps down from the center so that the ears are thinner.

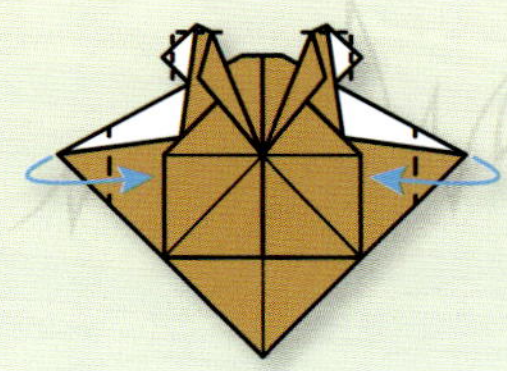

60 Fold in the corners to round the ears. Fold in the right and left sides to round the face.

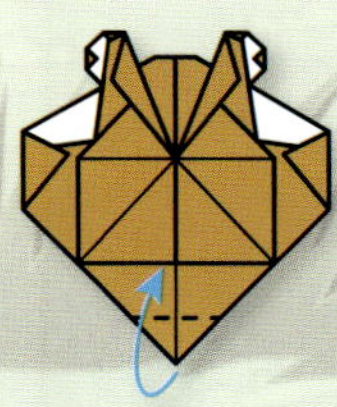

61 Fold the bottom corner up.

62 Turn the paper over.

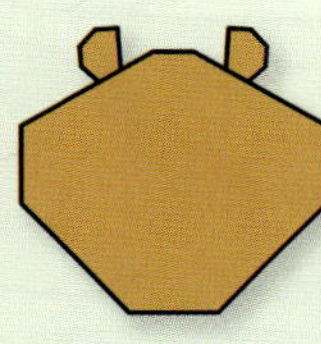

63 Bidoof's head is complete.

Assembling Bidoof

64 Squeeze a little glue to the back of the head.

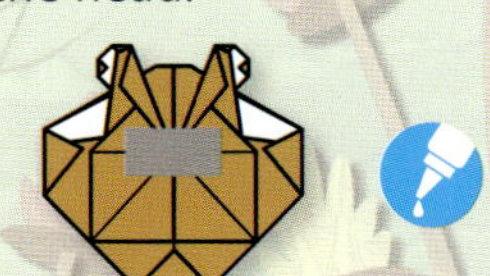

65 Attach Bidoof's body to the head so the top of the body lines up with the markers. Turn the paper over.

66 Unfold Bidoof's feet. Squeeze a little glue on the feet and the tail piece.

67 Attach Bidoof's head and body to the feet and tail piece, then glue the feet in place and fold back the sides.

68 Bidoof is complete!

Emolga

Emolga flutters and glides through the air with its cape-like membrane and crackles with electricity. Keep your eyes on it as you fold it—Emolga is cute, but it's a bit of a troublemaker.

TYPE: Electric / Flying **HEIGHT:** 1'4" / .4 m **WEIGHT:** 11 lbs. / 5 kg

INTERMEDIATE

How To Make Emolga

Emolga is folded from four pieces of paper: one large square becomes its body, and three small squares become its head, ears, and tail. You can find the templates on pages 93 and 97. Carefully cut out the pieces.

Folding the Body

Make sure to start with the large square template arranged so the asterisk is at the top.

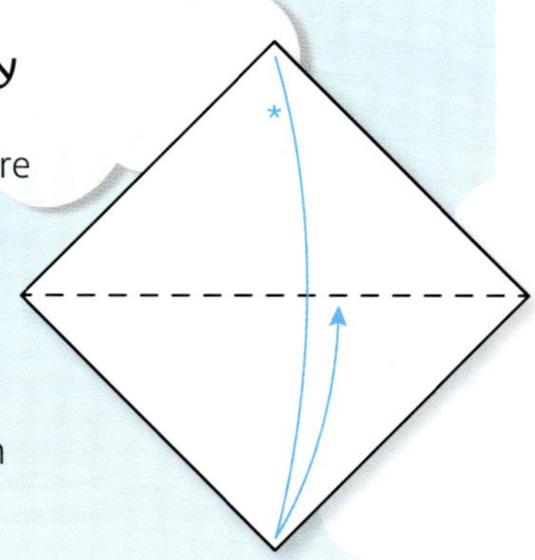

1 Fold in half from top to bottom, then unfold.

2 Fold the top and bottom corners into the centerline.

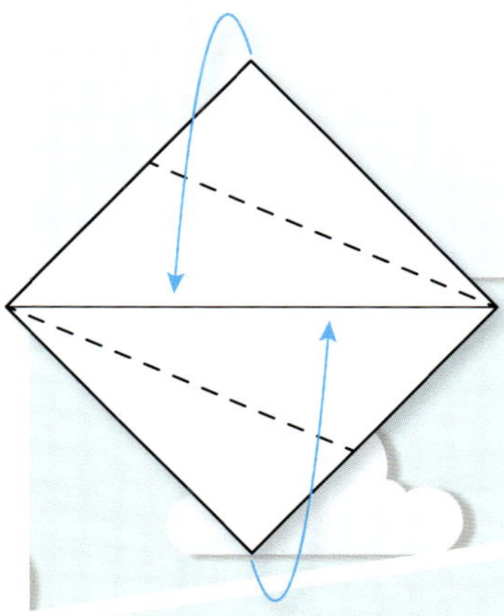

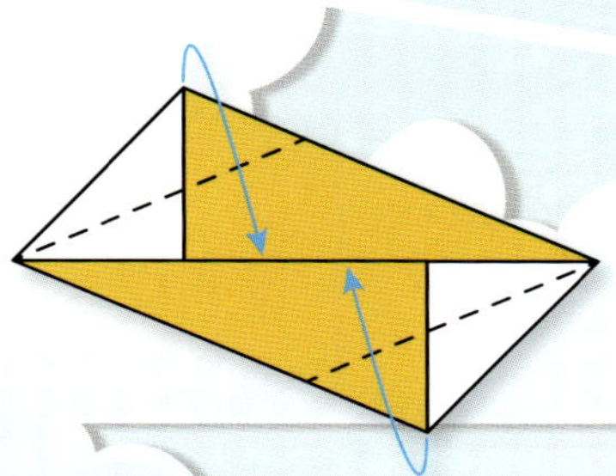

3 Fold the new top and bottom corners into the centerline.

4 Fold in half sideways, then unfold.

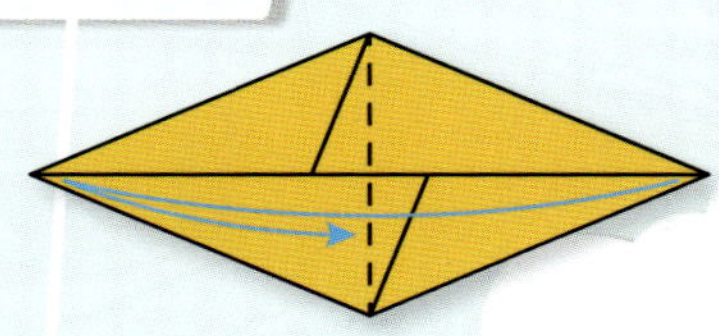

5 Fold the top and bottom corners to the center.

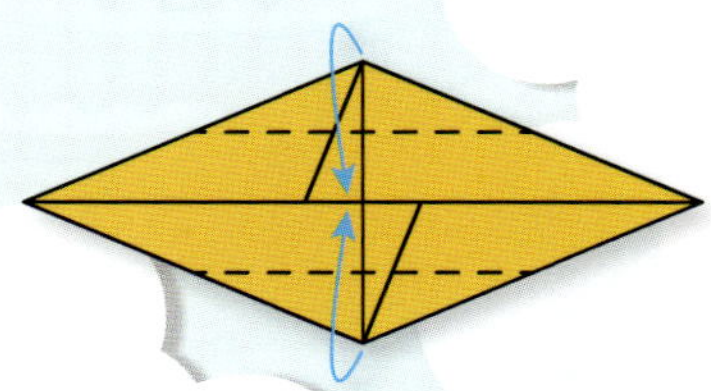

6 Fold the right corner to cover the fold from Step 3, but stay on the centerline (marked with a circle).

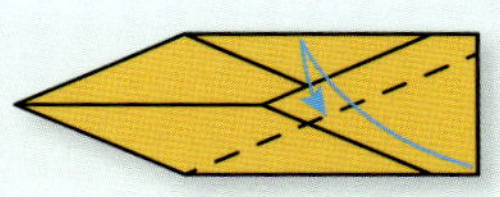

7 Fold the bottom-right corner up along the edge of the flap underneath, then unfold.

8 Fold the edge of the flap down along the crease (the upper-right corner will lift slightly).

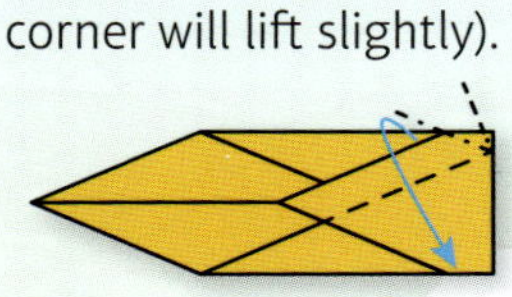

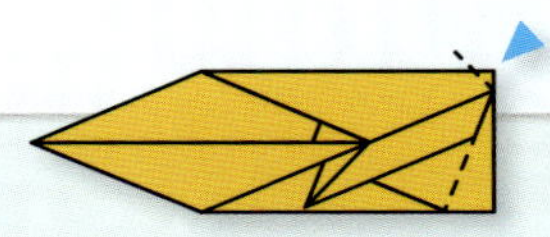

9 Carefully flatten the upper-right corner down.

10 Fold the flap back up.

11 Now fold the flap down so the centerline is perpendicular to the bottom edge (turn over to check foot placement).

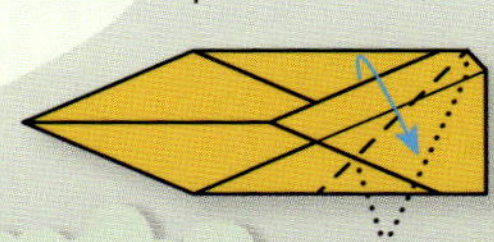

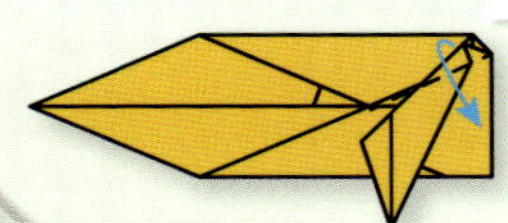

12 Fold the upper-right corner of the flap down.

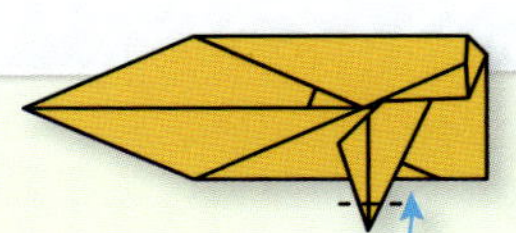

13 Fold the bottom tip up to the edge.

14 Fold the foot in half, carefully pulling out the extra paper from the fold above (check foot placement on the opposite side).

15 Fold the top-left corner to the marking.

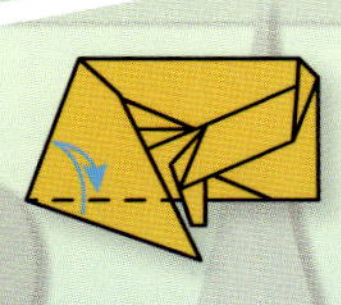

16 Fold the flap up along the bottom layer, then unfold.

17 Fold the bottom corner up to the crease, then unfold.

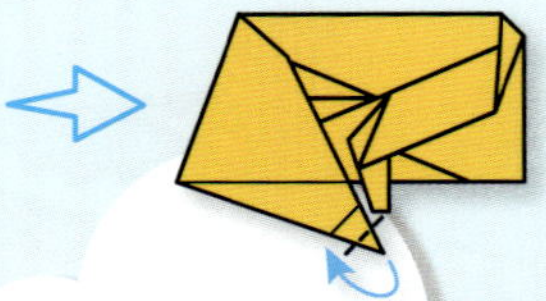

18 Fold the bottom corner up to the new crease.

19 Fold the bottom flap up along the crease.

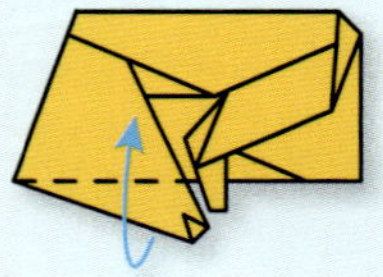

20 Fold the flap back down, even with the flap on the right (turn over to check foot placement).

21 Fold the flap in half and flatten the pocket. Again, turn over to check foot shape and position.

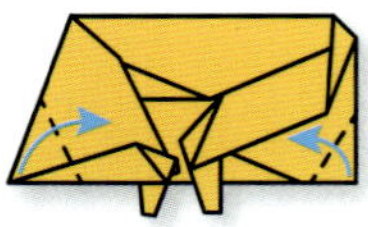

22 Fold the bottom corners in.

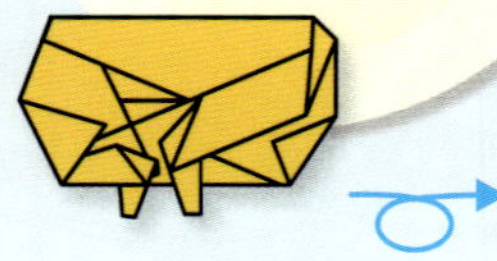

23 Turn the paper over.

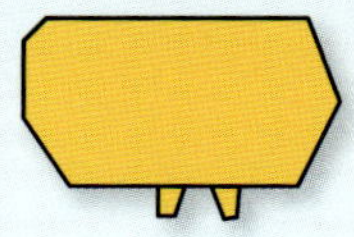

24 Emolga's body is complete.

Folding the Head

Make sure to start with the small square template arranged so the asterisk is at the top.

25 Fold in half sideways, then unfold.

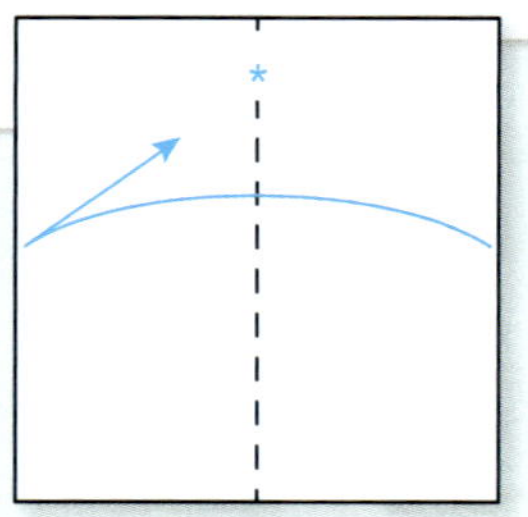

26 Fold in half from top to bottom, then unfold.

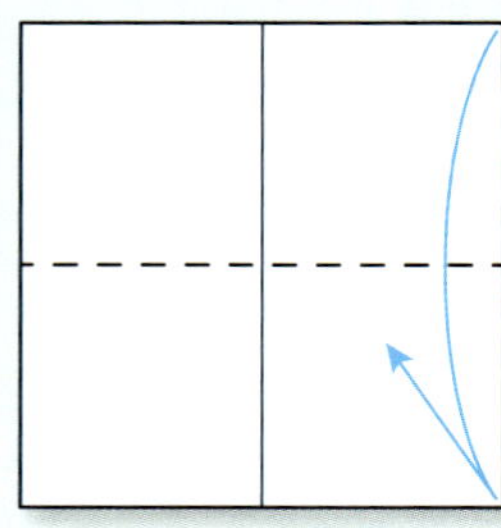

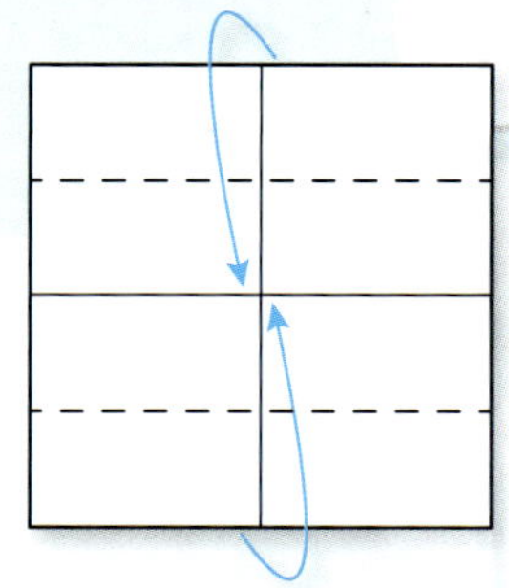

27 Fold the top and bottom edges into the centerline.

28 Fold the left corner of the top flap up.

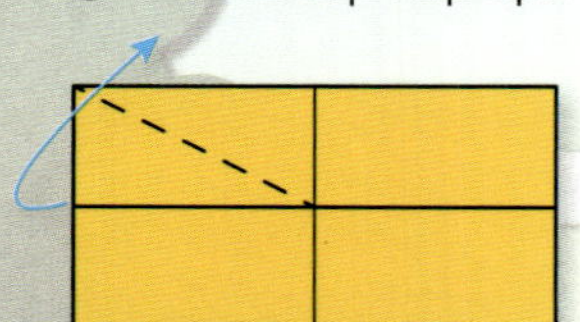

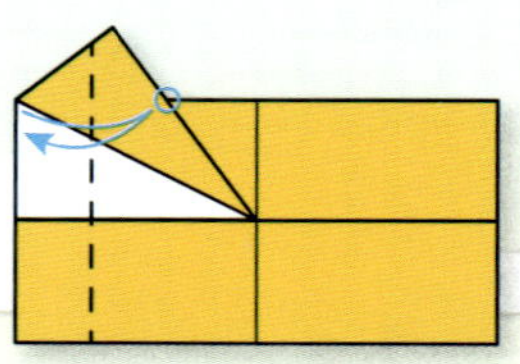

29 Fold the left side to the marking, then unfold.

30 Unfold the flap.

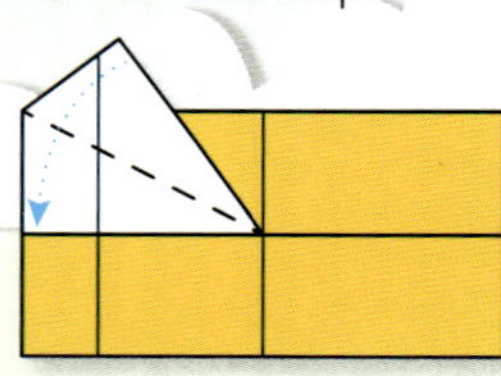

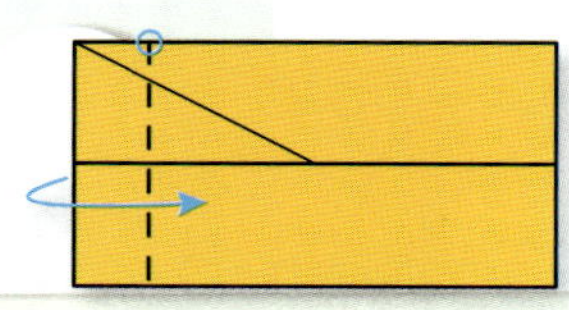

31 Fold the left edge in along the crease.

32 Fold the right edge in—almost to the centerline.

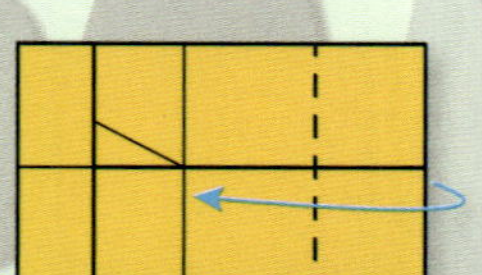

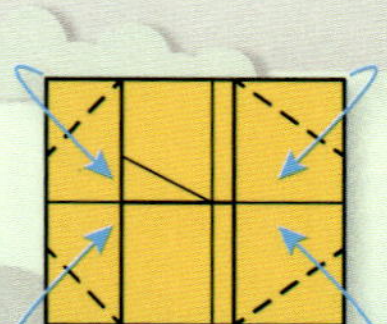

33 Fold all the corners in.

34 Turn the paper over.

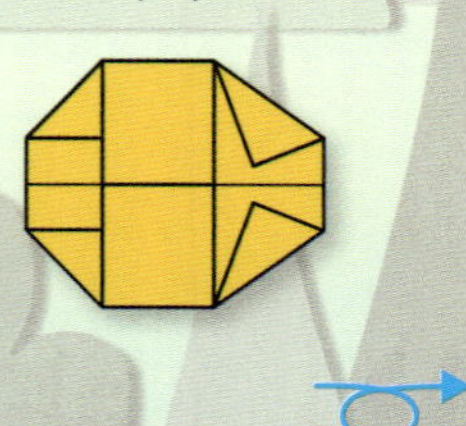

35 Emolga's head is complete.

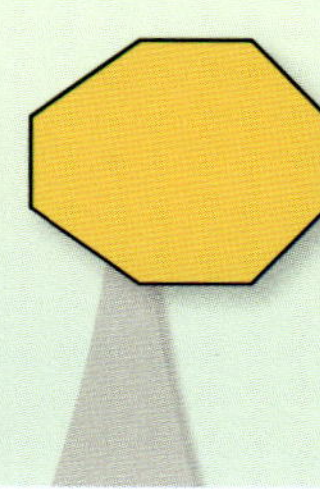

Folding the Ears

Make sure to start with the small square template arranged so the asterisk is at the top.

36 Fold in half along both diagonal lines, then unfold.

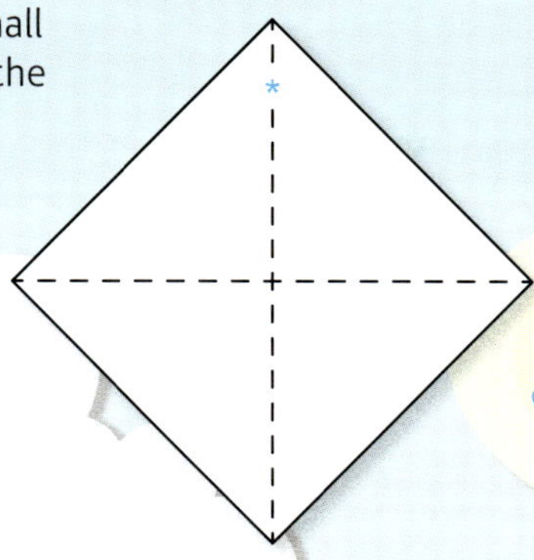

37 Fold the left and right corners into the center.

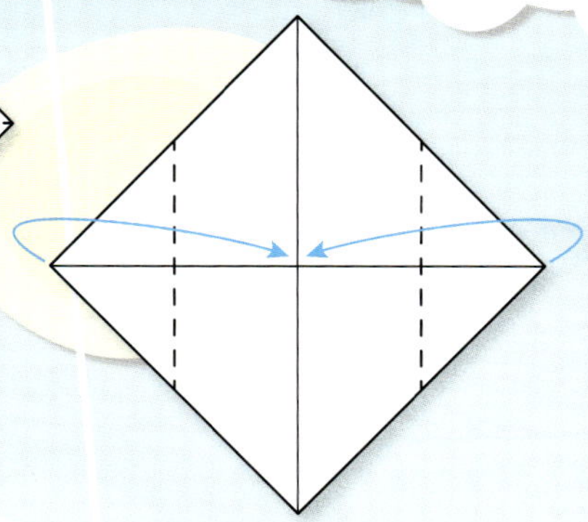

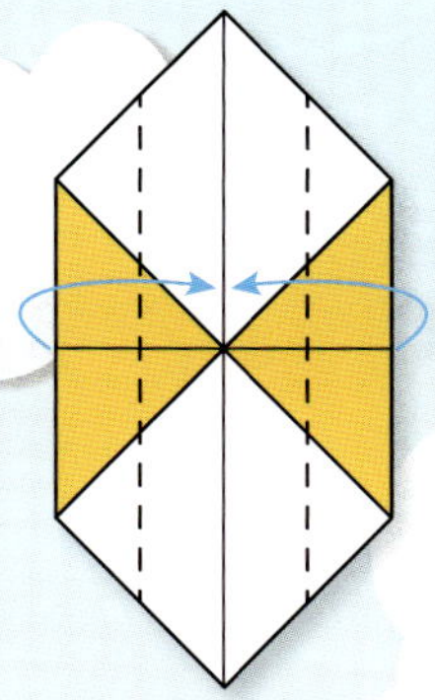

38 Fold the left and right edges into the center.

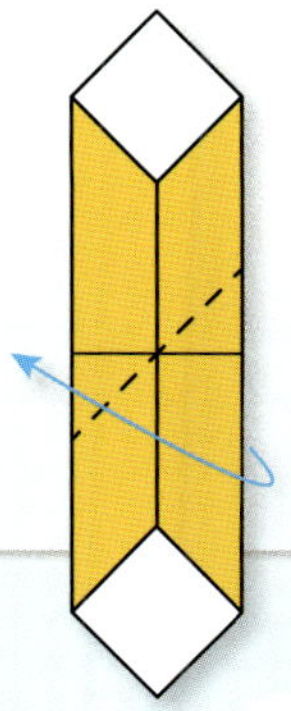

39 Fold the bottom corner up (through the centerline) to the left.

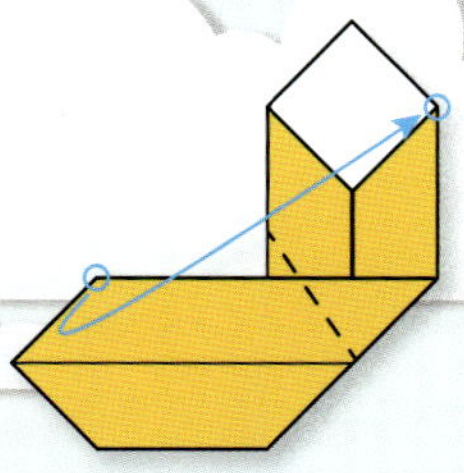

40 Fold the left corner up to the marking. Turn over to align the left ear.

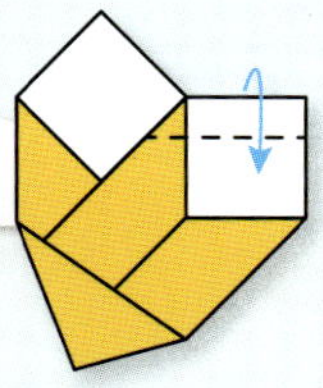

41 Fold the upper-left edge down about halfway.

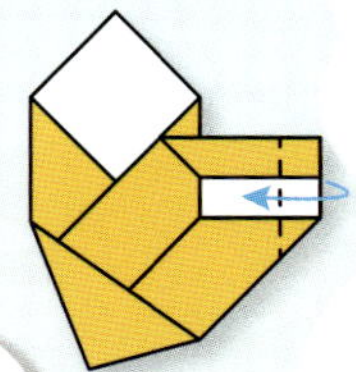

42 Fold the right edge in.

43 Turn the paper over.

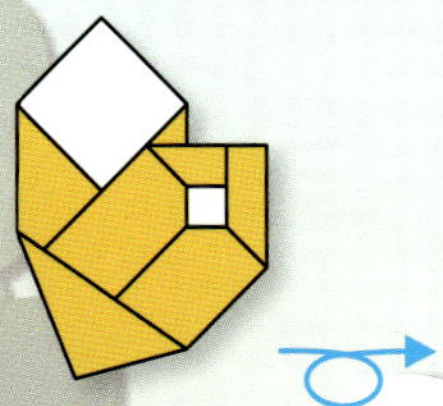

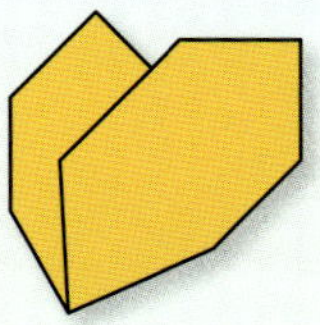

44 Emolga's ears are complete.

Folding the Tail

Make sure to start with the small square template arranged so the asterisk is at the top.

45 Fold in half from top to bottom, then unfold.

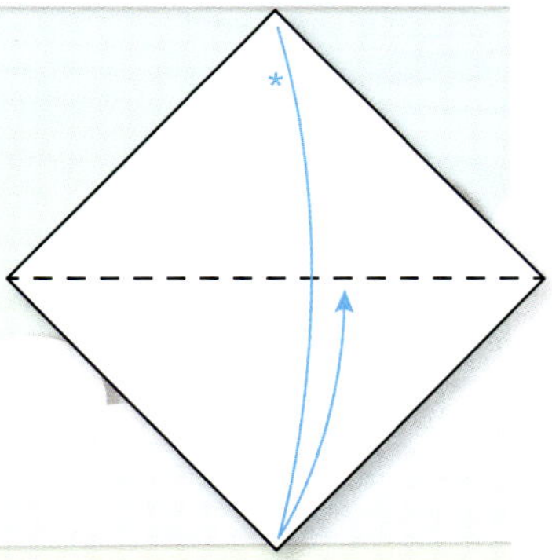

46 Fold the upper- and lower-right edges into the centerline.

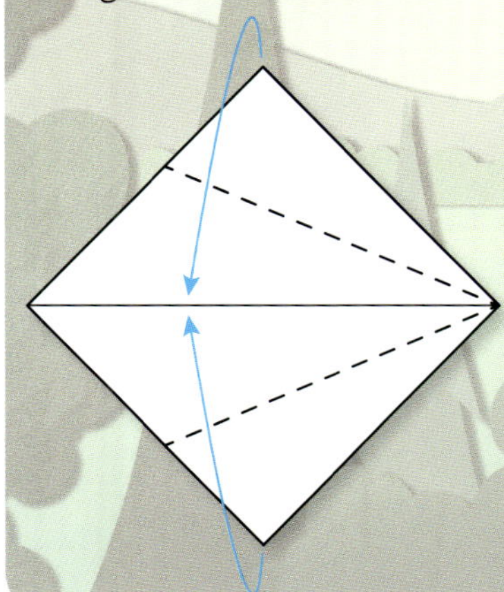

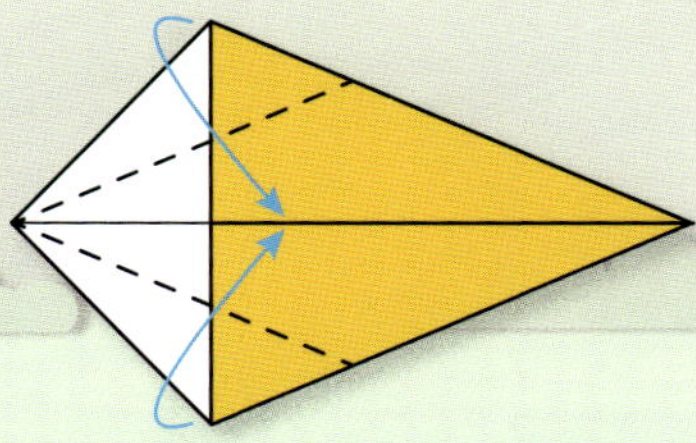

47 Fold the upper- and lower-left edges into the centerline.

48 Fold the left side along the edge from Step 47, then unfold.

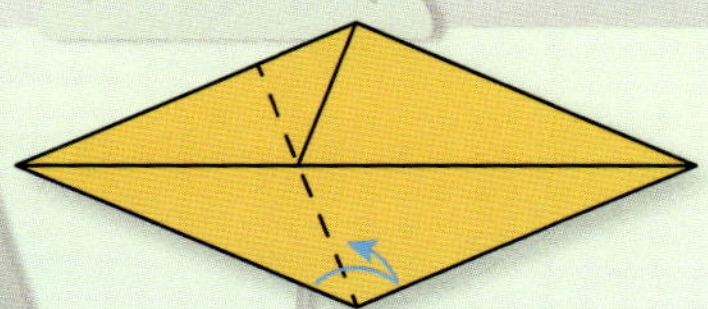

49 Fold the right side up along the edge, then unfold.

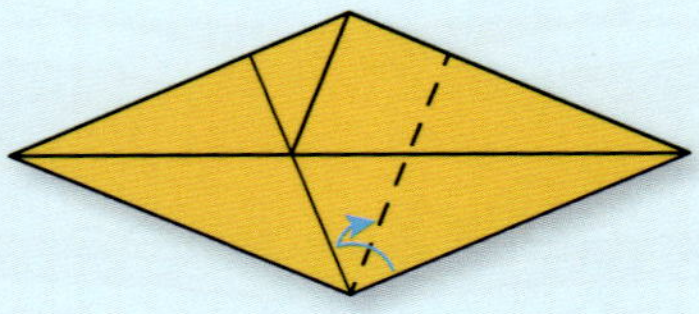

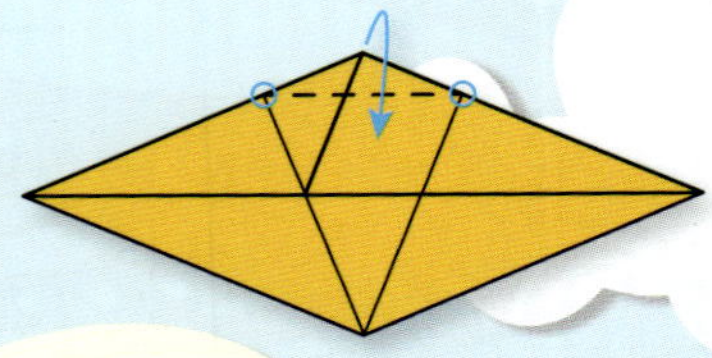

50 Fold the top corner down (as marked).

51 Fold the left corner in along the edge.

52 Turn the paper over.

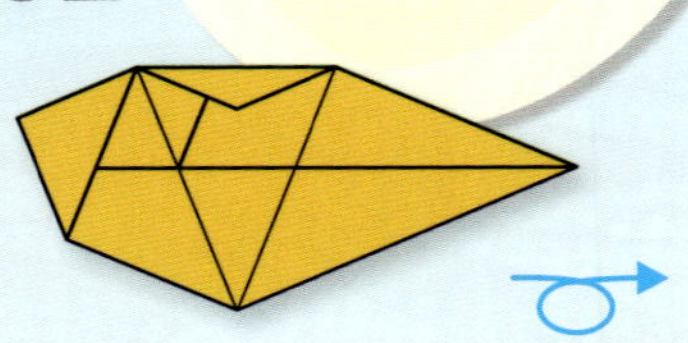

53 Emolga's tail is complete.

Assembling Emolga

54 Squeeze a little glue on the front side of the ears.

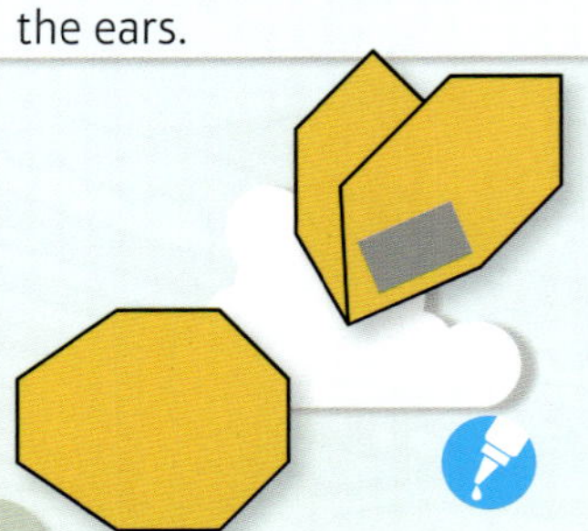

55 Attach the head to the ears (as shown). Align the ears as necessary.

56 Squeeze a little glue on the back of the head.

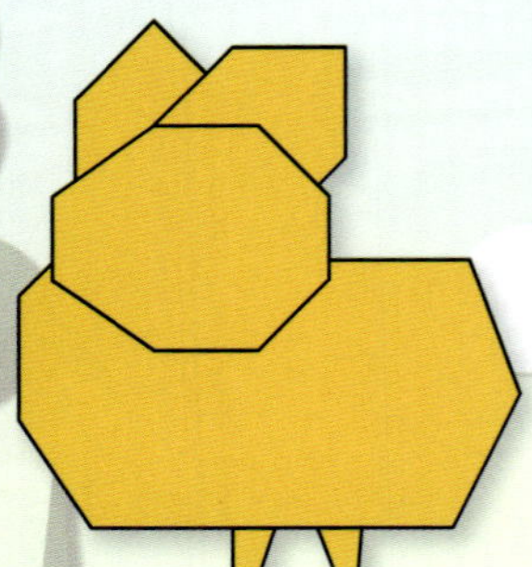

57 Attach the head to the body (as shown). Align the tops of the arms.

58 Squeeze a little glue on the back of the body.

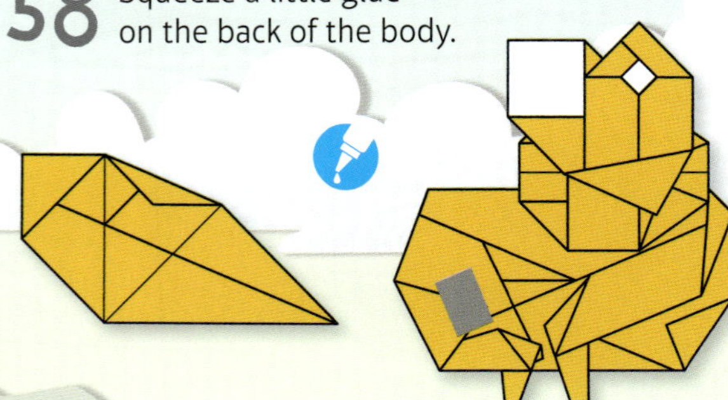

59 Attach the tail to the body (as shown), just above the bottom edge. Turn the paper over to align the tail.

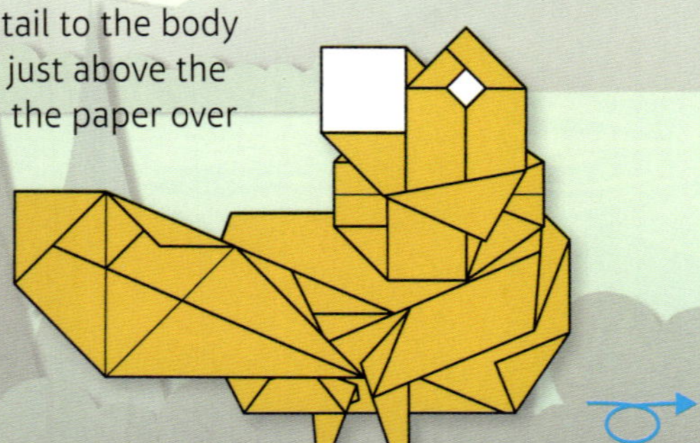

60 Emolga is complete!

Vivillon

Vivillon are found throughout many different regions. The patterns on this Pokémon's wings vary depending on the climate they live in. Fold your Vivillon to discover what pattern its wings have!

TYPE: Bug / Flying **HEIGHT:** 3'11" / 1.2 m **WEIGHT:** 37.5 lbs. / 17 kg

ADVANCED

How To Make Vivillon

Vivillon is folded from three pieces of paper. One large triangle becomes its wings, one small triangle becomes its head and antennae, and one small square becomes its body. You can find the templates on page 101. Carefully cut out the pieces.

Folding the Wings

Make sure to start with the large triangle template arranged so the asterisk is at the top.

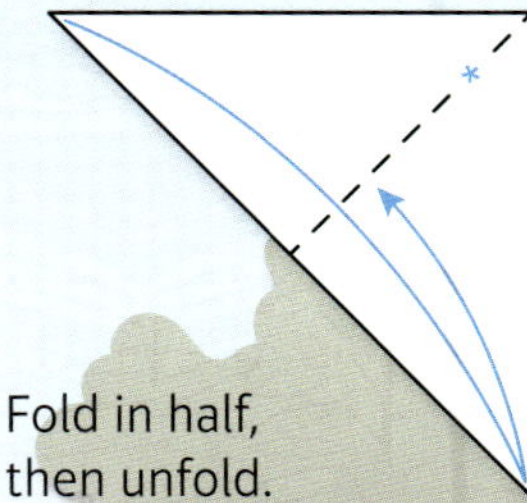

1 Fold in half, then unfold.

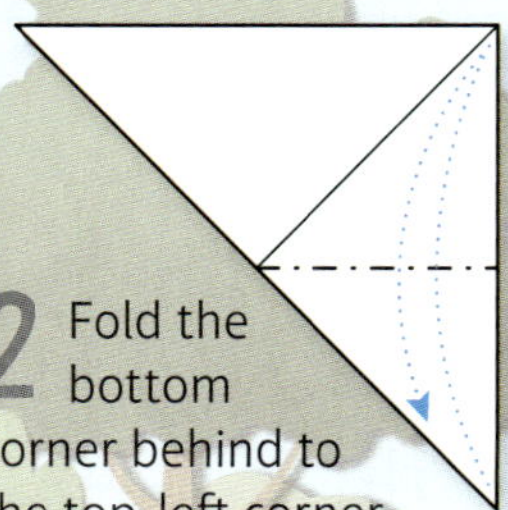

2 Fold the bottom corner behind to the top-left corner, then unfold.

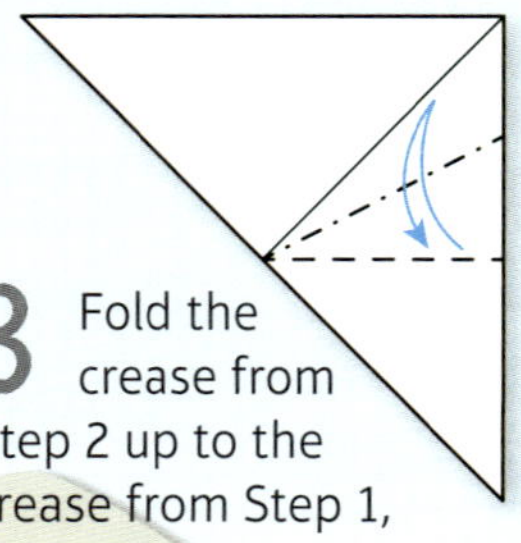

3 Fold the crease from Step 2 up to the crease from Step 1, then unfold.

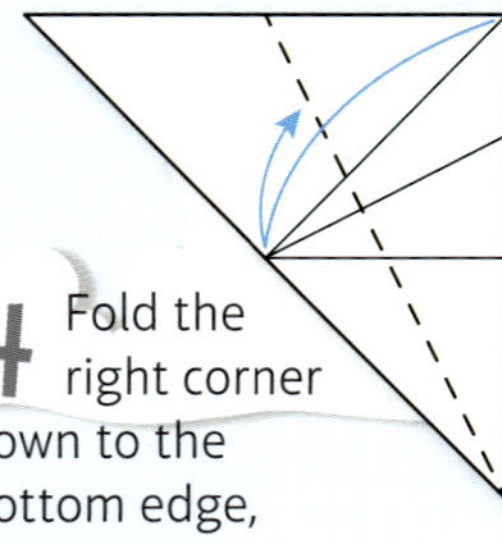

4 Fold the right corner down to the bottom edge, then unfold.

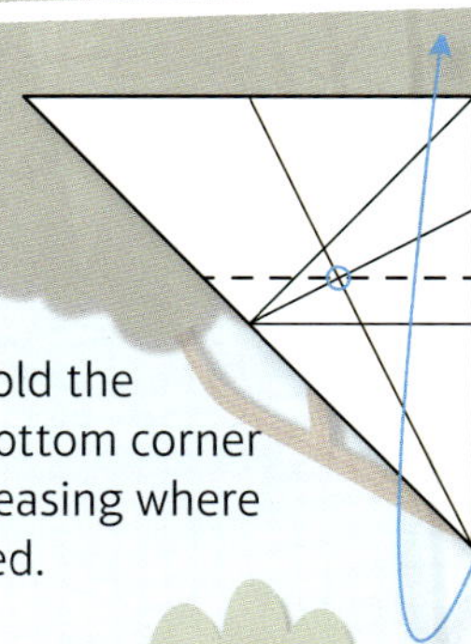

5 Fold the bottom corner up, creasing where marked.

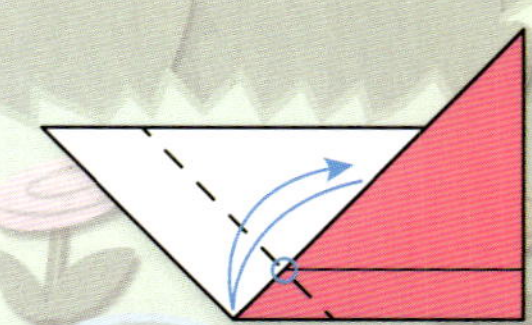

6 Fold the left edge in (as shown), then unfold.

7 Fold the top-left corner to the crease (marked with a circle).

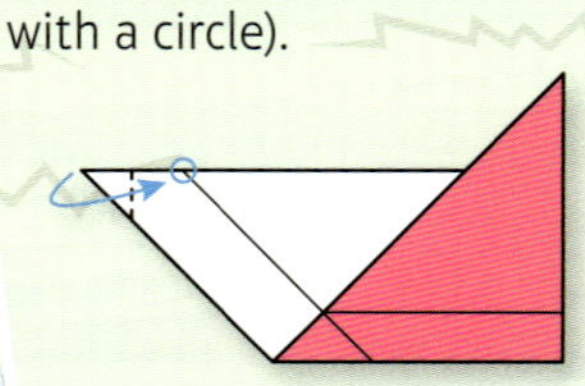

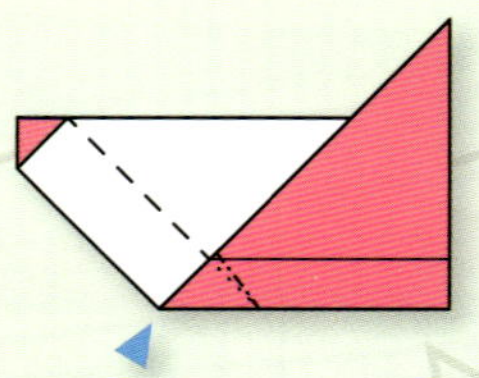

8 Reverse fold the bottom-left corner inside out.

9 Fold the left side behind, along the crease. Align the wings on the opposite side.

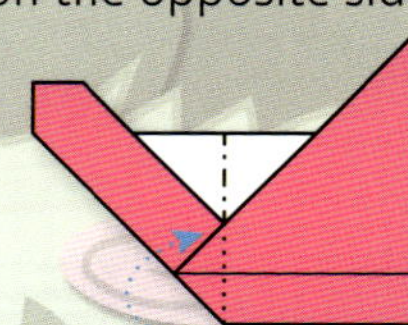

10 Fold the left corner in, then unfold.

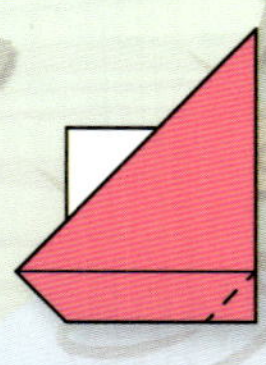

11 Reverse fold the bottom-right corner inside out.

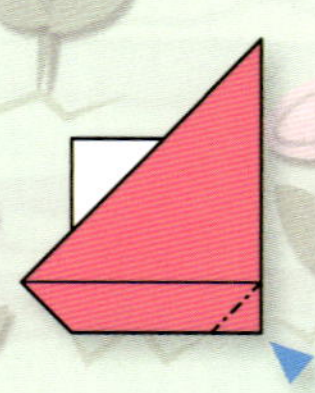

12 Fold the top-right corner down, along the existing crease.

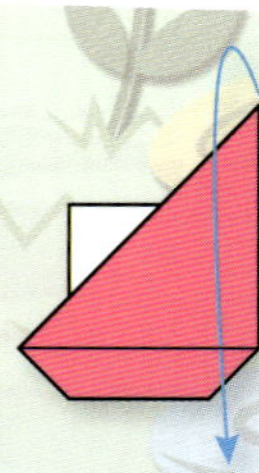

13 Fold the right edge of the flap in along the crease, then unfold.

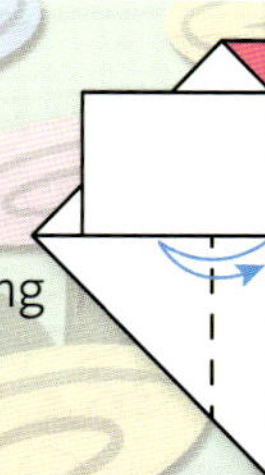

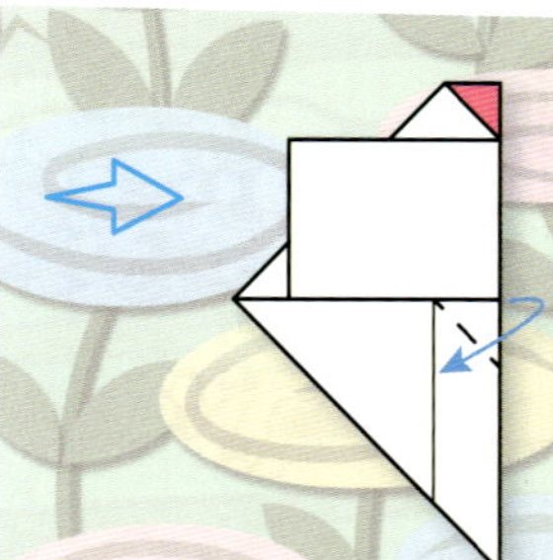

14 Fold the right corner of the flap to the crease.

15 Fold the bottom corner up (as shown).

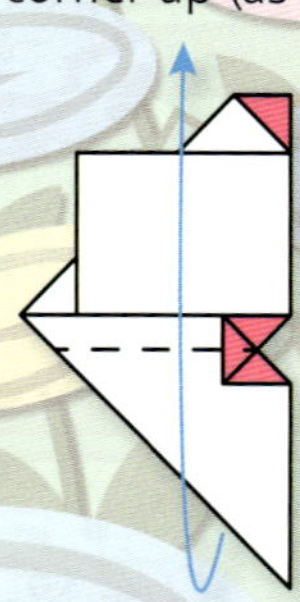

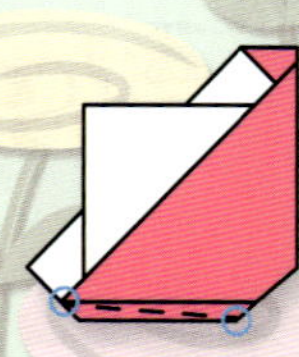

16 Fold the bottom edge up (marked with circles).

17 Tuck in the folded edge.

18 Fold the bottom-right corner up and tuck in.

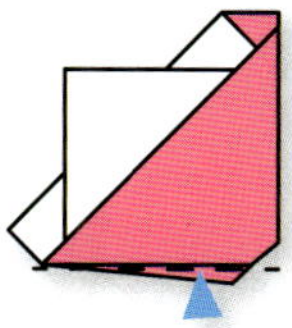

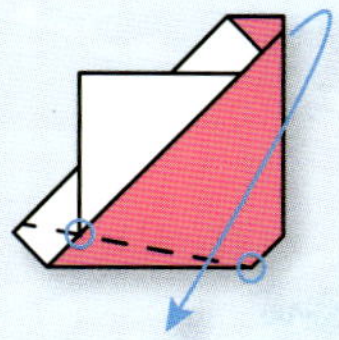

19 Fold the upper-right corner down (as shown).

20 Fold the bottom corner up to the right corner (marked with a circle), then unfold.

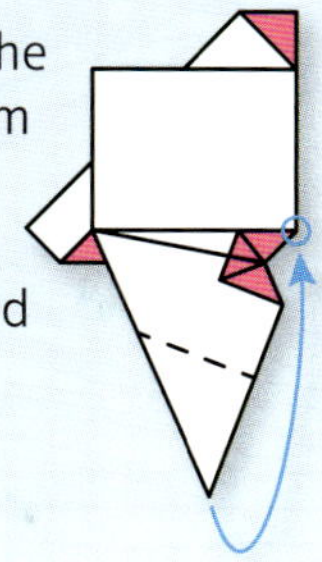

21 Fold the bottom corner up to the crease.

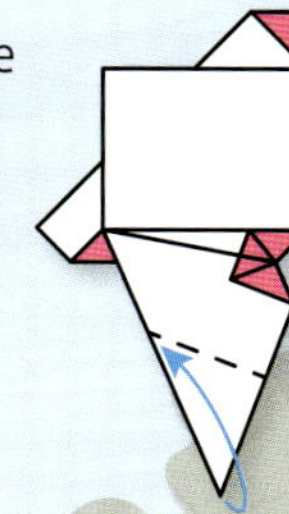

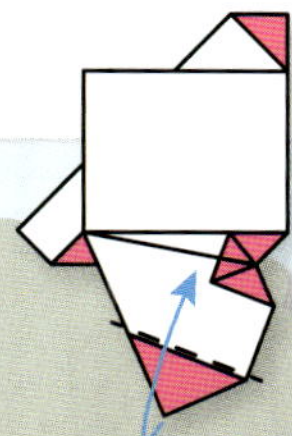

22 Fold the bottom corner up along the crease.

23 Fold the top-right corner down, then unfold.

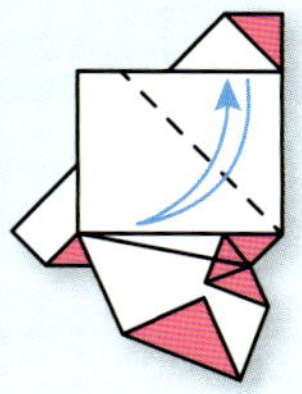

24 Fold the top-right corner down along the crease, then unfold.

25 Fold in the top-right corner (as shown).

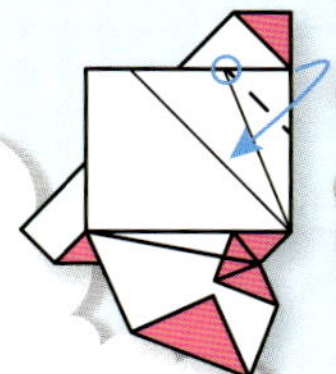

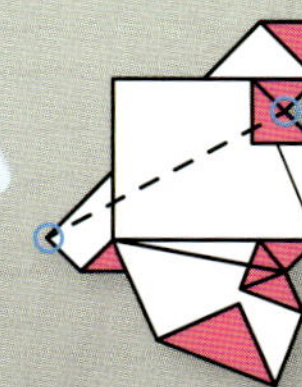

26 Fold up the entire bottom-right half of the wing (as shown).

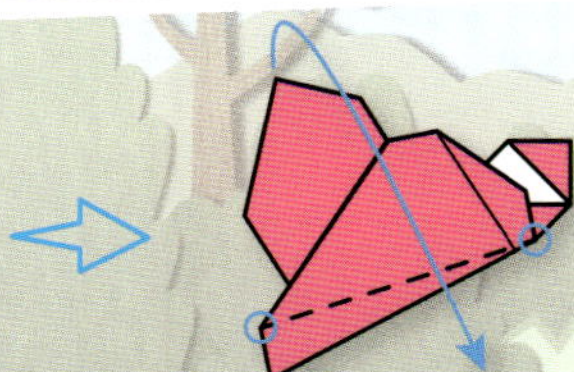

27 Fold the top-left flap down (marked with circles). Turn over to align the wings.

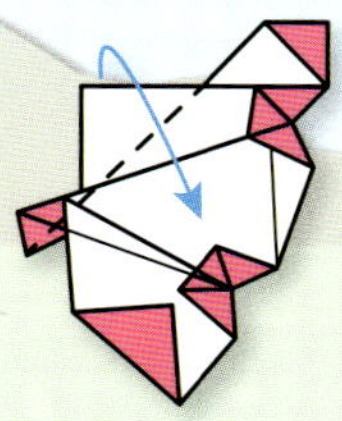

28 Fold the left corner down, along the edge.

29 Fold in the bottom-left corner.

30 Fold in the bottom-right corner.

31 Fold in the bottom-right edge.

32 Fold in the bottom-right corner.

33 Turn the paper over.

34 Fold the edges of the middle part of the wing back, so it's slightly more rounded.

35 Fold the tip of the wing to the back. Turn the paper over.

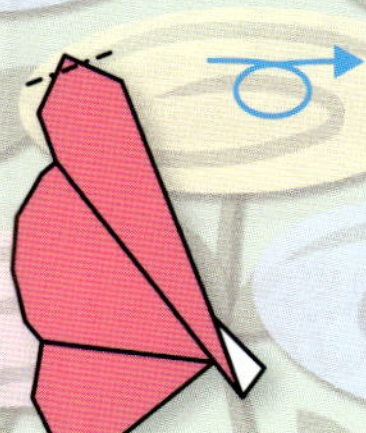

36 Fold the left edge down.

37 Fold the bottom-left tip in (as shown).

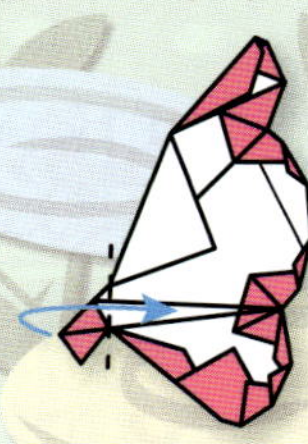

38 Turn the paper over.

39 Vivillon's wings are complete.

Folding the Head & Antennae

Make sure to start with the small triangle template arranged so the asterisk is at the top.

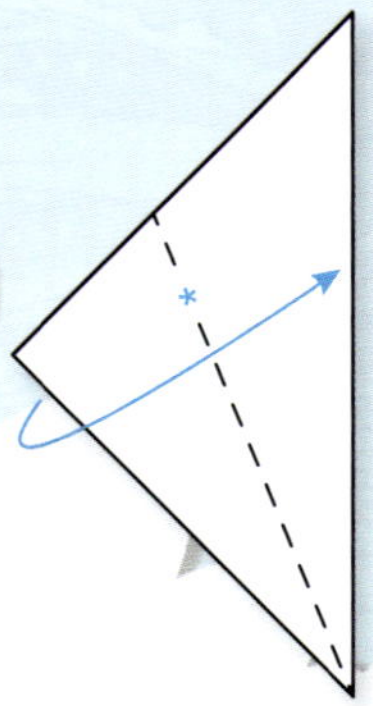

40 Fold the left corner to the right edge.

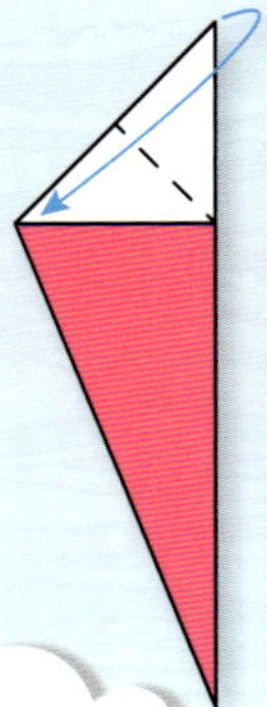

41 Fold the top corner down to the left corner.

42 Fold the top corner down to the edge, then unfold.

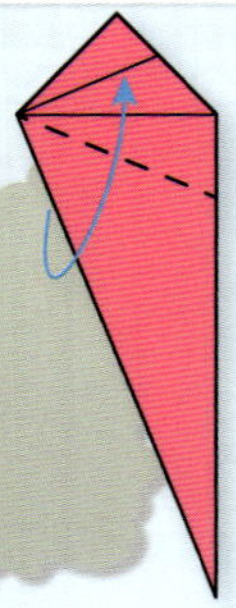

43 Fold the lower-left edge up to the crease from Step 40.

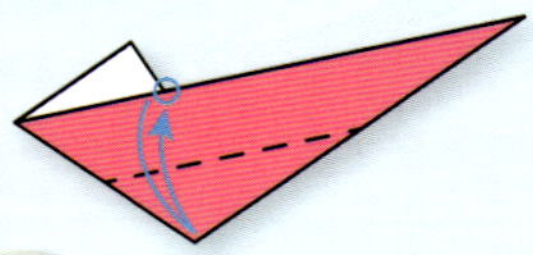

44 Fold the bottom corner up to the edge (marked with a circle), then unfold.

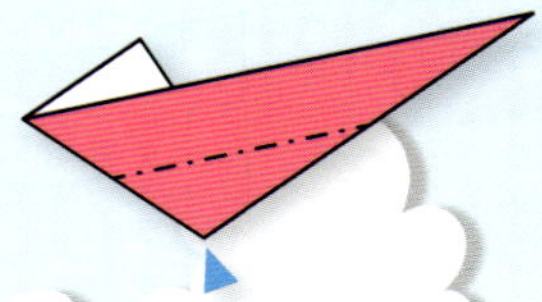

45 Reverse fold the bottom corner behind the back face flap.

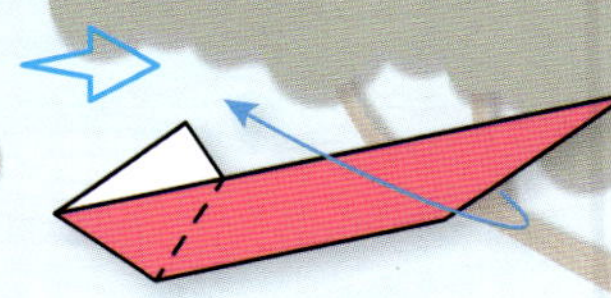

46 Fold the right corner to the left—along the crease.

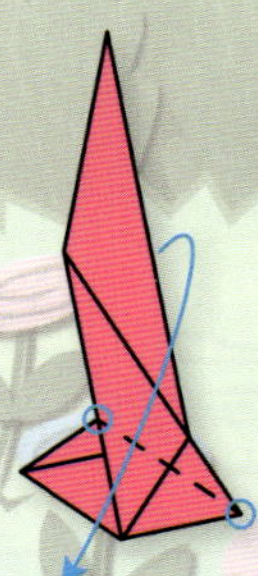

47 Fold the top corner down to the left (as shown).

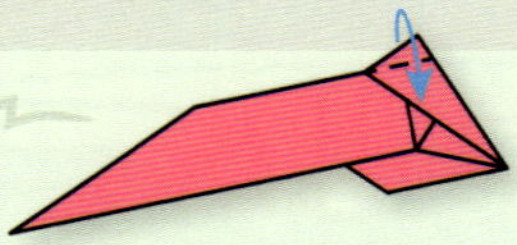

48 Fold the top corner down slightly.

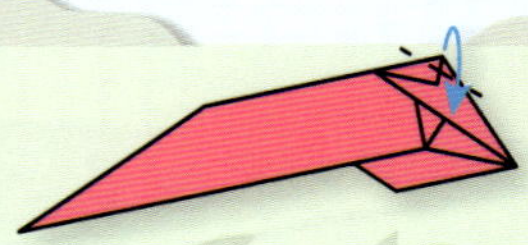

49 Fold the right edge in slightly (to round the head on the opposite side).

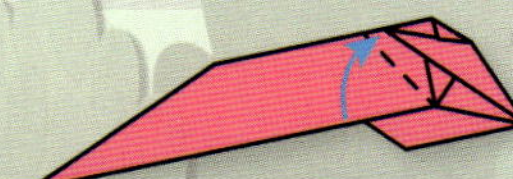

50 Fold the left corner up along the edge (turn over to align the antennae).

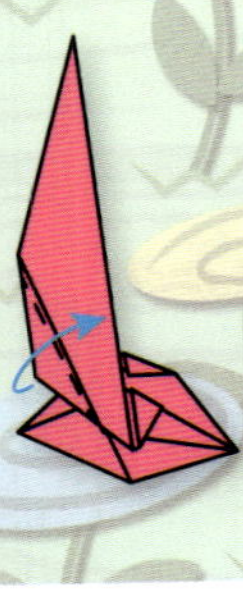

51 Fold the left edge of the flap in (as shown).

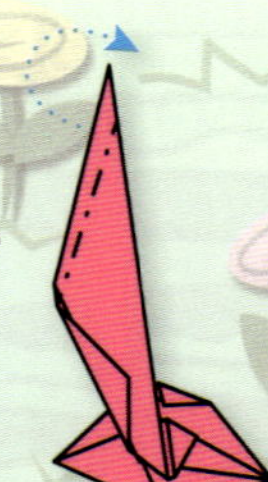

52 Fold the upper-left edge back.

53 Fold the left corner in (as shown).

54 Turn the paper over.

55 Fold the right corner back to shape the head.

56 Open the triangle at the top and carefully flatten the pocket.

57 Vivillon's head and antennae are complete.

Folding the Body

Make sure to start with the small square template arranged so the asterisk is at the top.

58 Fold in half from top to bottom, then unfold.

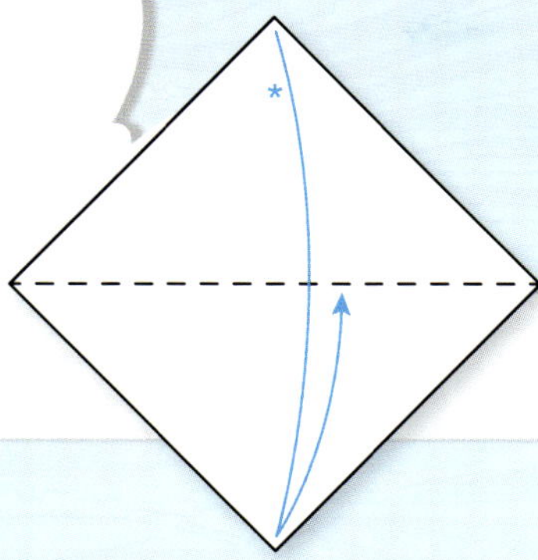

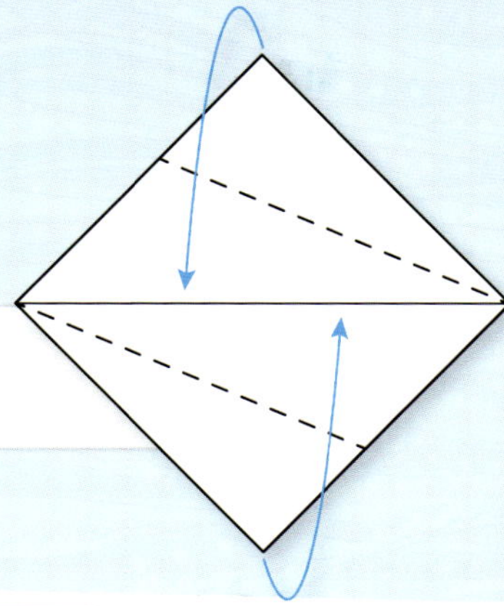

59 Fold the top and bottom corners into the centerline.

60 Fold the new top and bottom corners into the centerline.

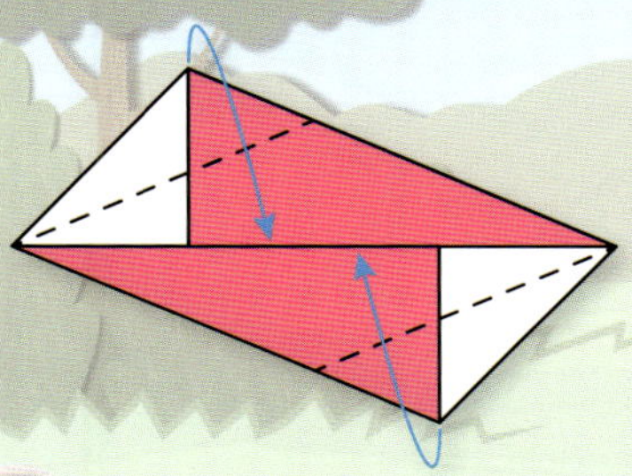

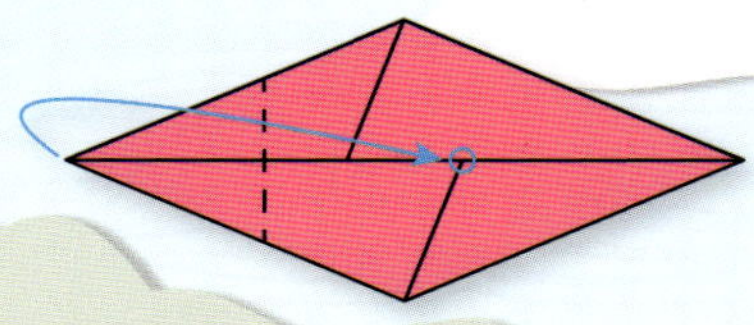

61 Fold the left corner over to the marking.

62 Fold the right corner over to the marking.

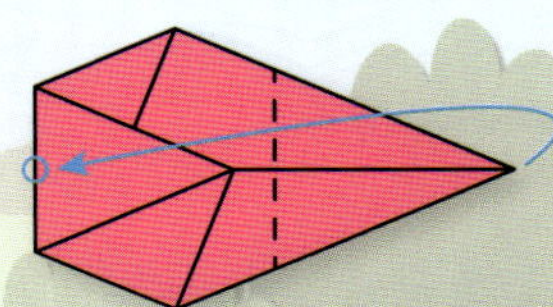

63 Fold in half from bottom to top.

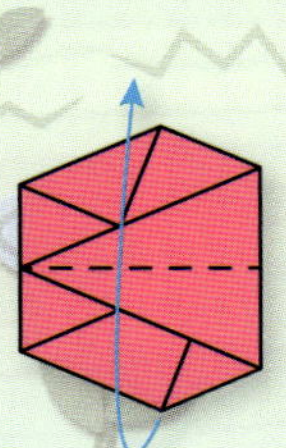

64 Fold the bottom corners back (paper will be thick).

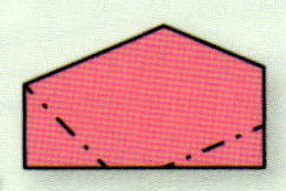

65 Vivillon's body is complete.

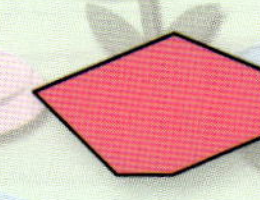

Assembling Vivillon

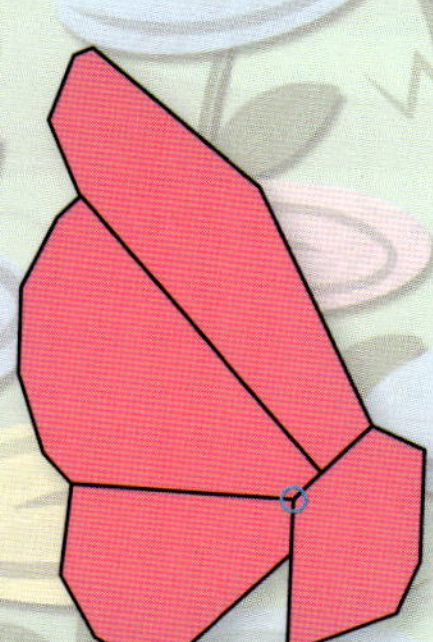

66 Place the wings inside the body (as marked). Align the lines on the wings.

67 Place the head on the body (as marked). Again, align the lines on the wings. Glue in place.

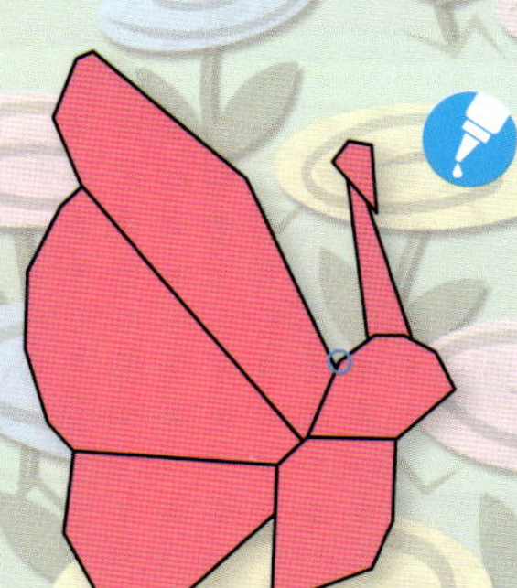

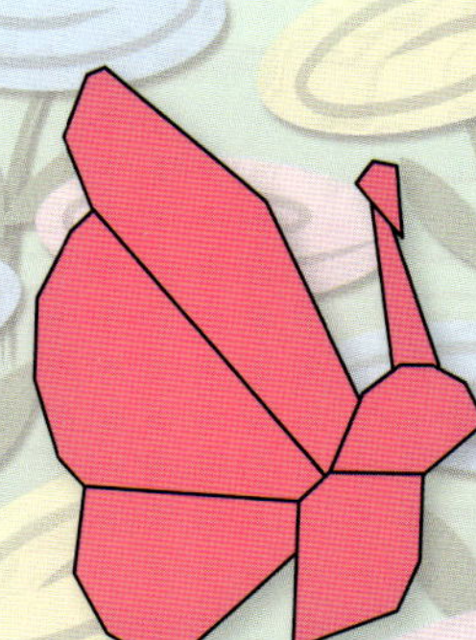

68 Vivillon is complete!

Alolan Diglett

Alolan Diglett lives underground, and it's powerful enough to dig right through volcanic rock. Dig into the directions for Alolan Diglett to create this origami version of the Mole Pokémon who's just popped its head out of the ground.

TYPE: Ground / Steel **HEIGHT:** 8" / .2 m **WEIGHT:** 1.8 lbs. / .8 kg

BEGINNER

How To Make

Alolan Diglett

Alolan Diglett is folded from two pieces of paper: one large square and one small triangle. The large square becomes its body; the small triangle becomes its hair. You can find the templates on pages 105 and 109. Carefully cut out each of the pieces.

Folding the Body

Make sure to start with the large square template, and arrange it so the asterisk is at the top.

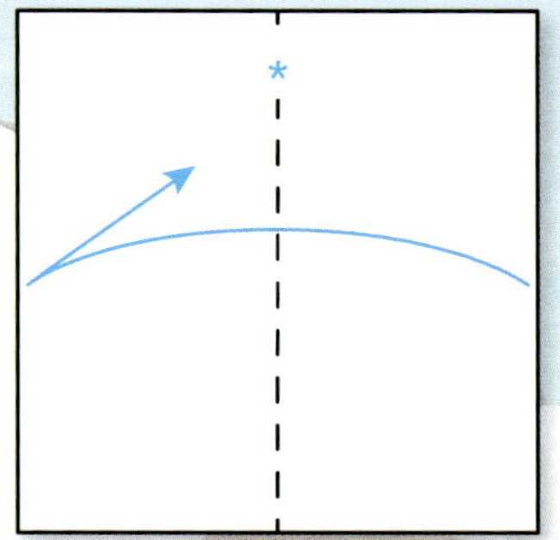

1 Fold in half sideways, then unfold.

2 Fold the left and right edges into the center, then unfold.

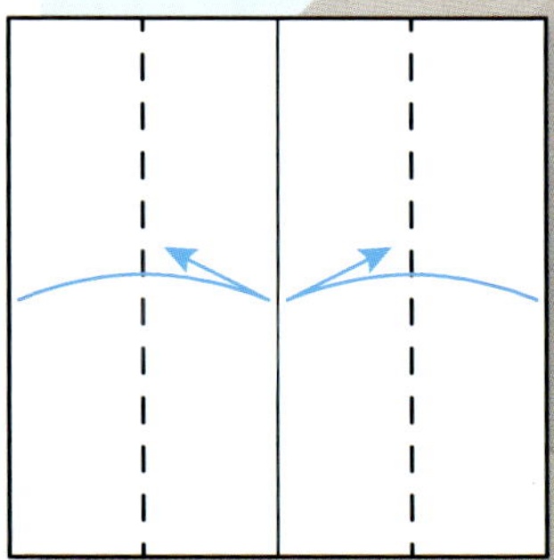

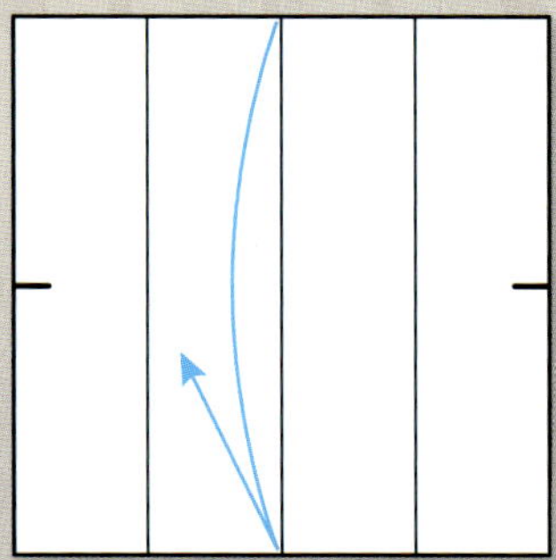

3 Fold in half from top to bottom. Create two reference points by making a crease at each of the two edges, then unfold.

4 Fold the bottom edge up to the reference points you made in Step 3, then unfold.

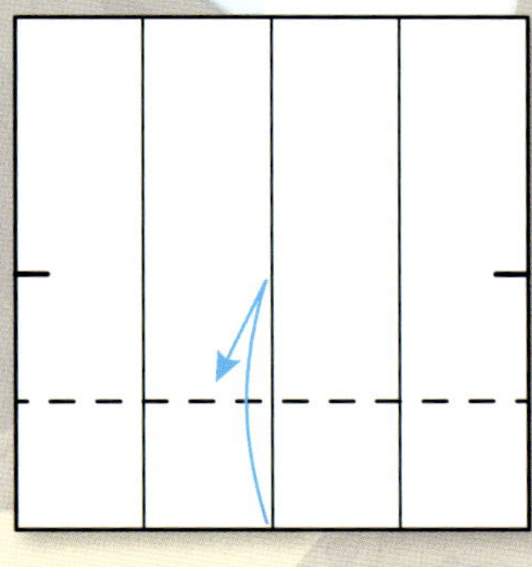

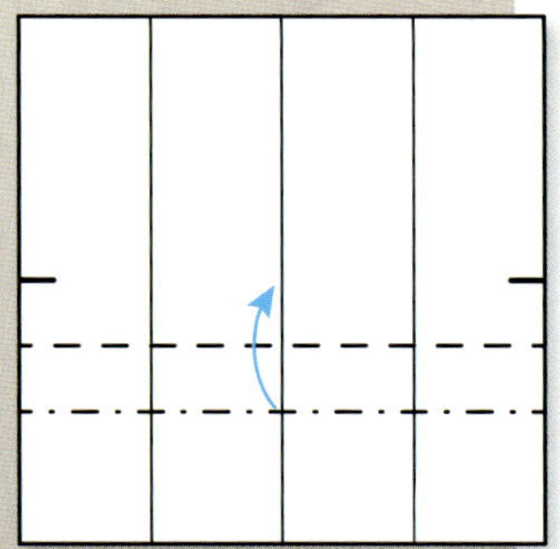

5 Fold the crease you made in Step 4 up to the reference points you made in Step 3.

6 This is what the result should look like, then unfold.

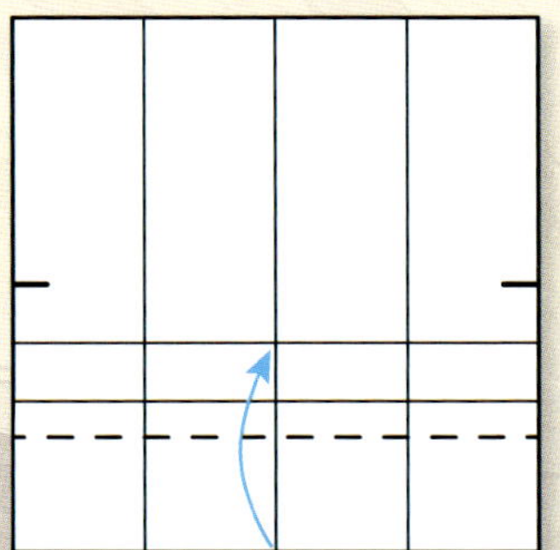

7 Fold the bottom edge to the crease you made in Step 6 to look like the next step.

8 Turn the paper over.

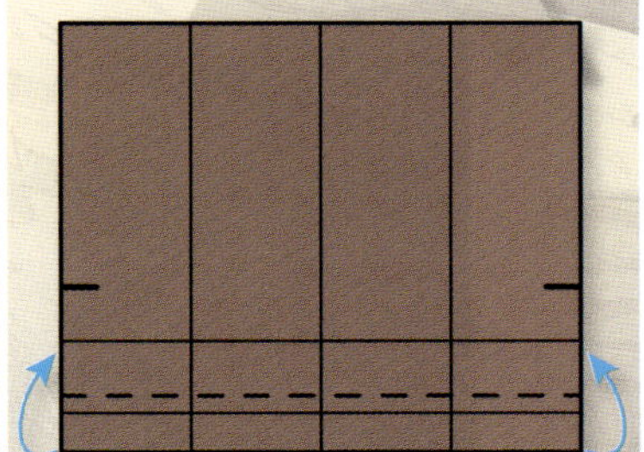

9 Fold the bottom edge to the crease you made in Step 5, allowing the layer at the back to swing into view.

10 Turn the paper over.

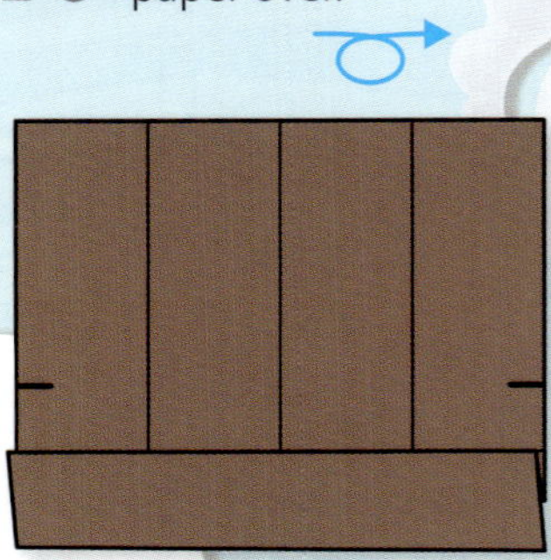

11 Fold the left and right edges into the center, using the existing creases.

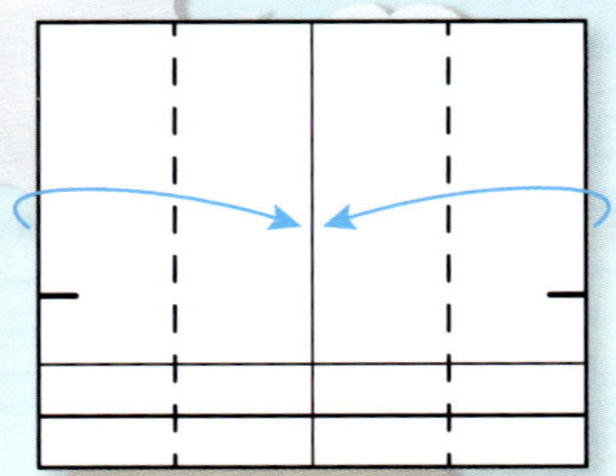

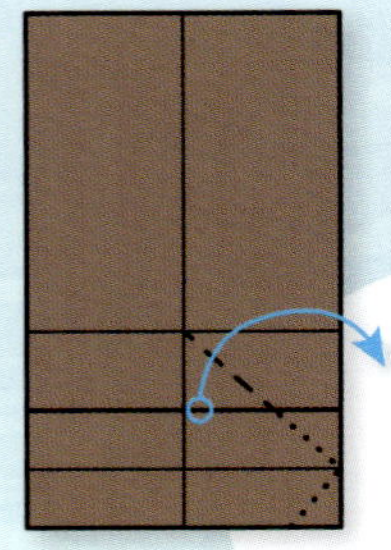

12 Swing out the inner-bottom corner (marked with a circle), and crease diagonally to look like the next step.

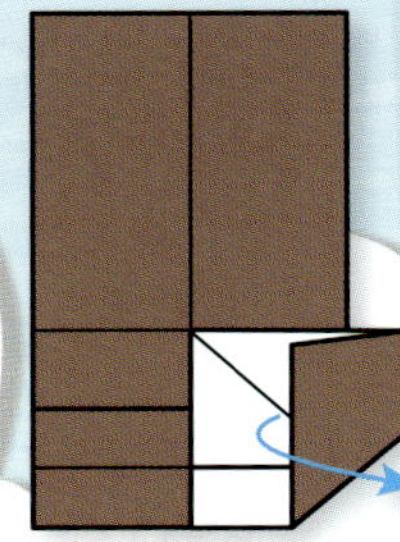

13 Gently open the flap out to the right.

14 Turn the top corner inside out so the two layers crease diagonally to form a pocket.

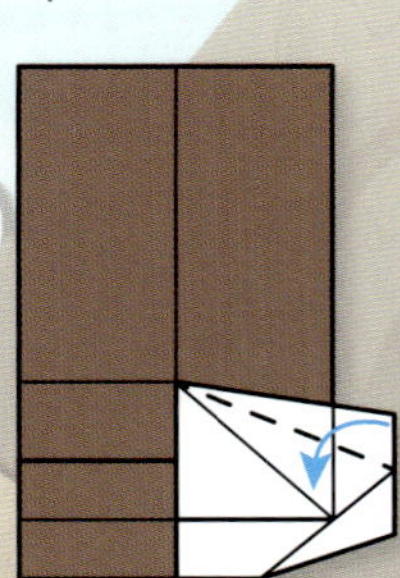

15 Flatten the pocket carefully.

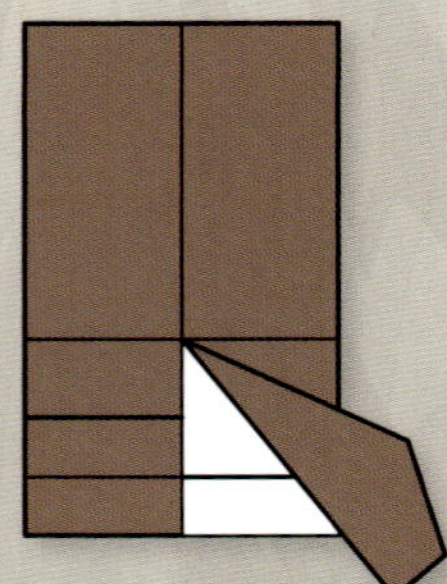

16 Repeat Step 12 on the left half of the paper.

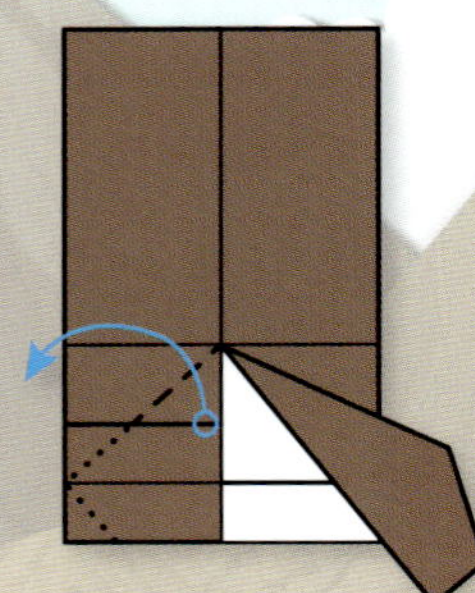

17 Gently open the flap out to the left, and crease diagonally to form a pocket.

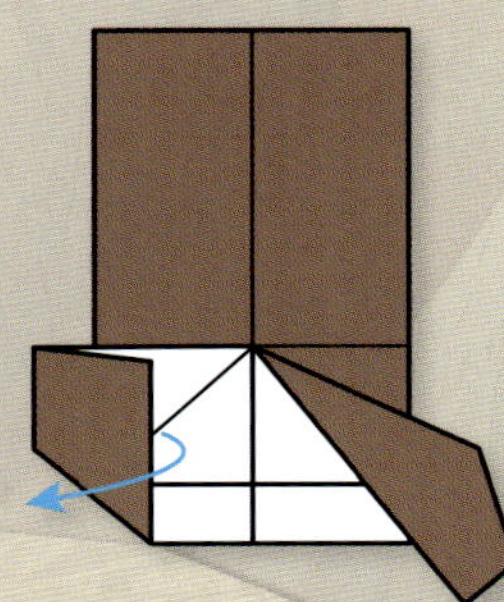

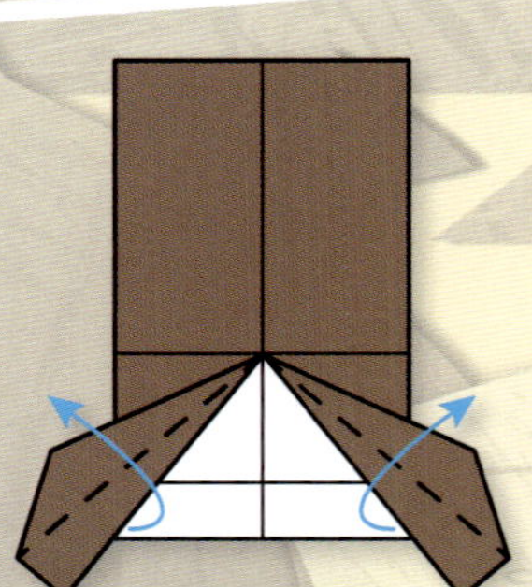

18 Fold the edges out to the sides, as shown.

19 Fold both top-inside corners of the front layer diagonally out toward the edges, then unfold.

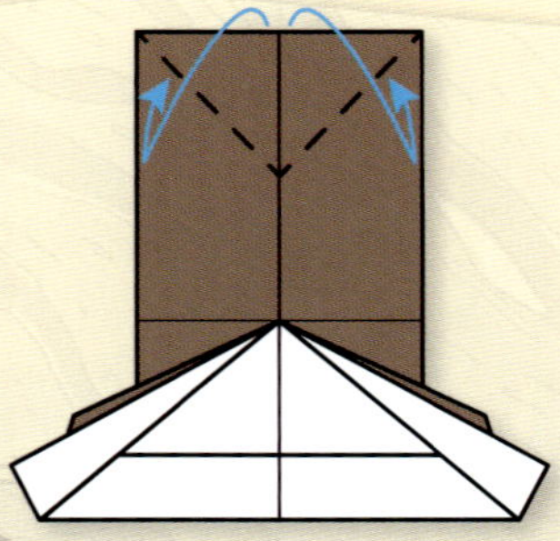

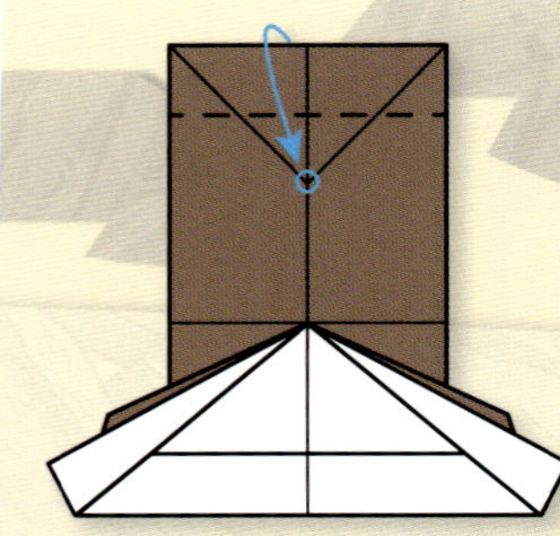

20 Fold the top edge down to where the creases from the folds you made in Step 19 meet—marked with a circle.

21 Fold both top-outside corners in, as shown.

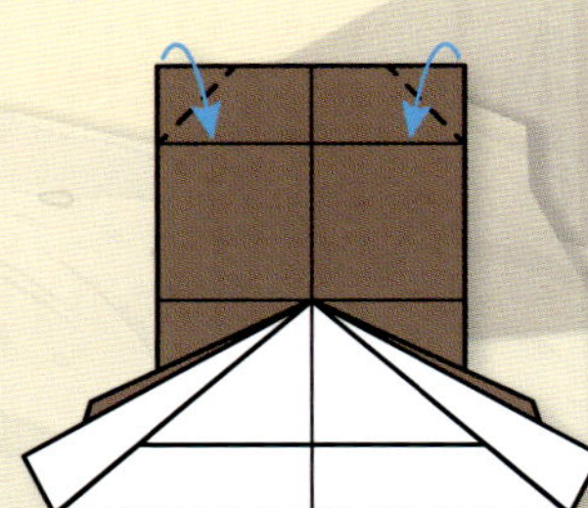

22 Turn the paper over.

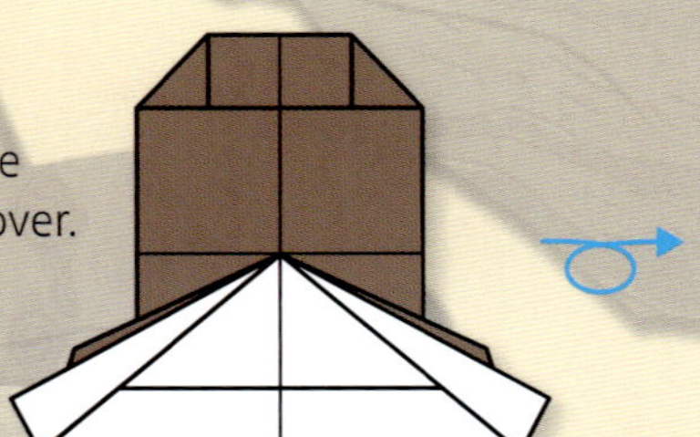

23 Alolan Diglett's body and dirt mound are finished.

Folding the Hair

Make sure you start with the small triangle template arranged so the asterisk is at the top.

24 Fold in half sideways, then unfold.

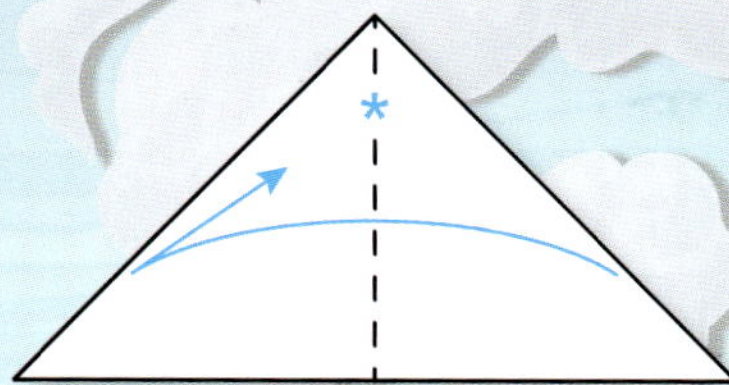

25 Fold the bottom corners up to the top corner.

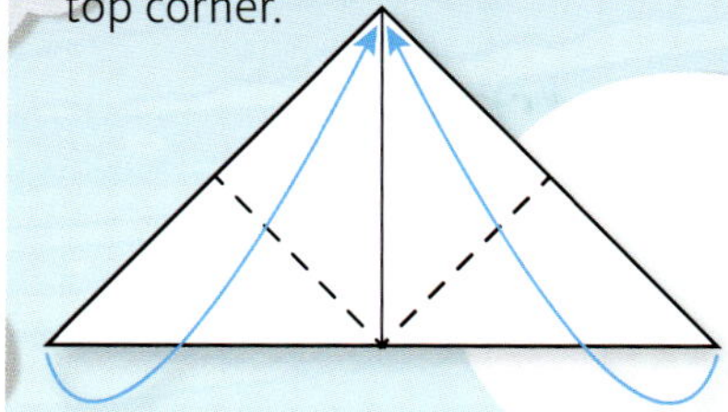

26 Fold the left and right edges into the center.

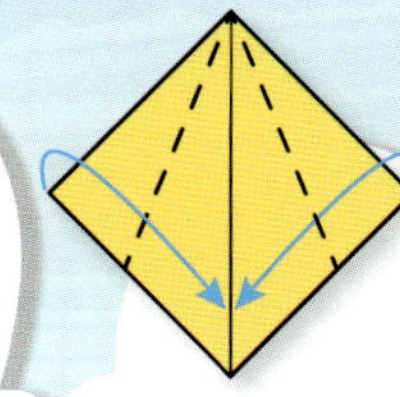

27 The result should look like this. Unfold completely.

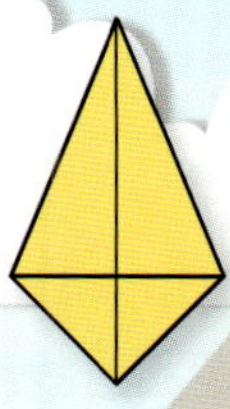

28 Fold the three corners in—just a bit.

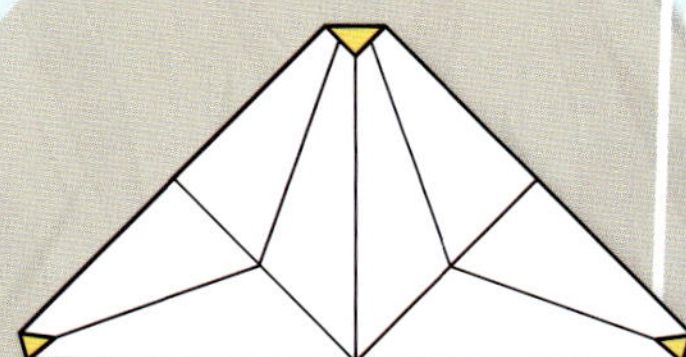

29 Reverse fold the left and right edges (marked with a circle) toward the center along the existing creases, as you fold the bottom corners up to the top corner.

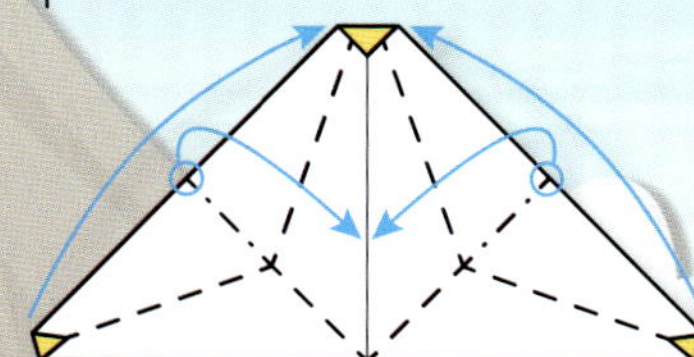

30 Where the diamond is at its widest (marked with a circle), make a small cut across the top two layers of the right-hand flap.

31 Fold down the right flap.

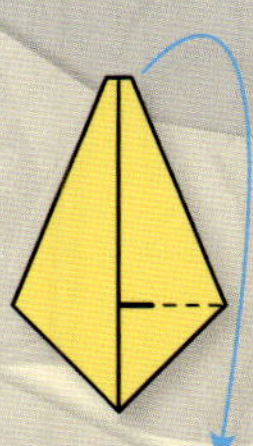

32 Fold over the cut portion of the flap to the right.

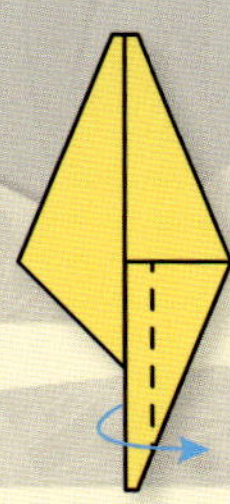

33 Fold the right flap up.

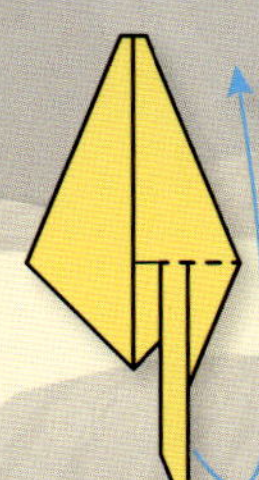

34 Fold the right half backward along the center crease.

35 Fold the top layer behind itself about one-third of the way down the right side.

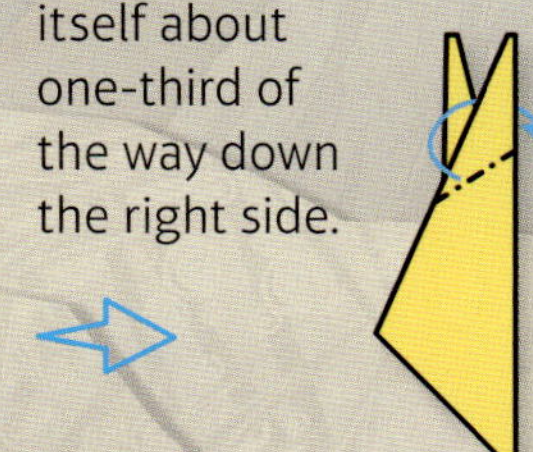

36 Fold the second layer behind itself about one-fourth of the way down the right side.

37 Fold back the tops of the front two flaps so that they are thinner.

38 Add a small zigzag pleat to the top of each flap.

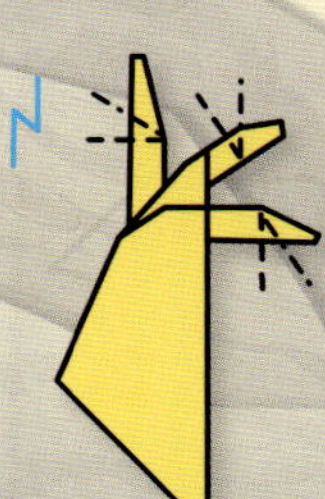

39 Alolan Diglett's hair is complete.

Assembling Alolan Diglett

40 Tape the hair onto the back of the head. Turn the paper over.

41 Alolan Diglett is finished.

Yamper

This Puppy Pokémon loves treats and playing chase. As it runs, its tail charges with electricity. Use your speed to fold Yamper, and then reward yourself with a treat—just like Yamper would!

TYPE: Electric **HEIGHT:** 1' / .3 m **WEIGHT:** 29.8 lbs. / 13.5 kg

ADVANCED

How To Make Yamper

Yamper is folded from three pieces of paper: one large square and two small squares. The large square becomes its body; one small square becomes its face, and the other small square becomes its ears. You can find the templates on pages 109 and 113. Carefully cut out each of the pieces.

Folding the Body

Make sure to start with the large square template; arrange it so the asterisk is at the top.

1 Fold in half sideways, then unfold.

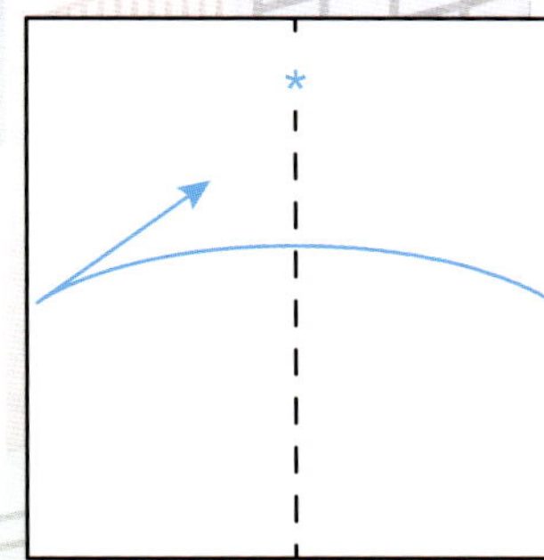

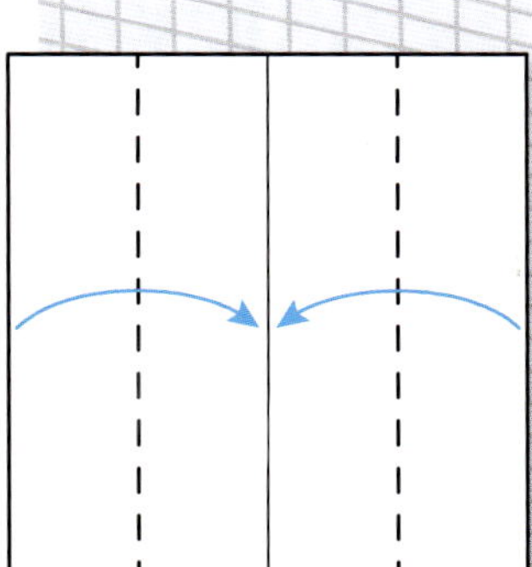

2 Fold the left and right edges into the center.

3 Fold both bottom-outside corners into the center.

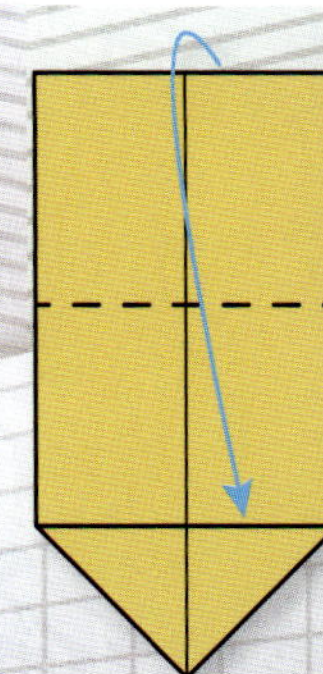

4 Fold the top edge down to the top of the flaps you made in Step 3.

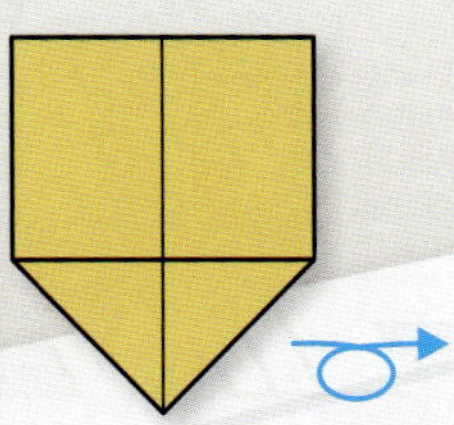

5 Turn the paper over.

6 Fold the top edge down to the corners, allowing the layer at the back to swing into view.

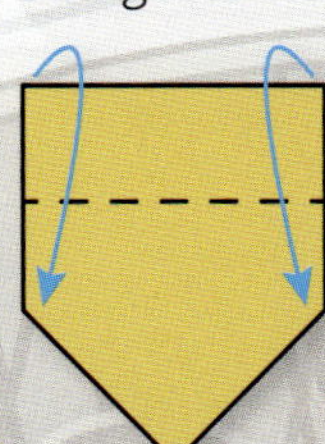

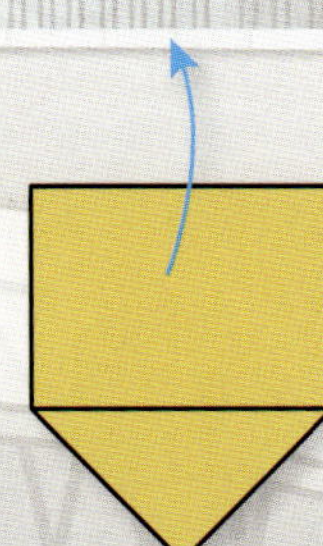

7 Undo Step 6, so the top layer swings to the back again.

8 Fold the two corners at the top to the crease you made in Step 6, then unfold.

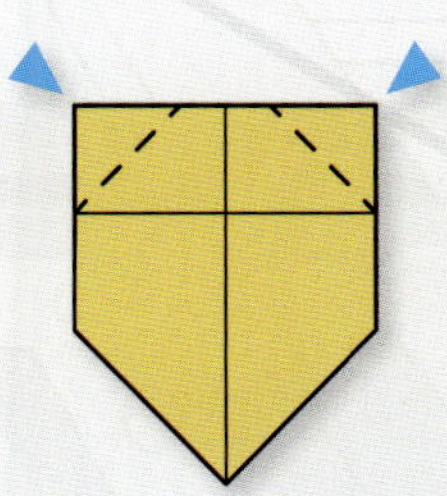

9 Reverse fold the two corners inside, using the creases you made in Step 8.

10 Fold the bottom corner up so the crease runs between the bottom corners (as shown).

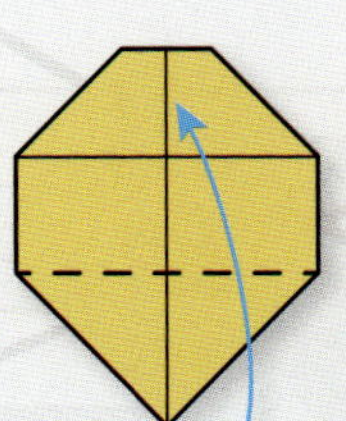

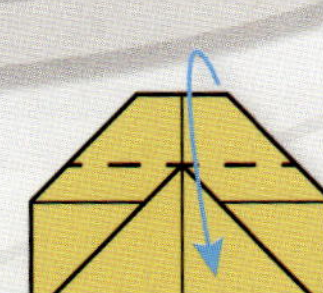

11 Fold the top edge down so the new crease runs along the top of the triangle (as shown).

12 Gently unfold the back layer up to the front (it will not lay flat).

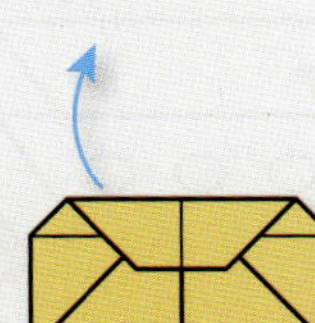

13 Turn the paper over.

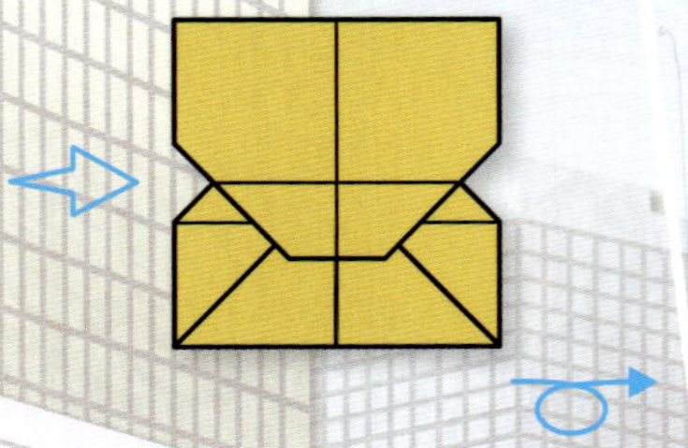

14 Flatten the two triangles carefully to look like the next step.

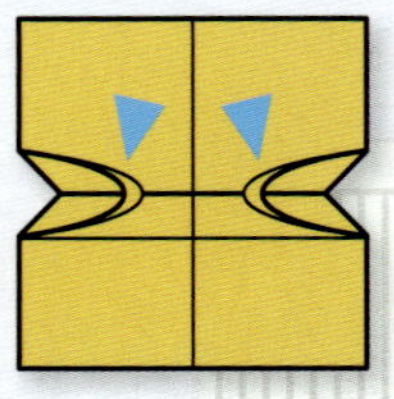

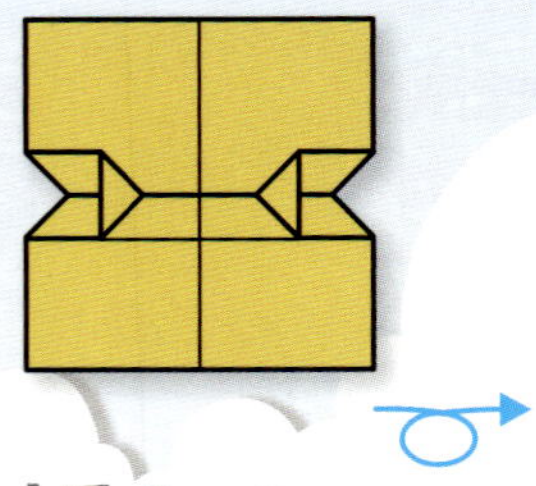

15 Turn the paper over.

16 Pull the point of the triangle to the front (see next step).

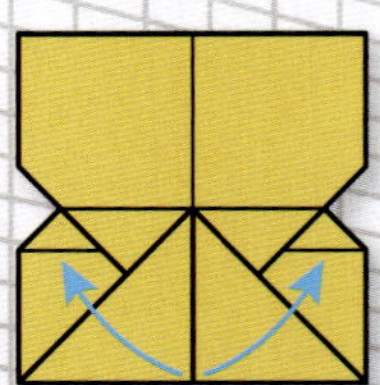

17 Unfold the smaller triangles.

18 Fold the top of the rectangle down to the bottom edge.

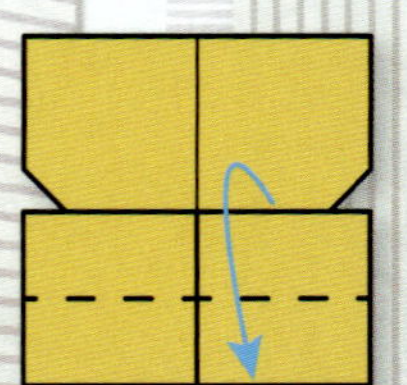

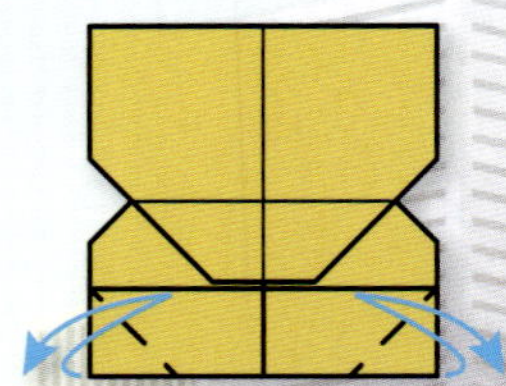

19 Fold in the bottom two corners to the crease, then unfold.

20 Fold the top layer of the bottom flap up, and flatten the sides along the creases (see next step).

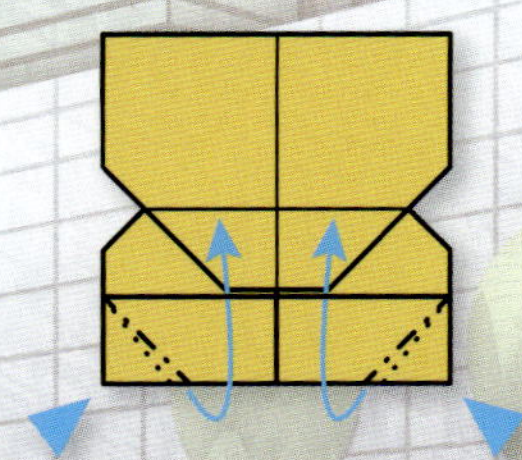

21 Fold the two bottom flaps up.

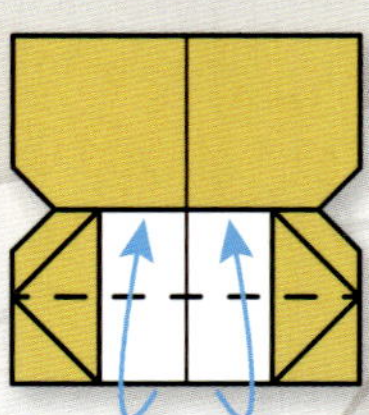

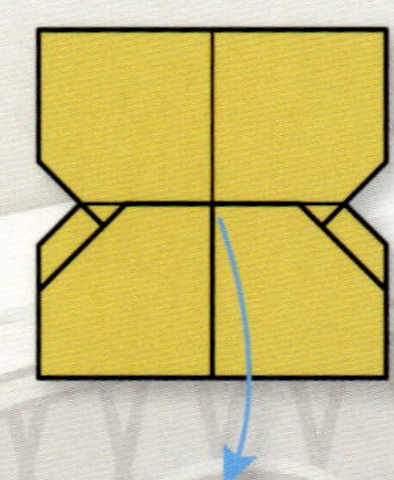

22 Unfold the flap.

23 Tuck the top layer up inside along the creases.

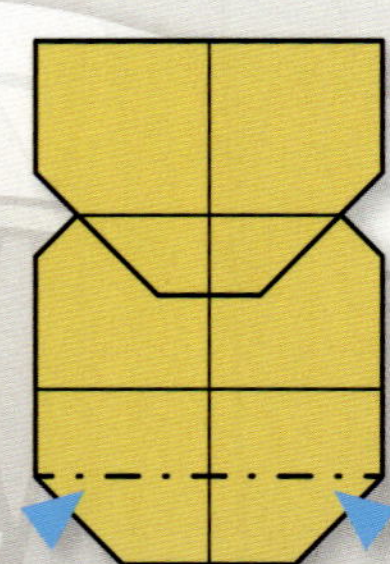

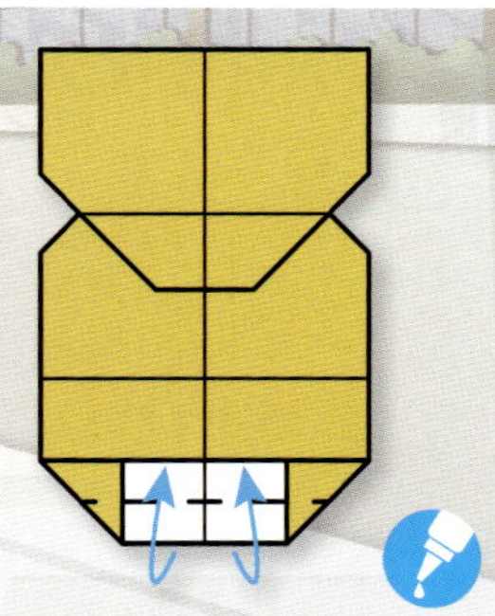

24 Fold the bottom two flaps up into the pocket. Glue them in place.

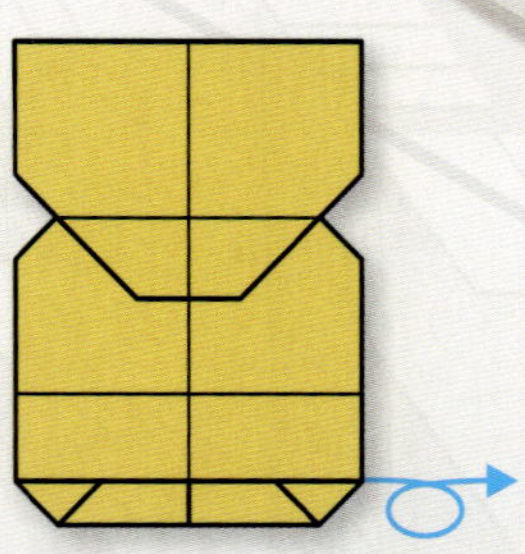

25 Turn the paper over.

26 Fold the middle crease up to the fold from Step 14.

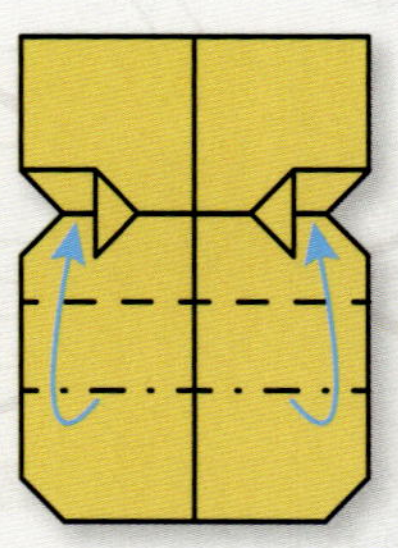

27 Fold the top edge one-third of the way down (as shown).

28 Fold down the two corners at the top.

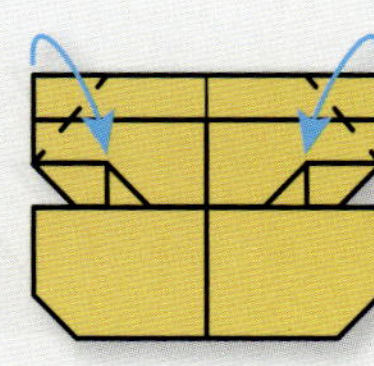

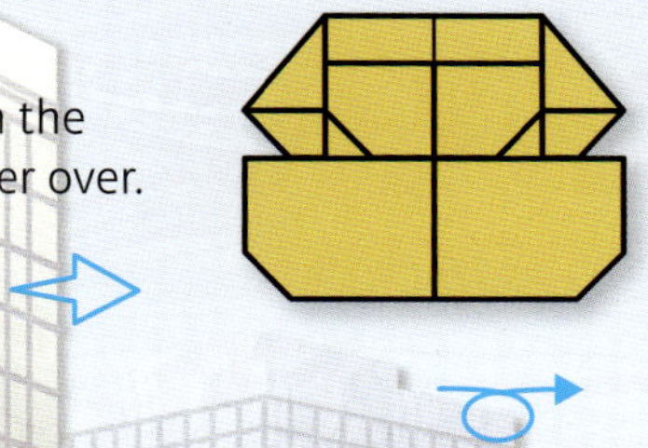

29 Turn the paper over.

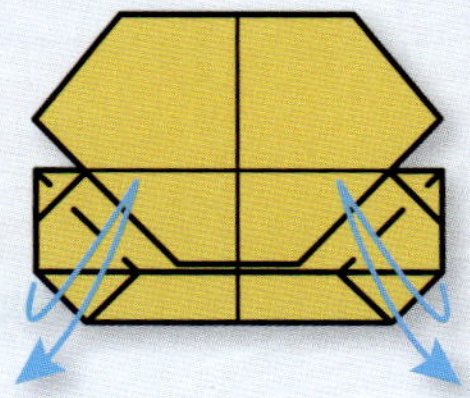

30 Fold the top layer of the bottom corners up, then unfold.

31 Using the creases you made in Step 30, reverse fold the two corners inside out.

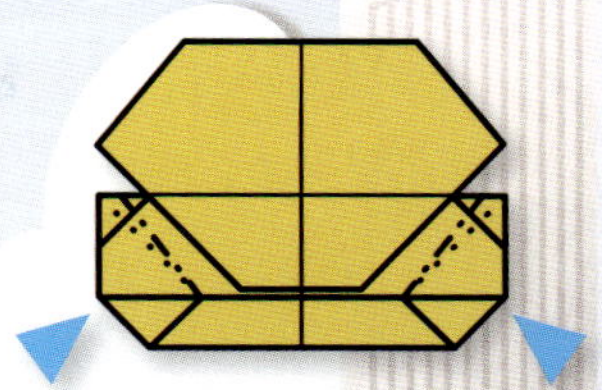

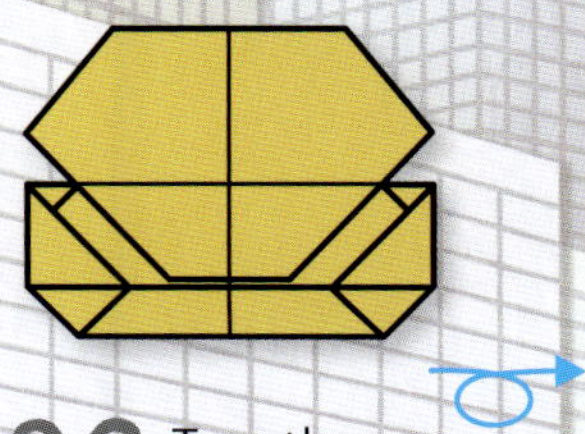

32 Turn the paper over.

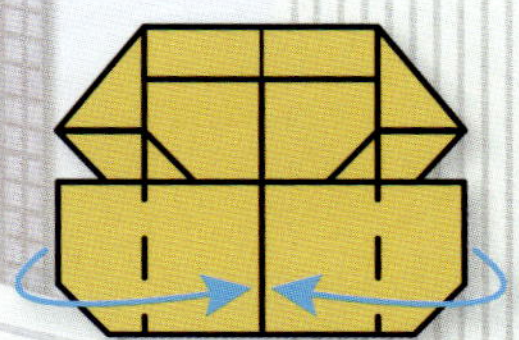

33 Fold the bottom flaps to the center.

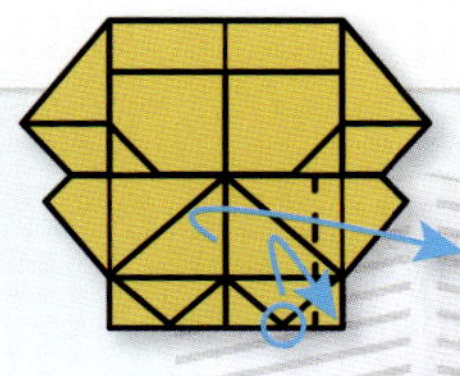

34 Fold inside point (marked with a circle) to the bottom-right corner.

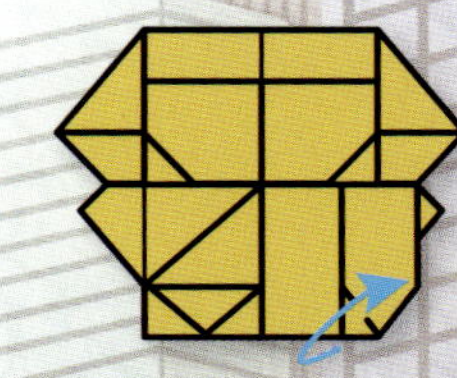

35 Fold out the edge (marked with a circle) to lock.

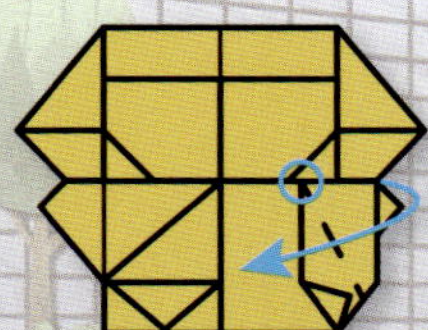

36 Fold the flap toward the center along its top-left corner (marked with a circle).

37 Fold out the bottom flap along its top-left corner.

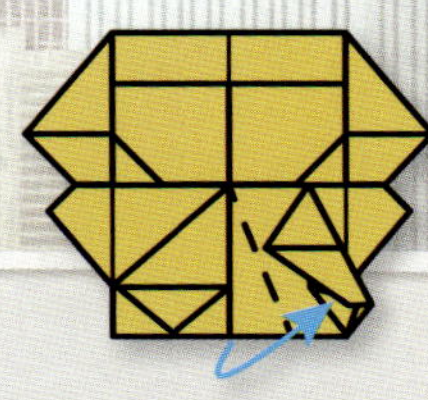

38 Repeat Steps 34–37 on the left side.

39 Fold the bottom corners toward the center.

40 Fold the inside corners to narrow.

41 Turn the paper over.

42 Fold the bottom edge behind the top layer to form the collar.

43 Fold back the four side corners to round the edges.

44 Yamper's body is complete.

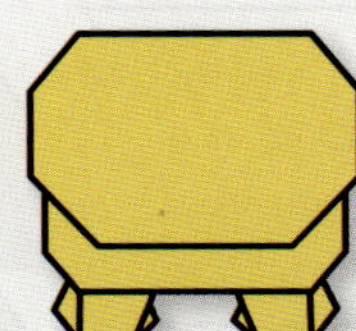

Folding the Head

Make sure to start with the smaller square head template, and arrange it so the asterisk is at the top.

45 Fold in half sideways, then unfold.

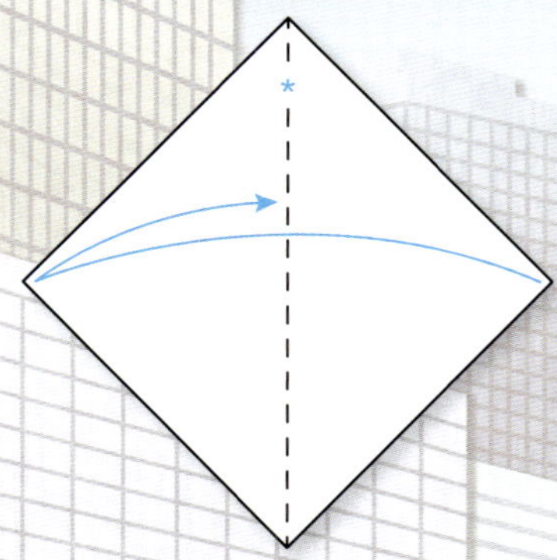

46 Fold the left and right edges into the center.

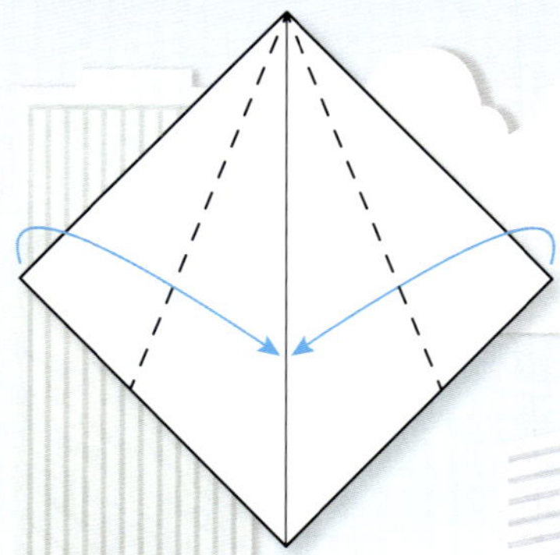

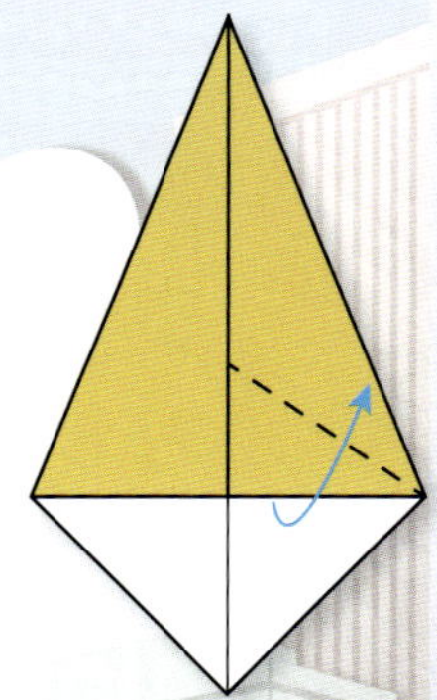

47 Fold the right-inside corner out to the right edge.

48 Fold the same flap to the crease from Step 47.

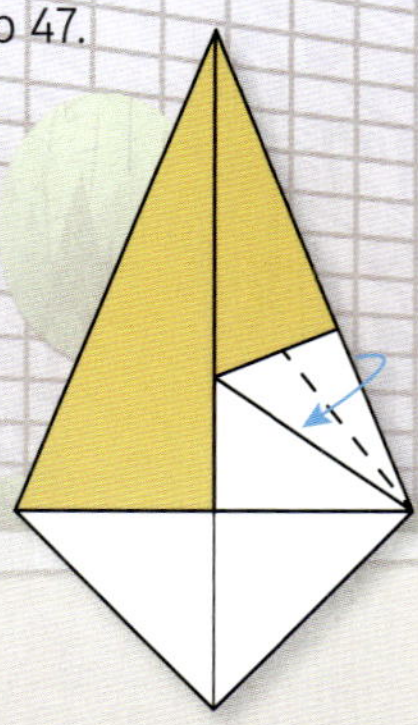

49 The result should look like this (see image). Then unfold.

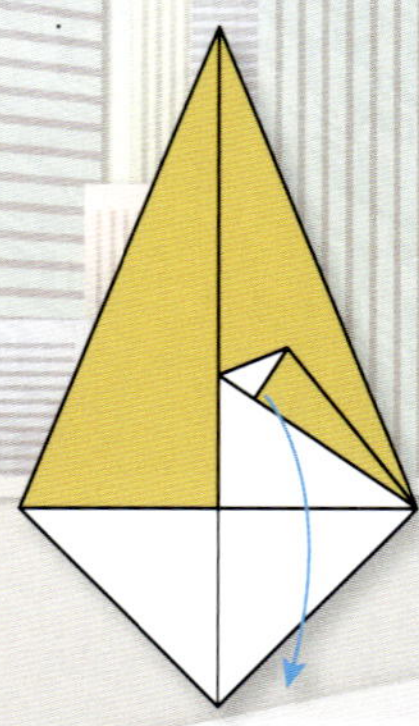

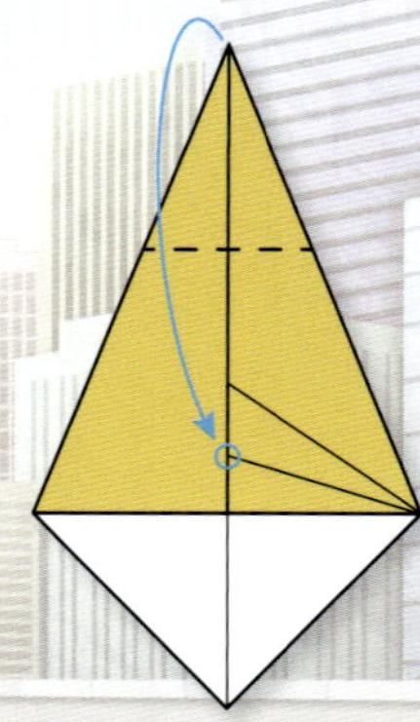

50 Fold the top corner down (marked with a circle). Turn over to crease the paper just above the head.

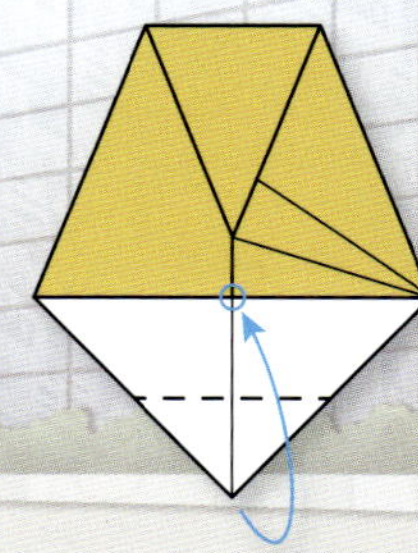

51 Fold the bottom corner up to the two center corners above (marked with a circle).

52 Slide the bottom up again so the crease lines up with the bottom of the flaps (see next step).

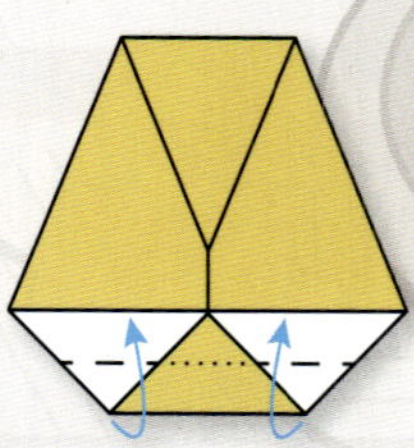

53 Tuck the corner under all the layers.

54 Fold the right and left corners in. Turn over to crease alongside the cheeks.

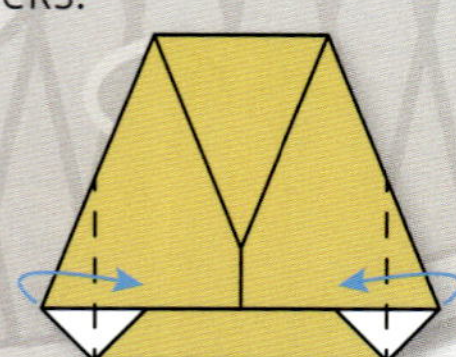

55 Fold the bottom corners in again (marked with circles).

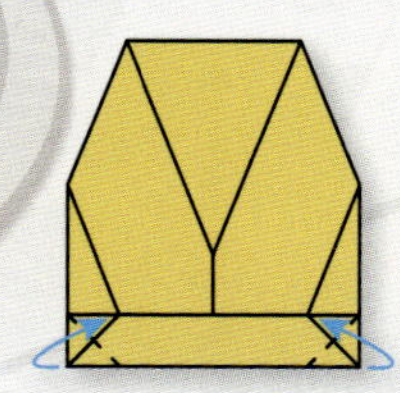

56 Fold the top corners in to round the edges.

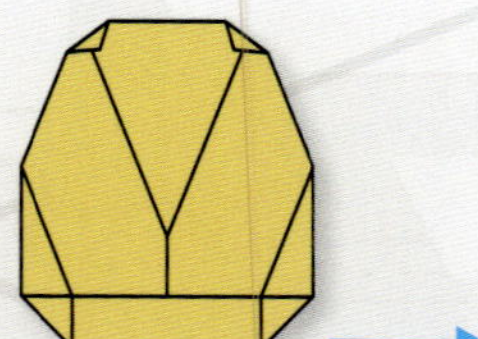

57 Turn the paper over.

58 Yamper's head is complete.

Folding the Ears

Make sure to start with the smaller square ear template; arrange it so the asterisk is at the top.

59 Fold in half along both diagonals, then unfold.

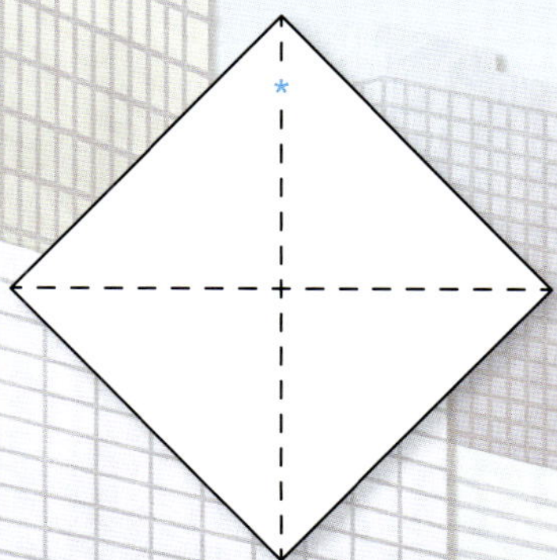

60 Fold the top and bottom corners into the center.

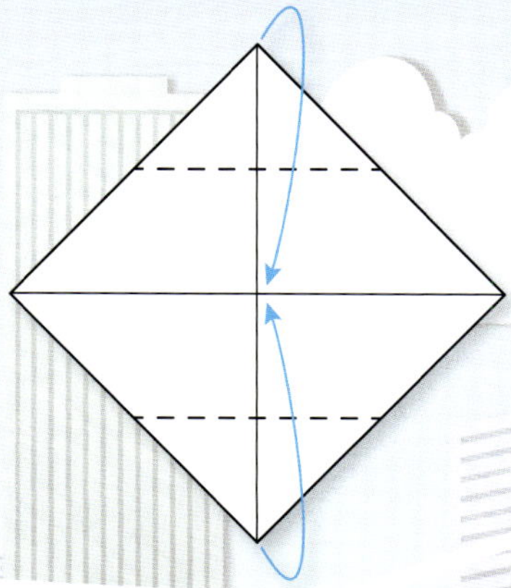

61 Fold the top- and bottom-right corners to the centerline (marked with circles) then unfold.

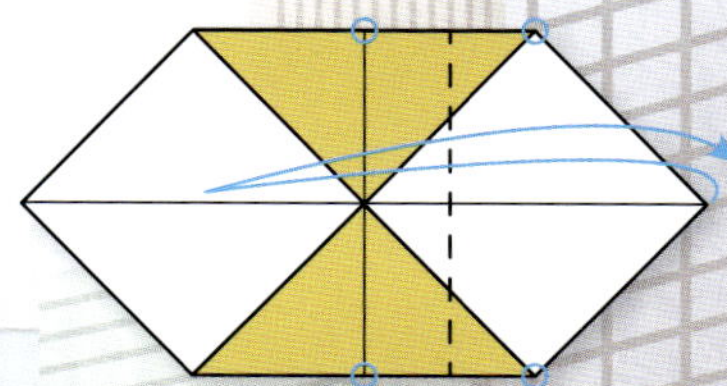

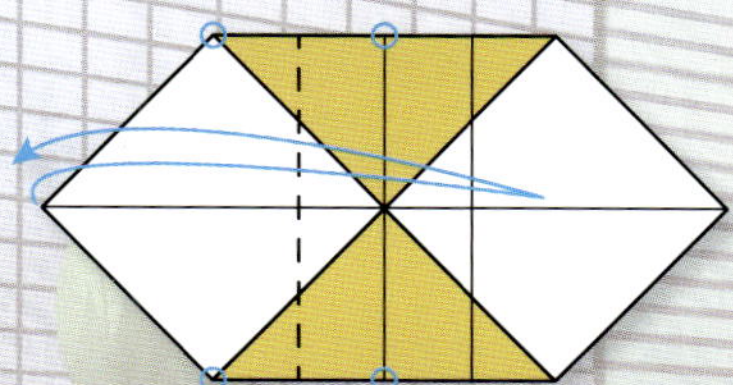

62 Repeat Step 61 on the left side.

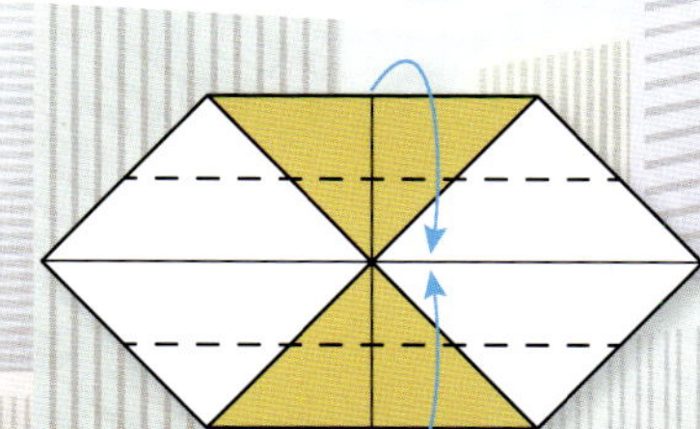

63 Fold the top and bottom edges to the center.

64 Cut along the creases up to the centerline (as marked).

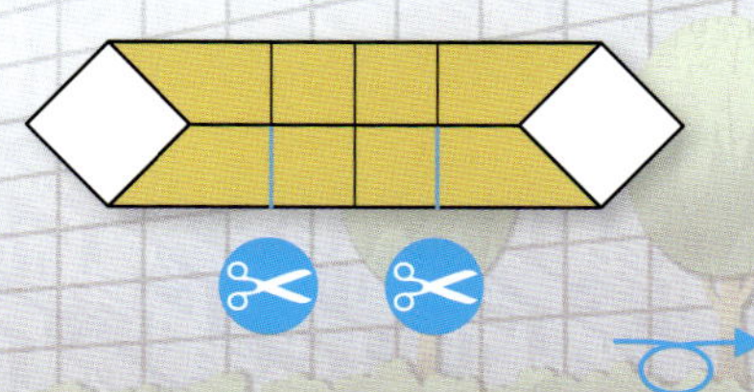

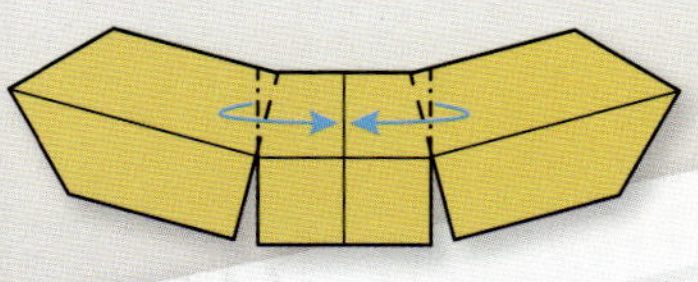

65 Pleat fold toward the center along the dotted lines on both sides.

66 Fold the bottom corners of the ears to the back.

67 Yamper's ears are complete.

Assembling Yamper

68 Squeeze a little glue onto the middle of the square.

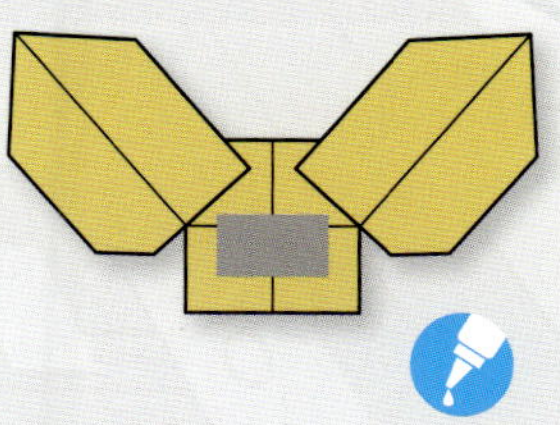

69 Attach Yamper's face to the ears by lining up the top of the head with the top of the central square. Adjust the ears as necessary.

70 Squeeze a little glue onto Yamper's body. Attach Yamper's head and ears by lining up the bottom of the head to the crease on the collar.

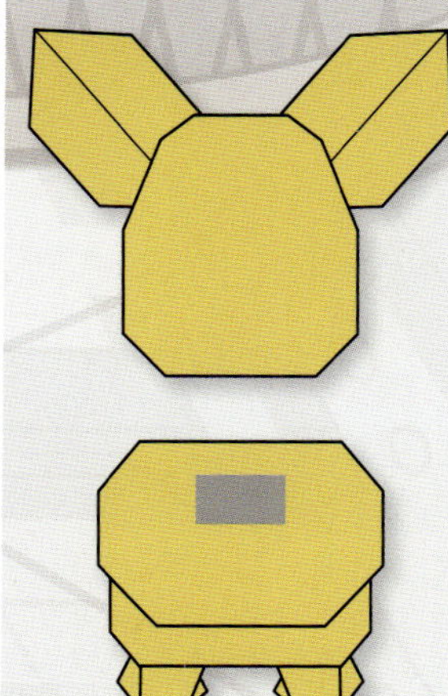

71 Yamper is complete!

Lechonk

Lechonk has an excellent sense of smell that helps it locate all its favorite berries to eat. Follow your nose and get lost in the detail of the folds. Before you know it, you'll have Lechonk by your side.

TYPE: Normal **HEIGHT:** 1'8" / .5 m **WEIGHT:** 22.5 lbs. / 10.2 kg

INTERMEDIATE

How To Make

Lechonk

Lechonk is folded from one large square of paper. You can find the template on page 117. Carefully tear out the piece.

Folding the Body, Head & Feet

Make sure to start with the large square template arranged so that the asterisk is at the top.

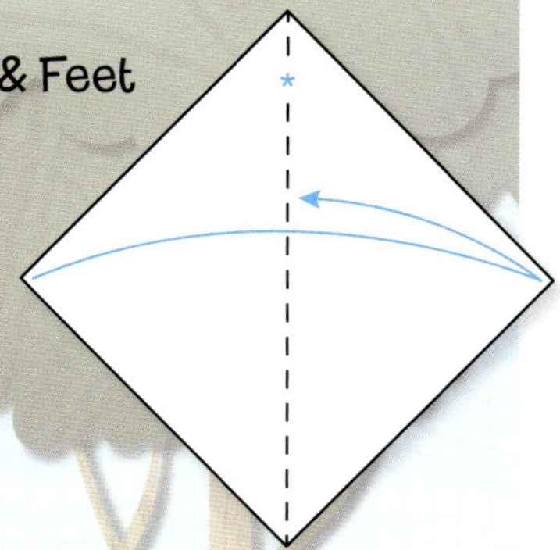

1 Fold in half sideways, then unfold.

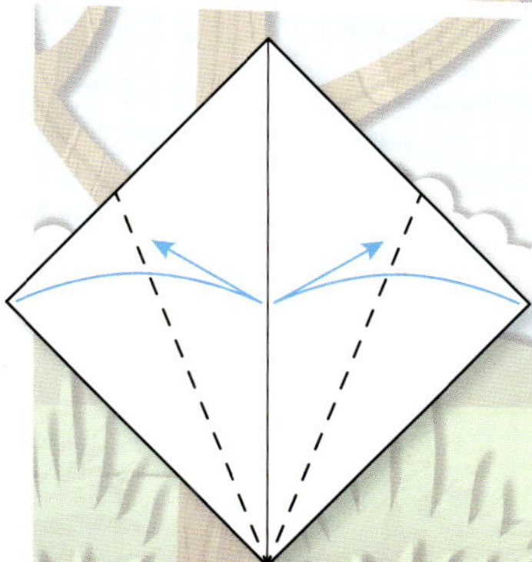

2 Fold the left and right edges to the centerline, then unfold.

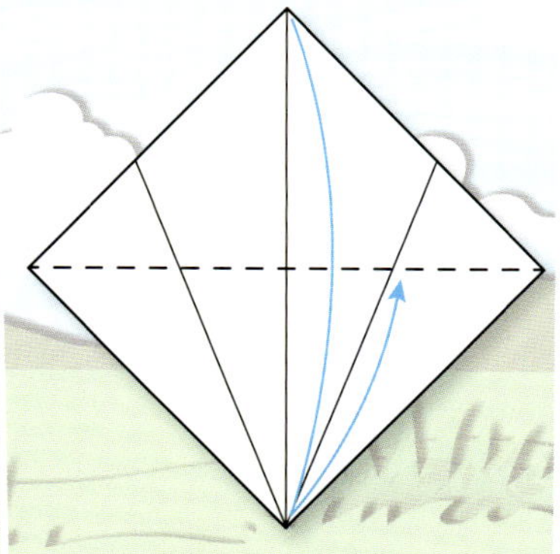

3 Fold in half from top to bottom, then unfold.

4 Fold the right edges to the centerline, then unfold.

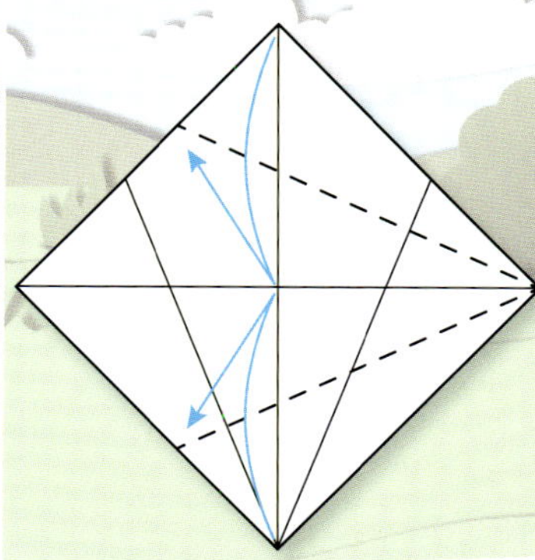

5 Fold the left edge to the centerline, then unfold.

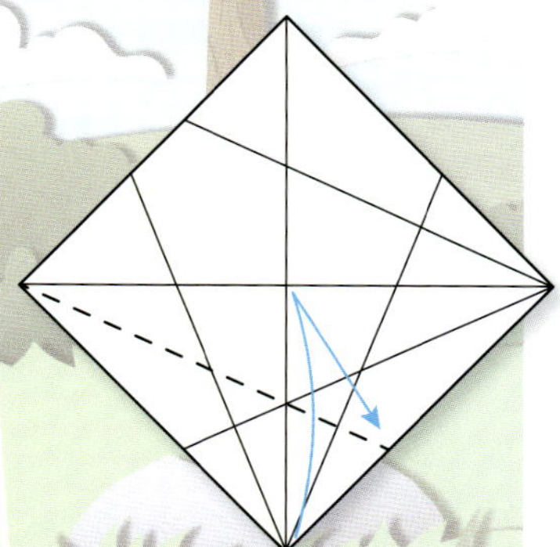

6 Fold the upper-right edge to the marker, then unfold.

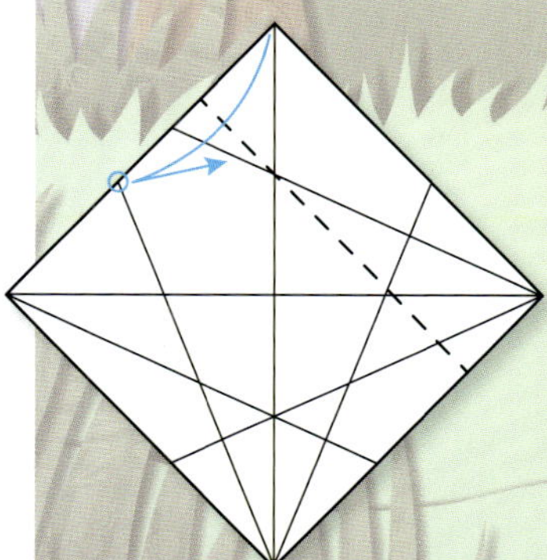

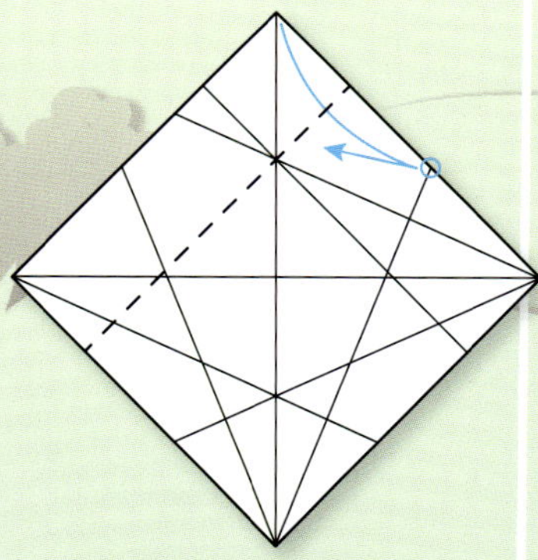

7 Fold the upper-left edge to the marker, then unfold.

8 Using the creases you made in Steps 6 and 7, fold the left and right edges in again, folding the top corner out into a flap. Fold the flap down toward the right.

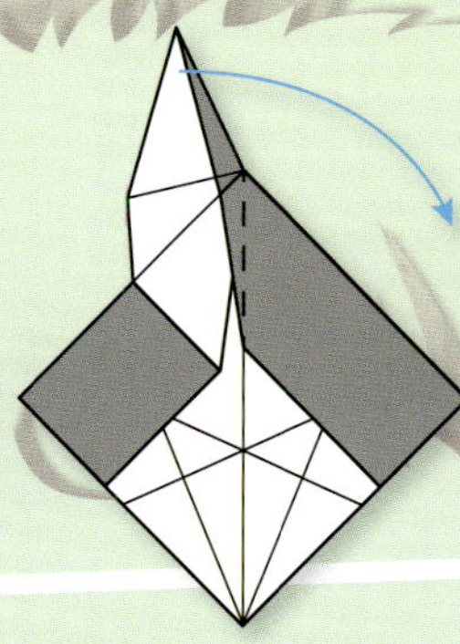

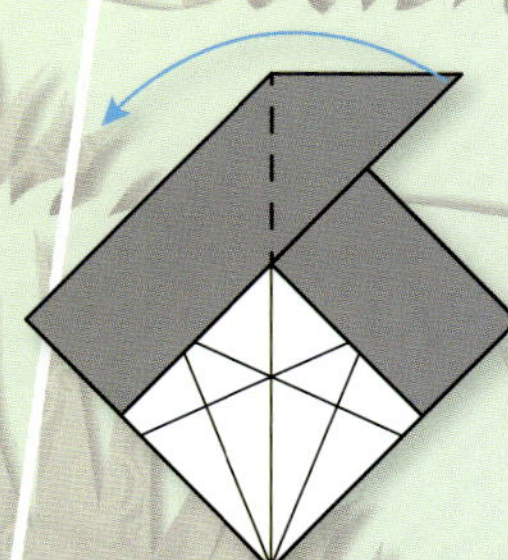

9 Fold the flap over to the left.

10 Using the existing creases, reverse fold the left and right corners up to the top corner.

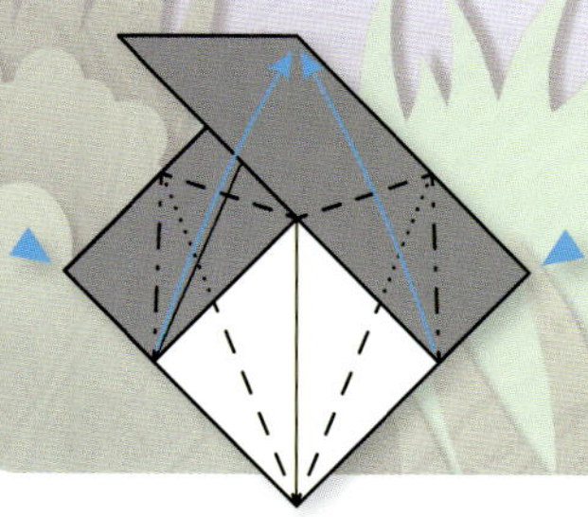

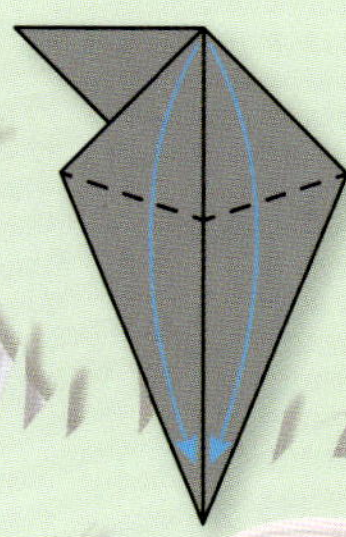

11 Fold the flaps down.

12 Fold the flap over to the right.

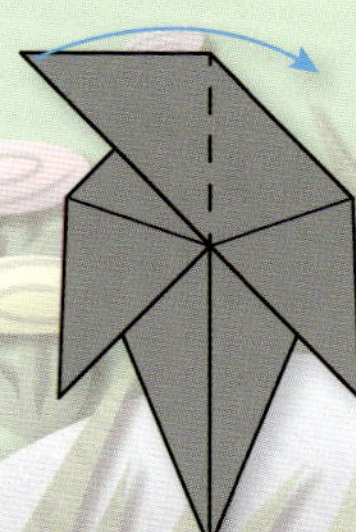

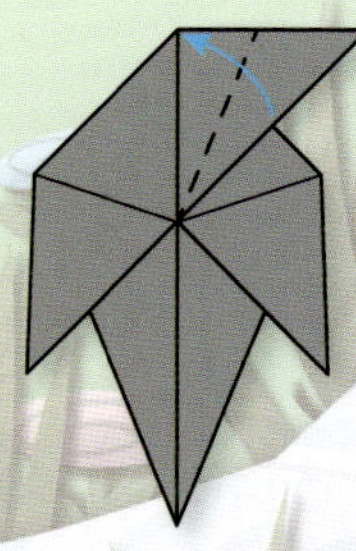

13 Fold the edge of the flap to the centerline.

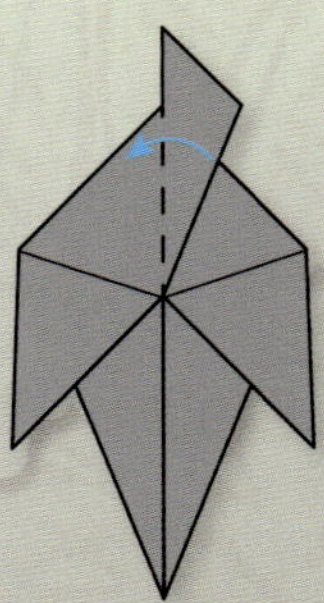

14 Fold the flap to the left.

15 Fold the top corner down to the marker.

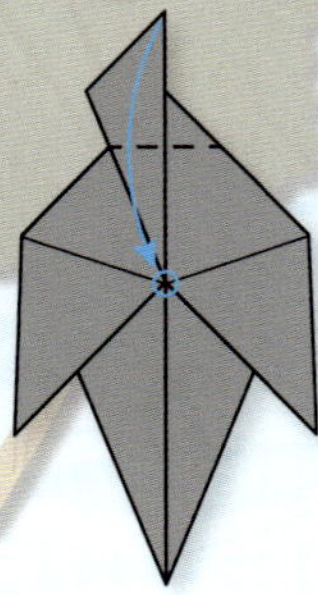

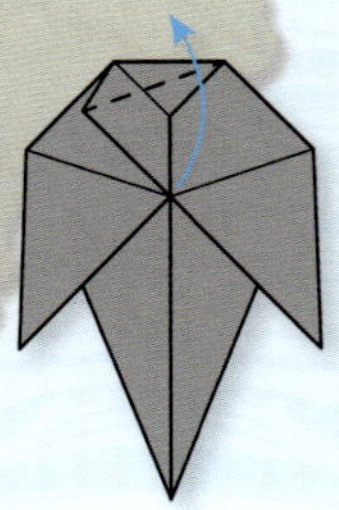

16 Fold the flap back up, creating a new crease (as shown). Turn over to place the front-left foot correctly.

17 Fold the left flap up at an angle (as shown). Again, turn over to place the back-left foot correctly.

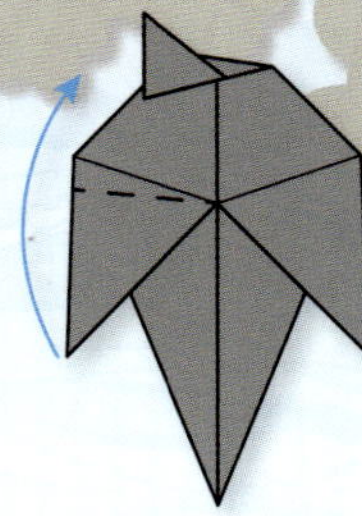

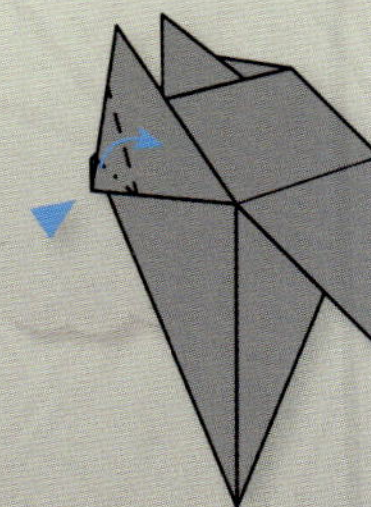

18 Pull the left corner inside slightly and fold (as shown).

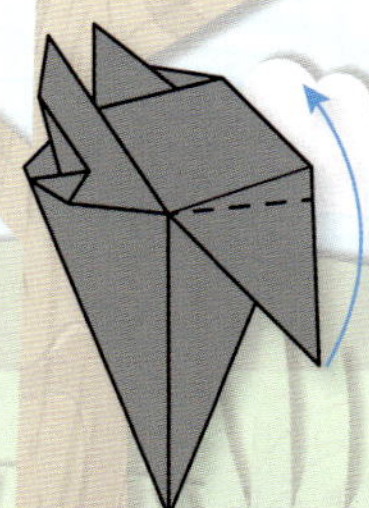

19 Fold the right flap up at an angle. Turn over to place the right foot correctly.

20 Pull the right edge of the flap inside slightly and fold (as shown).

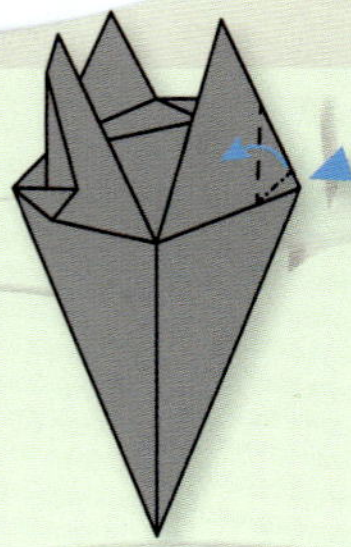

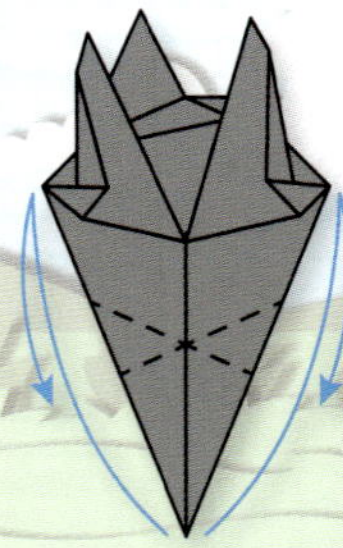

21 Fold and unfold along existing creases.

22 Fold the left and right corners in slightly.

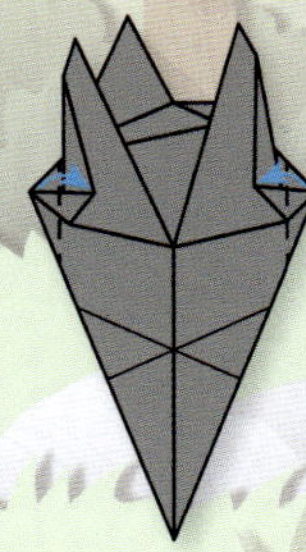

23 Pinch the tail in half to the right…

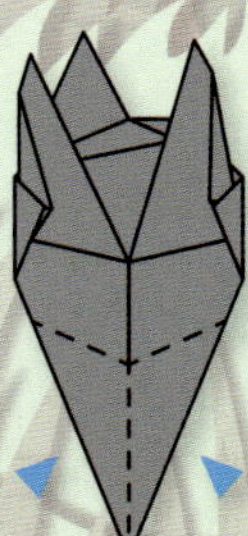

24 …and then fold to the left.

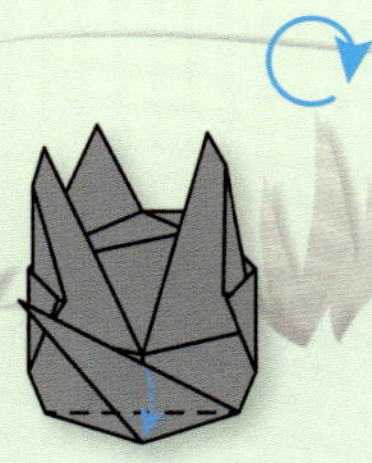

25 Fold the flap down. Rotate so the tail is on top.

26 Fold the tail flap down, then unfold.

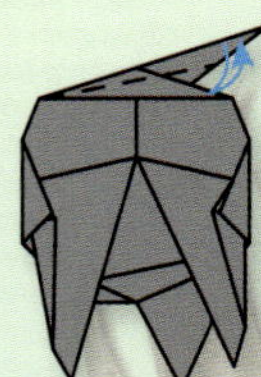

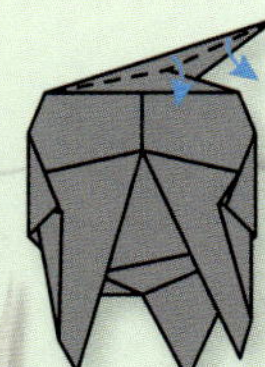

27 Fold the top of the flap down, as you fold the tip of the tail in half.

28 Curl the tail.

29 Turn the paper over.

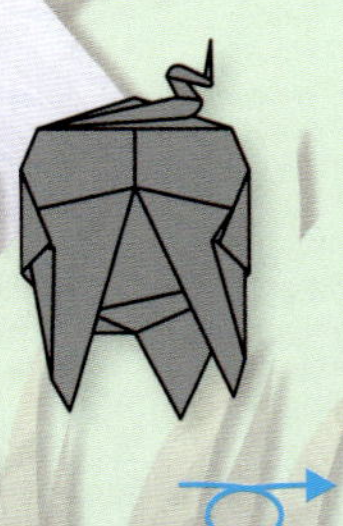

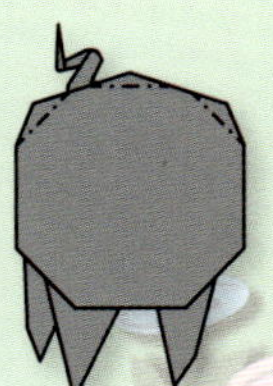

30 Fold back the top and side corners to round the shape.

31 Fold back the feet.

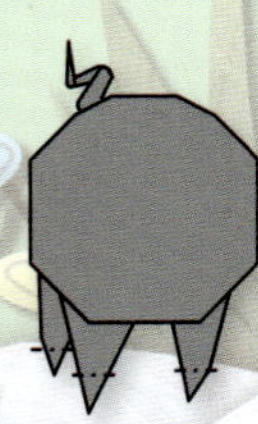

32 Lechonk is complete!

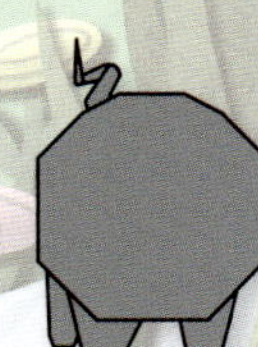

Pikachu

Pikachu is folded from four pieces of paper. You'll find the other pieces on pages 61 and 89. **See instructions on page 6.**

Pikachu's Head

Pikachu's Body & Feet

Pikachu's Head

Pikachu's Body & Feet

Snorlax's Belly

Pikachu's Tail

Here is Snorlax's belly.
See instructions on page 14.

Here is Pikachu's tail.
See instructions on page 6.

Snorlax's Belly

Pikachu's Tail

Snorlax

Snorlax is folded from four pieces of paper.
You'll find the other pieces on pages 61 and 69.
See instructions on page 14.

Snorlax's Feet

Snorlax's Feet

Snorlax's Head

Here are Snorlax's head and arms. **See instructions on page 14.**

Snorlax's Arms

Snorlax's Head

Snorlax's Arms

Larvitar

Larvitar is folded from two pieces of paper. You'll find the other piece on page 85.
See instructions on page 20.

Larvitar's Body & Right Foot

Larvitar's Body & Right Foot

Spheal

Spheal is folded from two pieces of paper.
You'll find the other piece on page 97.
See instructions on page 25.

Spheal's Body

Spheal's Body

Bidoof

Bidoof is folded from three pieces of paper. You'll find the other pieces on pages 85 and 89.

See instructions on page 29.

Bidoof's Head

Bidoof's Head

Bidoof's Feet & Tail

Here are Bidoof's feet and tail.
See instructions on page 29.

Larvitar's Tail & Left Foot

Here are Larvitar's tail and left foot.
See instructions on page 20.

Bidoof's Feet & Tail

Larvitar's Tail & Left Foot

Bidoof's Body

Pikachu's Arms

Here is Bidoof's body.
See instructions on page 29.

Here are Pikachu's arms.
See instructions on page 6.

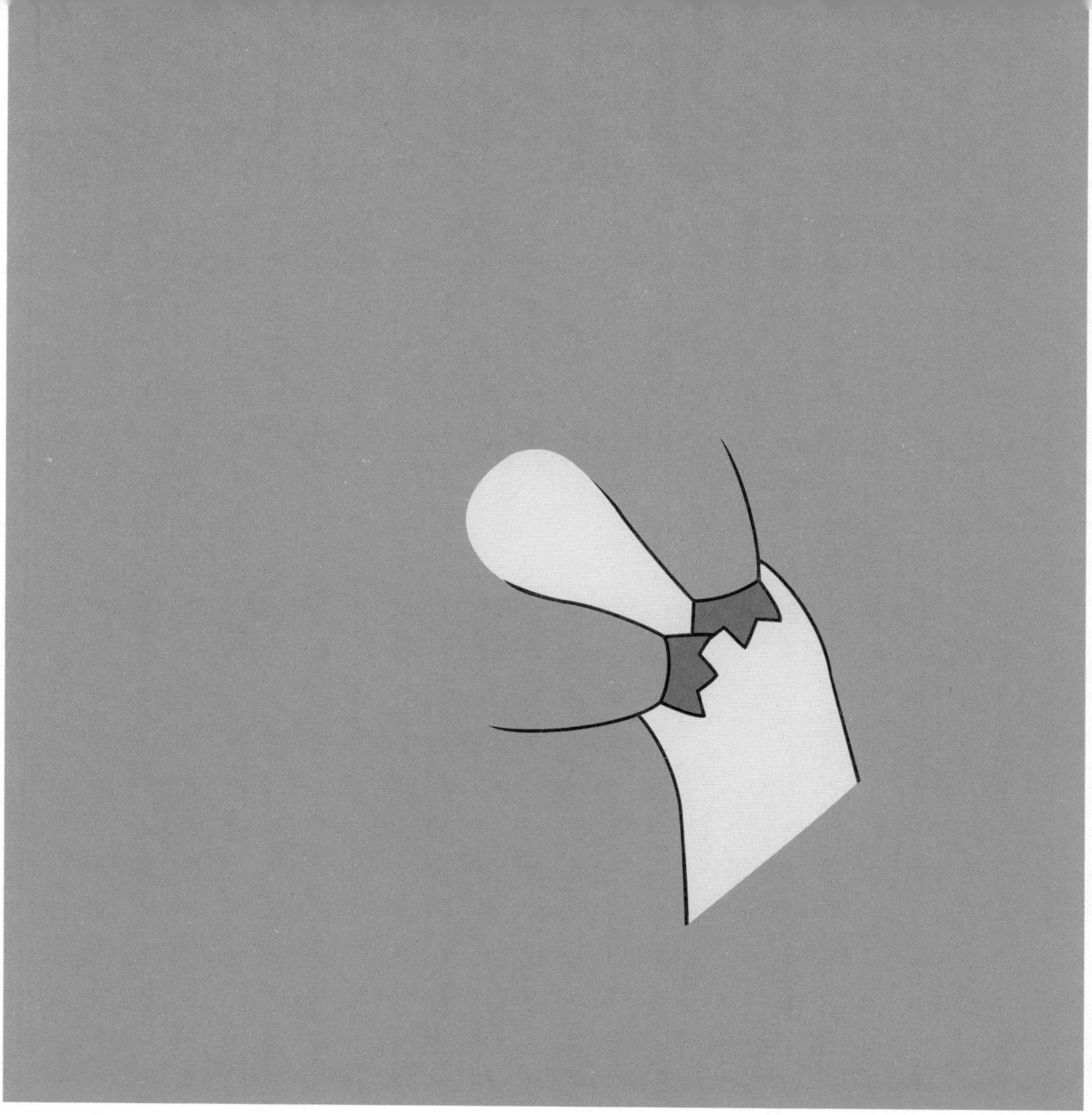
Bidoof's Body

Pikachu's Arms

*

*

Emolga is folded from four pieces of paper. You'll find the other pieces on page 97.
See instructions on page 34.

Emolga's Body

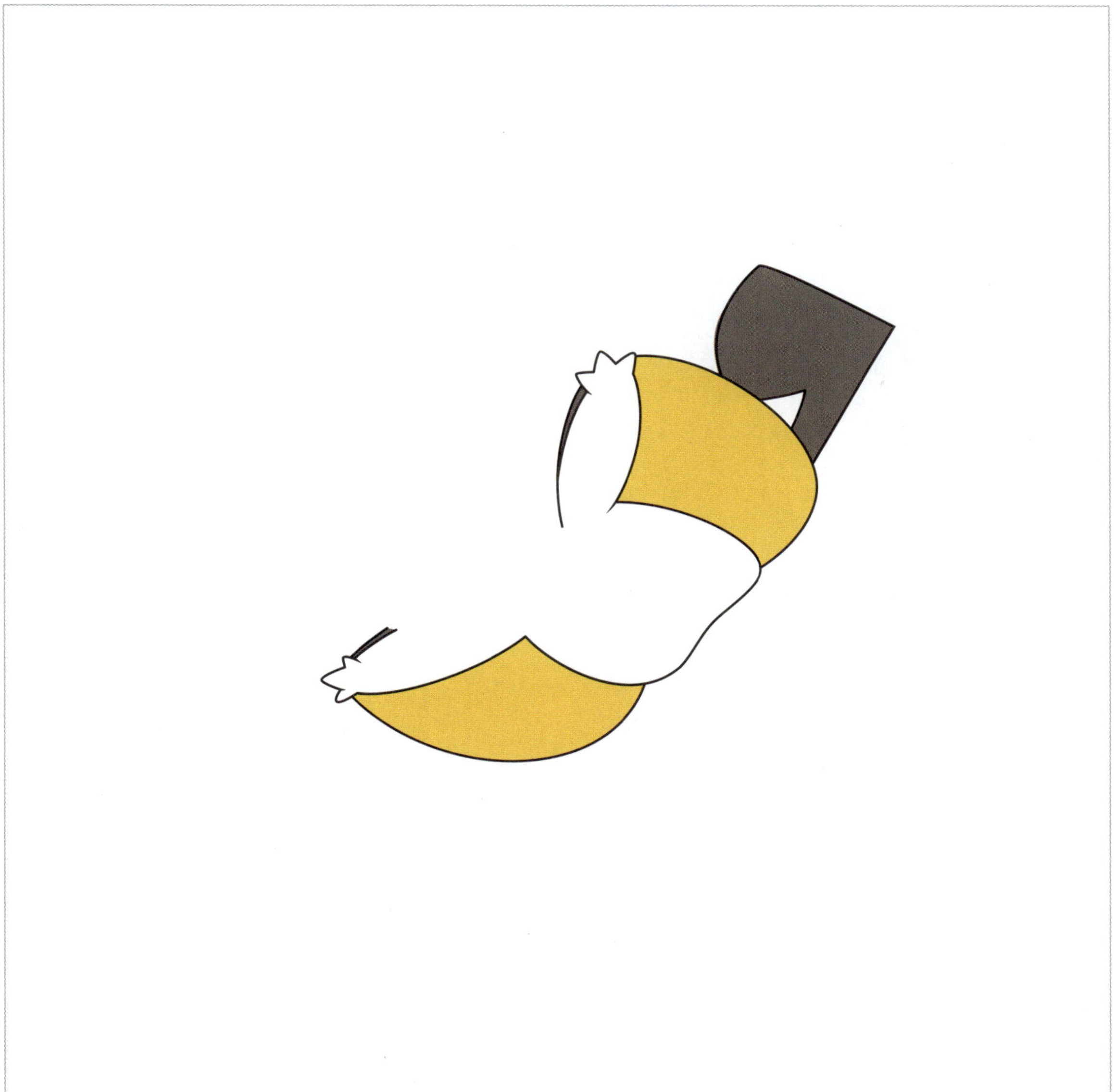

Emolga's Body

Emolga's Head

Emolga's Ears

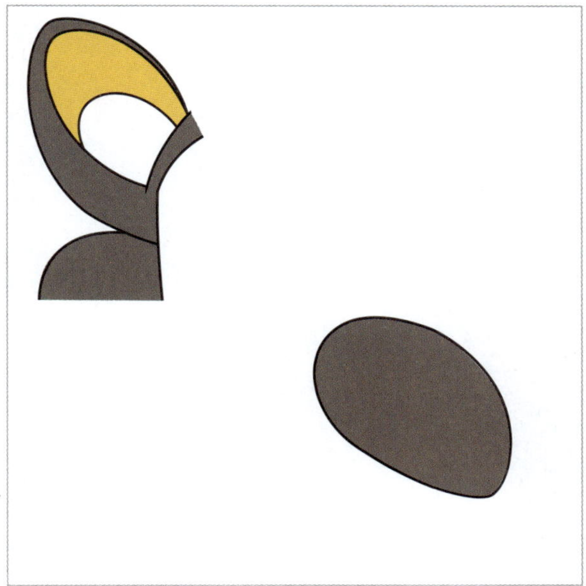

Emolga's Tail

Here are Emolga's head, ears, and tail.
See instructions on page 34.

Here are Spheal's tail and right leg.
See instructions on page 25.

Spheal's Tail & Right Leg

Emolga's Head

Emolga's Ears

Emolga's Tail

Vivillon

Vivillon is folded from three pieces of paper.
See instructions on page 39.

Vivillon's Body

Vivillon's Wings

Vivillon's Head & Antennae

Vivillon's Body

Vivillon's Wings

Vivillon's Head & Antennae

Alolan Diglett

Alolan Diglett is folded from two pieces of paper. You'll find the other piece on page 109.
See instructions on page 44.

Alolan Diglett's Body

*

Alolan Diglett's Body

*

Here is Alolan Diglett's hair.
See instructions on page 44.

Yamper's Head

Yamper's Ears

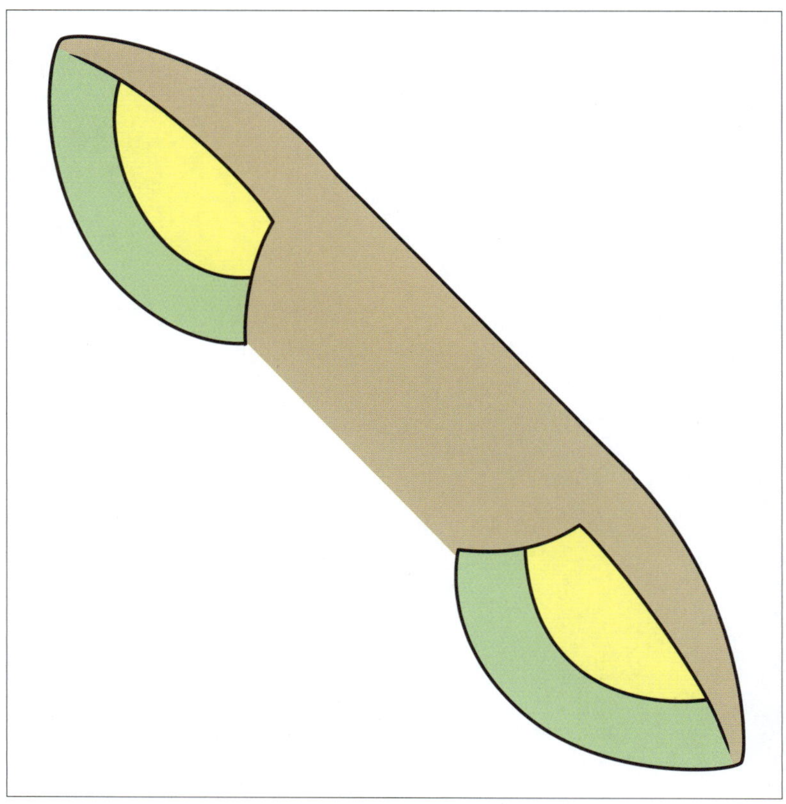

Here are Yamper's head and ears.
See instructions on page 48.

Alolan Diglett's Hair

Yamper's Head

Yamper's Ears

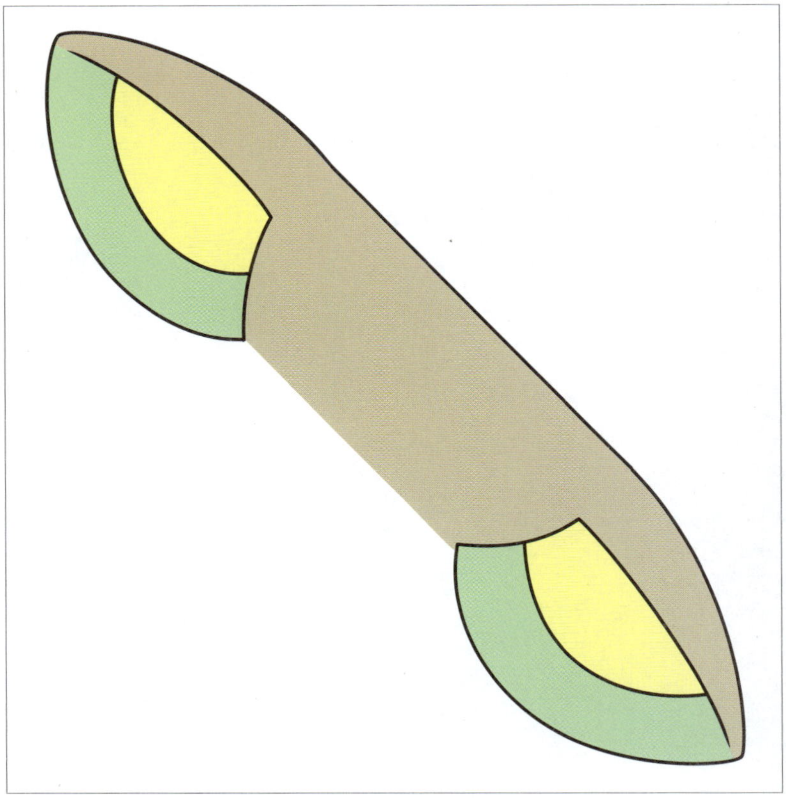

Yamper

Yamper is folded from three pieces of paper. You'll find the other pieces on page 109.
See instructions on page 48.

Yamper's Body

*

Yamper's Body

( ) ( )

Lechonk

Lechonk is folded from one piece of paper.
See instructions on page 54.

Lechonk's Body, Head & Feet

Lechonk's Body, Head & Feet